MATLAB®

Advanced GUI Development

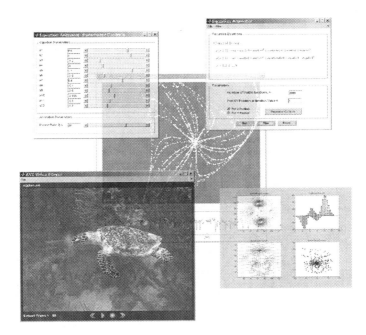

SCOTT T. SMITH

OpenGL® is a registered trademark of Silicon Graphics Inc.
Solaris® is a registered trademark of Sun Microsystems Inc.
Mac OS-X® is a registered trademark of Apple Computer Inc.
MS Windows® is a registered trademark of Microsoft Corporation

MATLAB® ,Handle Graphics®, and GUIDE® are registered trademarks of The MathWorks, Inc. and are used with permission. The MathWorks does not warrant the accuracy of the text or exercises in this book. This book's use or discussion of MATLAB® software or related products does not constitute endorsement or sponsorship by The MathWorks of a particular pedagogical approach or particular use of the MATLAB® software.

For MATLAB® and Simulink® product information, please contact:

The MathWorks, Inc.
3 Apple Hill Drive
Natick, MA, 01760-2098 USA
Tel: 508-647-7000
Fax: 508-647-7001
E-mail: info@mathworks.com
Web: www.mathworks.com

First published by Dog Ear Publishing
4010 W. 86th Street, Ste H
Indianapolis, IN 46268
www.dogearpublishing.net

dog ear
PUBLISHING

ISBN: 1-59858-181-3

This book is printed on acid-free paper.

Printed in the United States of America

Dedication

*To Alia, For Continuous Support, Understanding, and Patience
During This Journey*

To My Family For Years of Encouragement

To All Those Who Teach Science and Engineering With Passion

Table of Contents

Exercises

x

Examples

Figures

Tables

Chapter I
Introduction

In 1977, Cleve Moler developed the first version of MATLAB® software using the FORTRAN computer language and it was designed for solving systems of linear equations and performing matrix calculations. At that time, MATLAB was a relatively simple application with a command line interface and an arsenal of about 80 functions. In the early 1980's, Jack Little, a former graduate from Stanford University, was introduced to Cleve's MATLAB software through colleagues at Stanford. Jack soon took interest in MATLAB and Jack and Cleve formed The MathWorks in 1984 to develop MATLAB into a commercial software application.

Throughout the 1980's and 1990's, MATLAB evolved from a FORTRAN based matrix-solving application into a universal computing toolset complete with thousands of built-in computational and graphical functions. In the mid 1990's, around the time when I was taking my first image processing course in engineering, The MathWorks incorporated graphical user interface, GUI, capabilities into MATLAB. Recent versions of MATLAB, such as versions 6 and 7 or later, have advanced GUI development and graphics capabilities including real-time graphics support, 2D and 3D hardware acceleration using OpenGL, and many of the standard user interface controls common to graphical operating systems.

This book is intended to introduce you to the capabilities of MATLAB for developing GUI applications, explain the details of MATLAB GUI development, and finally cover advanced GUI topics such as designing multiple figure GUIs and real-time graphics and animation. The intended audience for this book ranges from novice MATLAB users who are looking for a complete guide for GUI development to veteran users who wish to learn more about advanced topics such as multiple figure GUIs and real-time event handling.

We start by investigating MATLAB's object-oriented Handle Graphics® programming structure and how simple GUIs can be built using Handle Graphics objects. Chapter 3 covers the high-level GUI development software included with MATLAB called GUIDE® that allows you to easily construct complex applications. Chapter 4 describes the structure of MATLAB GUIs such as the handles structure, event processing, graphical layout, and dialog boxes while Chapter 5 covers advanced topics such as multiple figure GUI applications, real-time graphics, timers, and controls.

1.1   Why Develop GUIs Using MATLAB?

One of the first questions you may ask regarding the topics covered in this book is: *Why should I develop GUI applications using MATLAB?* This is an excellent question since, after all, there are many advanced programming tools available for GUI based operating systems that allow you to create GUI applications. There are several compelling arguments for using MATLAB as a GUI development tool and this section explains these arguments in detail. The following list shows some of the important reasons why you may want to develop GUIs in MATLAB:

- High-Level Script Based Development
- Seamless Integration with Existing MATLAB Computational Power
- Operating System Independent GUI Applications
- User Interactivity and Real-time Measurements

1.1.1   High-Level Script Based Development

If you are already familiar with MATLAB as a computational tool, then you have likely realized the benefits of MATLAB's high-level script language capabilities. Unlike conventional languages such as C, MATLAB scripts do not require compilation, do not require rigorous instantiation of variables, and do not require low-level memory management. Therefore, code development time can be much shorter and often the complexity of your code is much simpler.

GUI application development can be a daunting task for scientists and engineers who do not have a strong background in software engineering. High-level script based development allows scientists and engineers to focus on the specific problems they are trying to solve rather than spending enormous amounts of time architecting a GUI application using a low-level language.

1.1.2   Seamless Integration with Existing MATLAB
         Computational Power

You may already be a committed MATLAB user and have libraries of functions and scripts for solving specific problems related to your field or perhaps you have acquired scripts and functions through the science and engineering community. Building your GUI using MATLAB means that all the code you have developed or acquired to solve complex problems may be directly used within your GUI. This form of seamless integration can be priceless for solving problems quickly with minimal programming effort.

1.1.3　Operating System Independent GUI Applications

MATLAB currently supports operating systems such as Solaris (UNIX), MS Windows, Linux, and Mac OS-X and this allows considerable flexibility for your code development. Since M-file scripts are not compiled, they may be executed using MATLAB that runs on any operating system supported. This is also true for GUI application development with a few exceptions for some properties. Generally, GUI development across operating systems is not a trivial task and MATLAB GUIs offer a simple solution using a common script language.

1.1.4　User Interactivity and Real-time Measurements

Although M-file scripts and functions are excellent for solving many problems, there are often situations where user interactivity with the application is integral for understanding or solving a particular problem. Some examples of where a GUI interface can help the user interact efficiently with an application are listed below:

- Video Applications
- Audio Signal Processing
- Communications Signal Processing
- Simulation of Complex Systems
- Instrumentation and Data Acquisition Interfaces
- Control Systems
- Real-time Financial Market Analysis
- Animation of 2D or 3D Graphical Data

The following figure shows an example of an interactive real-time simulation application that is developed in Chapter 5 of this book:

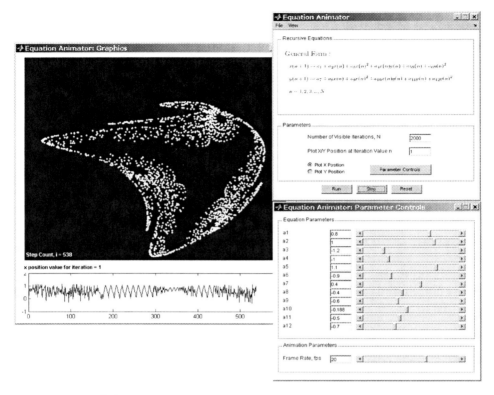

Figure 1.1 - EquationAnimator multiple figure GUI example

This multiple figure GUI application plots data in real-time and allows the user to modify parameters on-the-fly using sliders. The data shown in the graphics figure above is the output of an iterative set of equations that changes over time. This specific example shows chaotic strange attractors that occur for a set of input parameters. The user can change the slider parameters while the system is running to visualize different output maps for the equations.

1.2   MATLAB Capabilities For GUI Development

One of the first key elements for understanding how to develop GUIs is to recognize features available in MATLAB that may be used for graphical user interface design. Creating specifications for an application and determining what is possible is much easier when you have detailed knowledge about the functions and tools available. Some of the most important MATLAB GUI architectural components, functions, and tools are listed below:

- Handle Graphics Objects

- Figures, Axes, and UIControls

- GUIDE, Graphical User Interface Design Environment

- Event Handling: Callback Functions, Timers, and Mouse/Keyboard Input

- Global Variables

- Stand-alone Executable GUIs

Each of the capabilities listed above will be explored in more detail throughout the remaining chapters of this book. The subsequent sections listed below briefly describe these capabilities to provide you with a general overview of what is available in MATLAB.

1.2.1   Handle Graphics Objects

MATLAB uses object-oriented structures to define graphics and GUI objects and these are generally referred to as Handle Graphics Objects, or HG Objects. Figures, Axes, and UIControls, such as edit boxes or sliders, are all considered Handle Graphics Objects. This object-oriented approach to creating and modifying graphical content simplifies your code architecture and allows you to design complex GUIs at a high level.

1.2.2   Figures, Axes, and UIControls

As mentioned in the previous section, Figures, Axes, and UIControls are objects that may be used to develop GUIs. Each of these objects has a set of properties that may be modified to alter the behavior of each component. For example, a **Figure Object** has a **Color** property that may be modified to change a figure's background color while an Edit Box UIControl has a **String** property that may be set to display text in its text box area. Figures, Axes, and UIControls are at the top of a hierarchy of Handle Graphics Objects and are the core components used for GUI development.

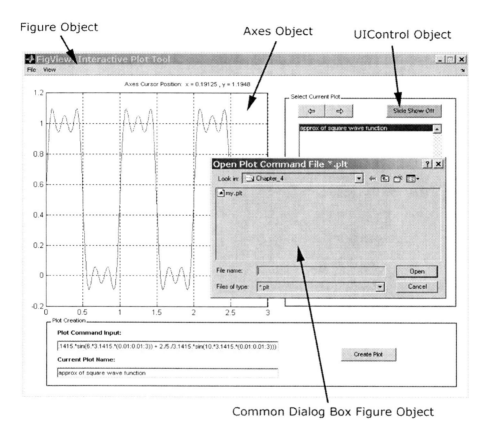

Figure 1.2 - Example GUI showing Figure, Axes, UIControl, and Dialog Box Figure Objects

1.2.3   GUIDE, Graphical User Interface Development Environment

MATLAB contains functions for low-level GUI development that allow you to create applications without the aid of a graphical layout tool. However, high-level GUI development is generally a much simpler approach since the layout of user interface components and defining properties for those components may be performed using a graphical layout tool.

The high-level GUI development tool included with MATLAB is called GUIDE, which stands for *Graphical User Interface Development Environment*, and this software allows you to easily construct your GUI design. GUIDE also allows you to manage properties with Property Inspector and has an option for automatically generating M-file code for your GUI. The figure below shows a snapshot of the GUIDE software and a simple GUI layout. Chapter 3 covers the details of learning how to use GUIDE to build your applications.

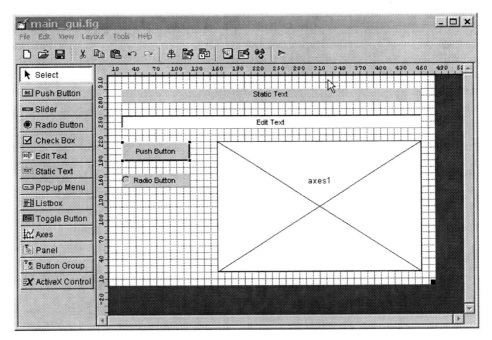

Figure 1.3 - Example high-level GUI layout using GUIDE

1.2.4   Event Handling: Callback Functions, Timers, and Mouse/Keyboard Input

Event handling is an essential aspect of GUI application development that includes management of input events such as mouse and keyboard events as well as using timers for real-time and periodic function calls. MATLAB uses Callback Functions for handling events that occur for user interface objects. For example, if your application has a pushbutton object, then there will be a callback function that is executed when the user clicks the mouse on the pushbutton.

MATLAB has the capability to handle or create most common events required to architect advanced GUI applications. You can track mouse motion in a figure or axes, create keystroke combinations for shortcuts, and use timer functions to manage animation rendering or control data acquisition events. Chapter 2 introduces you to callback functions and chapters 4 and 5 cover event processing and advanced uses of callback functions in detail.

1.2.5   Global Variables

Most common architectures for MATLAB GUI applications use a local handle object data structure to communicate user interface parameters across callback functions. This is the default structure used by GUIDE for automatic code generation for a GUI design. Although this is an effective way to develop single figure GUI applications, it limits the possibilities for expanding your GUI to include multiple figures that interact within a single application.

MATLAB includes global variable instantiation that allows you to extend the capabilities of GUI development to multiple figure architectures. This is very useful for applications that require graphics or plot figures that are separate from a main GUI figure that contains user interface controls. Chapter 5 discusses multiple figure GUI architectures using global variables.

1.2.6   Stand-alone Executable GUIs

Often a goal of creating a GUI in MATLAB is to allow many users to run your application. If your user audience does not have access to MATLAB, then there is no possibility of running you application in native M-file and figure file form. The MATLAB Compiler add-on tool allows you to convert your GUI into an executable program that may be distributed to users without dependence on running a MATLAB session. This is essential if you plan to development an application that you wish to deploy to a large audience or distribute as a commercial software product.

1.3   Where To Download M-files

Each example and exercise throughout this text shows the complete M-file code used to develop each GUI or application. In order to speedup your understanding of MATLAB GUI development, all M-file code and figure files used by GUIDE are available for download from the following website: ***www.mat-gui.com***

Chapter 2
Handle Graphics Programming

2.1   Introduction To Handle Graphics Objects

Similar to other object-oriented languages and techniques, MATLAB uses a hierarchy of objects called **Handle Graphics Objects** that are used to build any form of graphical user interface or graphical output object. You may already be familiar with Figures and Plots in MATLAB; these are examples of Handle Graphic Objects or *HG Objects*. Each HG Object contains a set of properties that define the appearance and behavior of the object. Development of GUI interfaces relies on the use of HG Objects to create GUI component objects and define the components' behavior. This chapter will introduce you to HG Objects and their associated properties, how to use HG Objects to create simple GUI interfaces, and demonstrate the use of the *handles* variable as an efficient data structure for GUI development.

2.1.1   HG Object Hierarchy

HG Objects are arranged in a parent-child hierarchy such that a child object must first have a parent to exist. This object-oriented structure is efficient for development of complex graphical objects and GUI applications. Figure 2.1 shows the full hierarchical organization of HG Objects within MATLAB and provides you with a snapshot overview of their parent-child dependence. This chart is not intended for you to memorize since MATLAB provides an excellent **Help** browser for HG Objects that should be used as your main programming reference. You can browse the HG Object hierarchy by starting **Help** and selecting **Handle Graphics Property Browser** under **Contents => MATLAB**. Figure 2.1 shows the Help window contents for the top of the hierarchy.

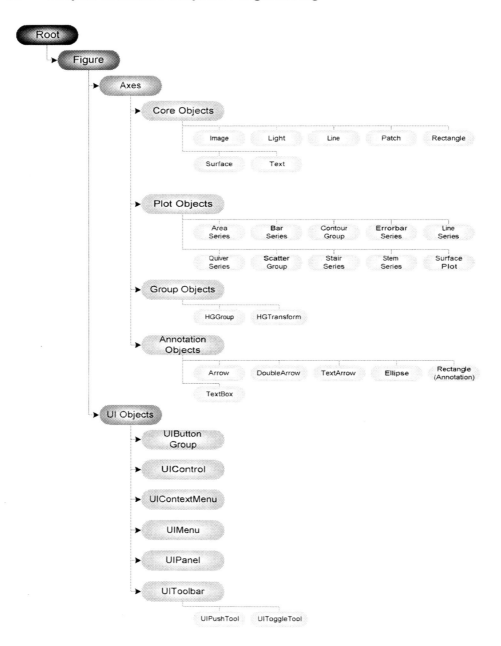

Figure 2.1 - HG Object Hierarchy

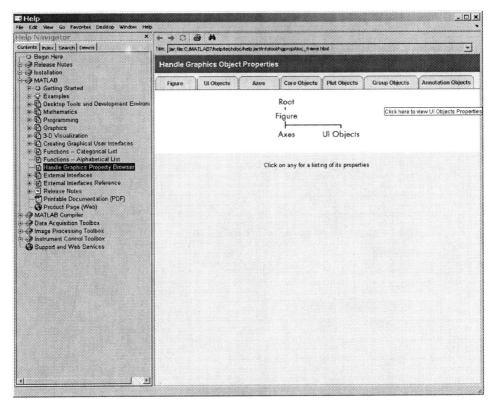

Figure 2.2 - HG Object hierarchy browsing using MATLAB Help

2.1.2   The Root Object

You will notice that the hierarchy starts with the **Root Object** and this represents the MATLAB session. The parent-child structure does not allow a figure window to be instantiated unless a MATLAB session is running. This principle applies to each HG Object that has a parent. For example, if you would like to create an **Image Object**, first a **Root**, **Figure**, and **Axes Object** must exist, the **Image Object** cannot exist on its own.

The **Root Object** is the only object that does not have a parent and is automatically instantiated when you start a MATLAB session. The **Root Object** contains several properties that are useful for GUI development such as **MonitorPositions** and **ScreenSize**. These properties contain information about your display monitor resolution that may be used for GUI initialization. For example, to determine the current display resolution setting of your video card hardware, you can type the following expression:

```
>> get(0)

        CallbackObject = []
        CommandWindowSize = [99 25]
        CurrentFigure = [1]
        Diary = off
        DiaryFile = diary
        Echo = off
        FixedWidthFontName = Courier
        Format = short
        FormatSpacing = loose
        Language = english
        MonitorPositions = [0 0 1600 1200]
        More = off
        PointerLocation = [585 334]
        PointerWindow = [0]
        RecursionLimit = [500]
        ScreenDepth = [32]
        ScreenPixelsPerInch = [96]
        ScreenSize = [1 1 1600 1200]
        ShowHiddenHandles = off
        Units = pixels

        BeingDeleted = off
        ButtonDownFcn =
        Children = [1]
        Clipping = on
        CreateFcn =
        DeleteFcn =
        BusyAction = queue
        HandleVisibility = on
        HitTest = on
        Interruptible = on
        Parent = []
        Selected = off
        SelectionHighlight = on
        Tag =
        Type = root
        UIContextMenu = []
        UserData = []
        Visible = on
```

Notice that a list of properties appears in the MATLAB command window. The *get()* function allows you to access all the properties of an HG Object. In the property list above you will find the following two statements:

```
MonitorPositions = [0 0 1600 1200]
```
and
```
ScreenSize = [1 1 1600 1200]
```

The **MonitorPositions** property provides you with current display monitor information for your primary and secondary monitors. The example above shows that a primary monitor on the system was found to have 1600x1200 pixel resolution. The [0 0] at the beginning of the vector denotes that the display is primary. If the system has a secondary display with resolution 1600x1200, then the return values for **MonitorPositions** and **ScreenSize** would show:

```
MonitorPositions = [0 0 1600 1200; 1601 0 3200 1200]
```
and
```
ScreenSize = [1 1 3200 1200]
```

These properties can be very useful for determining current display resolution limits for you GUI program.

The **Root Object** is always defined with a handle number of zero such that all properties may be accessed with the following syntax:

```
get(0, 'Property')
```

where '*Property*' defines the property you wish to access. The details of how to retrieve and change HG Object properties are discussed in the next section.

2.2   Handle Graphics Objects and Properties

In section 2.1 you were introduced to the highest level HG Object in the hierarchy, the **Root Object**, and a couple of associated properties. In addition, it was shown that the **Root Object** has a handle number zero. This section introduces the concept of handles as storage variables for HG Objects and their associated properties. We will also discuss common and specific sets of properties that are defined for each type of HG Object. You will also learn how to set and get properties from each type of HG Object.

2.2.1   Retrieving and Storing Properties Using s*et( )* and *get( )*

All properties for all HG Objects may be accessed using the *set()* and *get()* functions. These two functions are used extensively for developing GUI applications. The basic syntax for these functions is show below:

Set Function:

```
set(handle_to_graphic_object, 'Property', property_value);
```

Get Function:

```
property_value = get(handle_to_graphic_object, 'Property');
```

where the *property_value* is the value defined for the property and the *handle_to_graphic_object* is the *handle* that points to the HG Object. There are several forms of the *set()* and *get()* function that allow you to perform specific tasks. For example, if you use the *set()* function with the following syntax you can view all the properties and their legal values for any HG Object:

```
>> handle_to_figure = figure;
>> set(handle_to_figure)
       Alphamap
       BackingStore: [ {on} | off ]
       CloseRequestFcn: string -or- function handle -or- cell array
       Color
       Colormap
       CurrentAxes
       CurrentCharacter
```

```
CurrentObject
CurrentPoint
DockControls: [ {on} | off ]
DoubleBuffer: [ {on} | off ]
FileName
IntegerHandle: [ {on} | off ]
InvertHardcopy: [ {on} | off ]
KeyPressFcn: string -or- function handle -or- cell array
MenuBar: [ none | {figure} ]
MinColormap

...

Parent
Selected: [ on | off ]
SelectionHighlight: [ {on} | off ]
Tag
UIContextMenu
UserData
Visible: [ {on} | off ]
```

The first command instantiates a **Figure Object** and assigns a handle named *handle_to_figure*. Next, the s*et()* function is used with the **Figure Object** handle without any properties to list all properties for the **Figure Object** (The list above is truncated to fit on the page). This is a quick method to list all properties for an HG Object. You are encouraged to view the help pages in MATLAB for the s*et()* and *get()* functions to familiarize yourself with their syntax.

Exercise 2.1: HG Object Manipulation Using set() and get()

Create a **Figure Object** using the *figure()* function and an **Axes Object** by using the *axes()* function. Make sure you generate a handle to each object. Then, create a sinusoidal plot using the *plot()* function and **Axes Object** handle. Next, use the s*et()* and *get()* functions to change the following properties of each object and then retrieve the property values to make sure they are set correctly:

Figure Property Changes:

　　　　Color = [0 0.3 0]

Pointer = 'Crosshair'

Axes Property Changes:

Color = [1 1 0.8]

XGrid = 'on'

YGrid = 'on'

When complete, you should have a figure that has a greenish background and a yellowish axes background. Also, you should see an X-Y grid appear in the axes and the mouse pointer should change to crosshair style when used in the figure window.

Exercise 2.1 Solution:

```
% create figure and axes objects
hfig = figure(1);
haxes = axes;

% create sinusoidal plot
x = 0:0.05:4*pi;
plot(x , sin(x));

% set new figure and axes properties
set(hfig,      'Color', [0.7 0.9 0.7], ...
               'Pointer', 'Crosshair');
set(haxes,     'Color', [1 1 0.8], ...
               'Xgrid', 'on', ...
               'Ygrid', 'on');

% get property values that were just set
get(hfig,      'Color')
get(hfig,      'Pointer')
get(haxes,     'Color')
get(haxes,     'XGrid')
get(haxes,     'YGrid')

Command Window Output:
>> ex2p2
ans =
      0.7000    0.9000    0.7000
```

```
ans =

     crosshair
ans =

     1.0000     1.0000     0.8000
ans =

     on
ans =

     on
```

2.2.2   Common HG Object Properties

Each HG Object contains a set of properties that is common for all objects. Common properties will be introduced here as a group to minimize your effort in trying to absorb all the properties for each object individually. Properties can be classified as either Settings or Callback Functions. Settings are properties that may be read to retrieve information about an object or written to modify information of an object. Callback Functions are properties that define a function that is called when a specific action occurs for an object such as a mouse button click over an object. The common HG Object properties consist of both Settings and Callback Functions and are listed in the two tables below as separate groups. Note that legal values in brackets refer to the MATLAB default value for the property.

Table 2.1: Common HG Object Property Settings

Property Name	Legal Values/Types	Brief Description
BusyAction	cancel | {queue}	Defines action for interrupting a callback function that is currently running
Children	handles to objects	List of handles containing all child objects of the current object
Clipping	{on} | off	Clips objects that are outside axes object boundaries
HandleVisibility	{on} | callback | off	Sets the visibility of object handles, can hide handles if desired
HitTest	{on} | off	Defines if current object can be selected by a mouse click
Interruptible	{on} | off	Allow callback functions and events to interrupt current object's callback function
Parent	handle to object	Defines the parent object of the current object, the parent can be changed if desired
Selected	on | {off}	Defines if the current object is selected
SelectionHighlight	{on} | off	Determines if selection box will be drawn around a selected object
Tag	string	Defines a label for the current object that allows easy access to the object for programming
Type	string	Defines the type of object such as 'Axes', can only be read
UserData	matrix	User defined data that you can attach to an object for your own use
Visible	{on} | off	Defines visibility of the current object on the display, you can hide objects by turning this off

Table 2.2: Common HG Object Callback Functions

Property Name	Legal Values/Types	Brief Description
ButtonDownFcn	function string or handle	Callback function routine that executes when mouse is placed over an object and a mouse button is clicked
CreateFcn	function string or handle	Callback function routine that executes when an object is instantiated
DeleteFcn	function string or handle	Callback function routine that executes when an object is deleted or closed

There are several Setting properties defined above that are important for developing GUI programs. The most important properties are:

BusyAction, Children, Interruptible, Parent, Tag, and **Visible.** The **BusyAction** and **Interruptible** properties define if an object can interrupt or be interrupted by another callback routine. These are important features for programming GUIs that require priority based control objects such as making sure certain object callback routines are finished before another object callback can start. The **Children** and **Parent** properties are useful for keeping track of object hierarchies, reordering objects, or redefining the parent of an object. The **Visible** property allows you to hide graphics objects from view but still maintain their existence under the current parent object. The **Tag** property is probably the most important property since it allows you to define a unique name to any graphics object. The **Tag** name for an object can be considered analogous to a variable name such that it allows you to access the contents of the object by referring to its **Tag** name. This will be explained in further detail in Chapter 3 when you learn how to develop GUIs using GUIDE.

Each of the callback functions defined for the core properties is useful for GUI development. The **ButtonDownFcn** is very useful for creating your own buttons or control objects that are not part of the standard set of user interface objects. This function is also useful for drag-and-drop applications such as region of interest boxes, etc ... The **CreateFcn** and **DeleteFcn** are important for defining initialization and shutdown code for your GUIs. For example, if you have a GUI that contains a main control figure window and a plot figure window and you wish to make sure both windows are closed when the main control window is closed, you can use the **DeleteFcn** of the main control figure to delete the plot figure when the main control figure window is closed.

Exercise 2.2: Using The Parent Property To Control Graphic Objects

As mentioned above, the **Parent** property may be used to reassign an object to a different parent object. This exercise will show you how to use the **Parent** property to shift an **Axes Object** from one figure to another.

1. Create two new figures and handles to the figures
2. Create an axes on the first figure and handles to the axes
3. Plot a simple function such as *sin(x)* in the axes
4. Next, use the **Parent** property to reassign the axes from the first figure to the second figure

When you enter the *set()* command that reassigns the **Parent** you should see your axes and plot move from the first figure to the second. This is a powerful method of manipulating graphics objects within the hierarchy.

Exercise 2.2 Solution:

```
>> h1 = figure(1);
>> h2 = figure(2);
>> set(0, 'CurrentFigure', h1);
>> a1 = axes;
>> plot(a1, sin(1:100));
>> set(a1, 'Parent', h2);
```

Note that you can use the **CurrentFigure** property of the **Root Object** to control the focus of the current figure. After you entered the second command instantiating *figure(2)*, the current figure is not the figure where you would like to create the axes. Setting the **CurrentFigure** property enables *figure(1)* to receive graphic object output.

2.3   Figure Object Properties

Exclusive properties for **Figure**, **Axes**, and **UI Objects** allow you to perform more complex object manipulation, initialization, and callback function event processing. This section describes object specific properties for **Figure Objects** and the basic functionality of each setting and callback function.

2.3.1   Figure Properties

The **Figure Object** has several unique properties that are specifically useful for GUI development. Similar to the common object properties that are defined for all objects, figure specific properties have both unique *settings* and *callback functions*. The tables below list the figure specific settings properties and callback function properties that are most useful for GUI development. You are encouraged to browse the MATLAB help pages for a more in depth description of all the Figure properties available. Some properties are not listed here since they are rarely used for GUI development.

Table 2.3: Figure Property Settings

Property Name	Legal Values/Types	Brief Description
BackingStore	{on} | off	Enables/disables an off-screen figure buffer for drawing figure contents, can speed up animations for some applications when BackingStore is enabled however it uses more memory for the off-screen buffer
Color	[R G B] matrix	Defines the background color of the figure
Colormap	m-by-3 matrix of RGB values	Defines the colormap for the figure which affects surface, image, and patch objects
CurrentAxes	handle of current Axes	Holds handle information for current Axes defined for the figure. This property can be set to target a specific Axes if multiple Axes exist. The gca command also can return this information.
CurrentCharacter	character	Holds character of the last key pressed in the figure, but only a single character, not a string.
CurrentObject	handle of object	Similar to CurrentAxes, holds information for current object for the figure. The gco command returns this value also.
CurrentPoint	[x, y] vector	X and Y position of the mouse during the last button click. The position is updated upon each mouse button click. If the WindowButtonMotionFcn is defined for the figure, then the CurrentPoint is updated each time the mouse is moved without the mouse button pressed.
DockControls	{on} | off	Enables the display controls used for docking the figure to the MATLAB session window. This is a feature added to MATLAB 7
DoubleBuffer	{on} | off	Enables off screen drawing surface that is used to update the figure graphics. This allows flicker free rendering of all graphics objects is essential for animation and video applications.
IntegerHandle	{on} | off	Enables the use of integer values for definition of figure objects. When disabled, figure handles will use non-integer values to define the figure that avoids drawing content to the wrong figure.
MenuBar	none | {figure}	Enables the display of the menu bar for the figure
Name	string	Defines the title of the current figure. If this property is not set, MATLAB uses the figure handle number as part of the title such as: Figure 1, Figure 2, etc ... When defined the title will appear as Figure x: <string> where <string> is the Name of the figure. You can disable the display of Figure x: by turning off the NumberTitle property.
NextPlot	new | {add} | replace	Defines the format of the next graphics output. New creates a new figure for output,

	| replacechildren	add uses the current figure, replace resets all figure properties except position, and replacechildren replaces all child properties such as Axes objects and does not reset figure properties.
NumberTitle	{on} | off (GUIDE default off)	Determines if the figure will display the figure number will appear in the title
Pointer	crosshair | {arrow} | watch | topl | topr | botl | botr | circle | cross | fleur | left | right | top | bottom | fullcrosshair | ibeam | custom	Establishes the current pointer shape for the figure window. When the mouse is moved over the active region of the figure window, the pointer will change to this shape
PointerShapeCData	16 x 16 matrix	Defines the pointer shape from a 16 x 16 user supplied matrix, the Pointer property must be set to custom
PointerShapeHotSpot	2 element vector	Sets the hot spot of the pointer when button is clicked
Position	4 element vector [left, bottom, width, height]	Holds the current figure position, this information may be used to set the figure position on the screen
Renderer	{painters} | zbuffer | OpenGL | None	Defines the rendering method for the figure. painters is usually the fastest renderer for basic 2D graphics, if your computer system has OpenGL hardware acceleration you may wish to set this to OpenGL
RendererMode	{auto} | manual	Allows MATLAB to select the best renderer for the current graphic task
Resize	{on} | off	Determines if the figure can be resized by the user. The ResizeFcn callback function may be used to define an action when a resize event occurs
Toolbar	none | {auto} | figure	Enables the figure toolbar, auto setting will remove the figure toolbar if UI control is added to the figure
UIContextMenu	handle of UIContextMenu object	Defines the UicontextMenu that will appear for the current figure
Units	{pixels} | normalized | inches | centimeters | points | characters	Determines the units for the values of other figure properties such as Position. Pixels are set as default so that Position values refer to screen pixels
WindowStyle	{normal} | modal | docked	Defines the window type for the figure. Modal windows stay in focus above other MATLAB windows and capture all events. Docked windows may be docked to the main MATLAB interface window
WVisual	{on} | off	**MS Windows systems only**, defines the pixel format for the figure such as RGB 16 bit, hardware accelerated. This property can only be set if WVisualMode is set to Manual

WVisualMode	{auto} | manual	**MS Windows systems only,** enables manual control of figure pixel format, the default is auto and in general you do not need to set this unless you are experiencing performance problems
XDisplay	{on} | off	**UNIX systems only**, defines the display output for the current figure, remote display identifiers may be defined
XVisual	{on} | off	**UNIX systems only**, defines the visual identifier output for the current figure, you can define different bit depth properties if desired
XVisualMode	{auto} | manual	**UNIX systems only**, enables manual setting of visual mode defined in the Xvisual property

Table 2.4: Figure Callback Functions

Property Name	Legal Values/Types	Brief Description
CloseRequestFcn	function string or handle	Callback function routine that executes when a *close(fig_handle)* or close all command is issued, or when the figure is closed using the mouse or if the MATLAB session is closed
KeyPressFcn	function string or handle	Callback function that executes when a key is pressed within the figure window
ResizeFcn	function string or handle	Callback function routine that executes when the figure is resized by the user
WindowButtonDownFcn	function string or handle	Callback function routine that executes when mouse button is pressed within a figure window
WindowButtonMotionFcn	function string or handle	Callback function routine that executes when mouse moved within a figure window
WindowButtonUpFcn	function string or handle	Callback function routine that executes when mouse button is depressed within a figure window

2.3.2   Settings

Many of the property settings available for **Figure** objects are easy to understand and manipulate to achieve the desired behavior. For example the **Color** property simply sets the background color for the figure while the **ColorMap** property defines a lookup table of RGB color values that are used to map data values for **Surface**, **Image**, and **Patch** graphics objects. The following code example shows how these properties may be used to tailor the color output of your figure:

```
c = (0:255)./255;
f = figure;
set(f, 'color', [0 0 0]);
[x, y, z] = peaks(50);
surf(x, y, z);
cmap = [c; c; c]';
set(f, 'colormap', cmap);
```

The above example creates a figure with a black background and a grayscale rendering of the built-in surface function *peaks()*. Note that an alternative and generally easier way to define a grayscale colormap for a figure is to use the built-in colormap function as follows:

```
set(0, 'currentfigure', f);
colormap(gray(256));
```

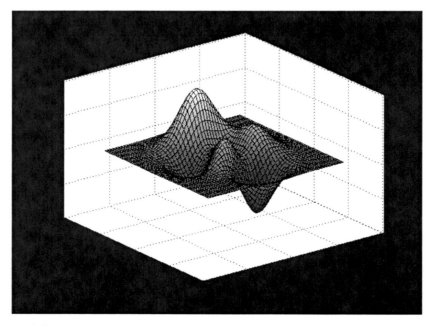

Figure 2.3 - Using the *set()* function to alter Figure Color and Colormap properties

There are several built-in color maps in MATLAB, the list below shows the name of each colormap that may be used directly with the *colormap()* function or when defining the colormap using the *set()* function to set the figure colormap property:

- Jet
- HSV
- Hot
- Cool
- Spring
- Summer
- Autumn
- Winter
- Gray
- Bone
- Copper
- Pink
- Lines

The number of colors defined for the colormap is the input argument when using the above list of predefined maps. For example, if you only want to display 8 colors on the surface of a plot using the Jet colormap, you can enter the following command:

```
colormap(jet(8));
```

Setting the colormap is especially important for defining image figures to ensure the image data is correctly displayed in the figure. The default colormap when a figure is instantiated is *jet(64)*. If you try to display a 256 level grayscale image with the default color map you will have a pseudo-color, 64 level, image that does not represent the original data correctly. This will be discussed further when GUI programming with images is covered in more detail.

Other important figure properties include **CurrentPoint, MenuBar, ToolBar, Name, NumberTitle, Pointer, PointerShapeCData, PointerShapeHotSpot, Position,** and **WindowStyle**. As mentioned in the property settings table, the **CurrentPoint** property may be used to return the mouse position within the figure window. When the **WindowButtonMotionFcn** callback function is not defined, then the **CurrentPoint** property is updated only when a mouse click occurs in the figure window. If you wish to track the position of the mouse as it moves within the figure without button clicks, you can define the **WindowButtonMotionFcn** and query the **CurrentPoint** property of the figure within the function.

Some application may require a figure window that shows graphic output only and you may not want the user to access the menu bar or tool bar. The **MenuBar** and **ToolBar** property allow you to disable these features of the figure such that only the graphic output portion of the figure window is displayed. You can also use the **WindowStyle** property in conjunction with the **Resize** property to create a non-resizable window that stays in focus above other MATLAB windows.

Pointer, **PointerShapeCData**, and **PointerShapeHotSpot** allow you to create your own mouse pointer for a figure and define the hot spot position of the pointer. You can also use the predefined pointer types as well. When defining the shape of a custom pointer, the following data value designators should be used for the 16x16 **PointerShapeCData** matrix:

- Black pixel = 1
- White Pixel = 2
- Transparent = Nan (not a number)

You can also create animated cursors by defining several shape matrices and periodically set the **Pointer** property with a new matrix in a repeating pattern.

The **Position** property is also very important for GUI development since it defines the physical location of the figure window on the display screen. Rather than allowing MATLAB to generate the initial position and size of a figure automatically, it is often advantageous to specify the location and size based on the display screen size parameters. For example, if you want to create a new figure window that is 400 x 400 pixels in area and opens in the center of the display screen, then you may use code similar to the following:

```
screen_size = get(0, 'ScreenSize');
hFig = figure('Position', [   screen_size(3)/2 - 200, ...
                              screen_size(4)/2 - 200, ...
                              400, 400 ]);
```

2.3.3   Callback Functions

Callback functions may be assigned to a figure using the following syntax:

```
figure('callback_function_type', @user_callback_function)
```

Callback function definitions require at least two input arguments to be passed from the source object to the function. The two input arguments are:

- Source handle of the object for the callback
- Event data from the object

The syntax for the callback function definition is as follows:

```
function user_callback_function(source, event_data)
```

where *source* and *event_data* are the required input arguments. For example, to define a callback function to track the motion of the mouse in a figure window you may generate code similar to the following:

```
function main_fcn
        % instantiate figure with callback function
        hFigure = figure(      'WindowButtonMotionFcn', ...
                            @hFigure_MotionFcn);


function hFigure_MotionFcn(hFigure, event_data)
        % get position of mouse
        mouse_pos = get(hFigure,'CurrentPoint')
```

Callback functions are not restricted to two inputs and often a third input parameter, *handles*, is passed to the function as well. Defining additional parameters for callback functions requires you to add the parameters using a cell array as follows:

```
        % instantiate figure with callback function and 2 user parameters
```

```
hFigure = figure(      'WindowButtonMotionFcn', ...
                       {@hFigure_MotionFcn, param1, param2});
```

The curly brackets are used to encapsulate the callback function name along with additional parameters you wish to pass to the function. The *source* and *event_data* parameters do not need to be explicitly defined.

Exercise 2.3: Creating Custom Figures Using Properties

Use the Figure properties to create a graphics output window with the following characteristics:

1. Set background color to black

2. Disable the **MenuBar** and **ToolBar**

3. Set the name of the figure to "Graphics Output Window" and make sure the Figure x number title property is not displayed

4. Set the cursor to the crosshair pointer

5. Use the **WindowButtonMotionFcn** callback function to track the cursor position and display the position of the mouse in a **UIControl** text object. Update the position of the mouse position text as the mouse moves.

Note: Use the *drawnow* MATLAB command directly after the figure is created to ensure the figure gets rendered before you use the *set()* function to change the properties. Some graphic properties may not be properly set if this command is not included.

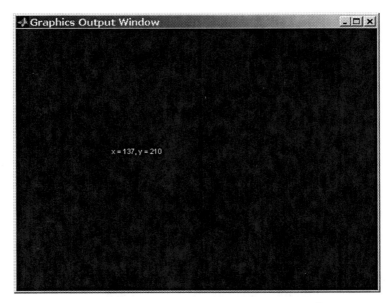

Figure 2.4 - Exercise 2.3 graphics output figure

Exercise 2.3 Solution:

```
% main function
function main_fcn

    % create figure
    hFigure = figure;
    % make sure figure is drawn before properties are set
    drawnow

    % create a text box ui control to display mouse position
    hText = uicontrol(hFigure,  'Style', 'text', ...
                                'BackgroundColor', [0 0 0], ...
                                'ForegroundColor', [1 1 1]);

    % set properties of figure and define mouse motion callback function
    set(    hFigure, ...
            'color', [0 0 0], ...
            'menubar', 'none', ...
            'toolbar', 'none', ...
            'name', 'Graphics Output Window', ...
            'numbertitle', 'off', ...
            'pointer', 'crosshair', ...
            'WindowButtonMotionFcn', {@hFigure_MotionFcn, hText});
```

```
% mouse motion callback function
function hFigure_MotionFcn(hFigure, event_data, hText)
      % get position of mouse
      mouse_pos = get(hFigure,'CurrentPoint');
   set(    hText, ...
            'Position', [mouse_pos(1) mouse_pos(2) 100 20], ...
            'String', ['x = ' num2str(mouse_pos(1)) ...
                    ', y = ' num2str(mouse_pos(2))]);
```

2.4   Axes Properties

Axes Objects also have many unique properties that are specifically useful for GUI development. The tables below list the Axes specific setting properties and callback function properties that are most useful for GUI development. The tables below are not a complete list of properties available for **Axes Objects** and you are encouraged to browse the MATLAB help pages for a more in depth description of all Axes properties available.

Table 2.5: Axes Property Settings

Property Name	Legal Values/Types	Brief Description
ActivePositionProperty	{outerposition} | position	Sets the position used by the resize function when the figure is resized
AmbientLightColor	ColorSpec	Defines a directionless, ambient, background light for a scene that shines uniformly on all current HG objects. Generally used for 3D plots where light shading is important
BeingDeleted	on | {off}	Determine if an HG object is currently being deleted from the axes
Box	on | {off}	Determines if the axes will be enclosed by a bounding rectangle (2D) or cube (3D). The plot command automatically enables the box property
CameraPosition	[x, y, z] axes coordinates	Defines the position of the camera using 3D coordinates, usually used for 3D plots to set the viewpoint
CameraPositionMode	{auto} | manual	Allows the user to set the camera properties when manual mode is set, otherwise MATLAB defines the viewpoint
CameraTarget	[x, y, z] axes coordinates	Defines the aiming point or direction in the axis where the camera points
CameraTargetMode	{auto} | manual	Manual mode allows user to define the

		CameraTarget
CameraUpVector	[x, y, z] axes coordinates	Defines the camera rotation around the viewing axis
CameraUpVectorMode	{auto} | manual	Manual mode allows user to select the CameraUpVector
CameraViewAngle	scalar greater than 0 and less than or equal to 180 (angle in degrees)	Defines the field of view of the camera using an angle value between 0 and 180 degrees
CameraViewAngleMode	{auto} | manual	Manual mode allows user to select the CameraViewAngle
Color	{none} | ColorSpec	Defines the background color of the axis, the default value is 'none' which allows the figure color to show through the axis
ColorOrder	m-by-3 matrix of RGB values	Defines the colors that plot commands will use for successive plots using the same axes
CurrentPoint	2-by-3 matrix	Returns the coordinates of the mouse with respect to the axes as a 3D line. This value is updated when a button click occurs.
DrawMode	{normal} | fast	Defines the object drawing method for the axes. Normal mode draws objects from back to front to handle hidden surfaces and object intersections. If the intended application only contains 2D information, then 'fast' mode may help increase drawing update speed.
FontAngle	{normal} | italic | oblique	Defines font angle for axes text
FontName	A name such as Courier or the string FixedWidth	Defines font name for axes text
FontSize	Font size specified in FontUnits such as point size, default is 12	Defines the font size for axes text
FontUnits	{points} | normalized | inches |centimeters | pixels	Defines the units used for the font size property
FontWeight	{normal} | bold | light | demi	Sets the weight of the font such as Bold
GridLineStyle	- | - -| {:} | -. | none	Specifies the line style to use for grid lines for the axes. In order from left to right of legal values, the line types are defined as: solid (-), dashed (--), dotted (:), dash-dot (-.), and 'none'.
Layer	{bottom} | top	Determines if axis lines will be drawn on top or bottom of plot data in the axes. This is useful for placing grid lines and other axis lines on images data.
LineStyleOrder	LineSpec (default: a solid line '-')	Similar to ColorOrder, this property defines the line styles that plot commands will cycle

		through when plotting on the same axes.
LineWidth	line width in points	Defines the width of axis lines in points, 0.5, 1, 2 , etc...
MinorGridLineStyle	- | - -| {:} | -. | none	Defines line style for minor grid lines
NextPlot	add | {replace} | replacechildren	Allows the user to define how plot objects are drawn onto the axis. 'Add' simply adds plot data on the current axes without resetting axes information or deleting previous plot data. 'Replace' resets the entire axes and 'ReplaceChildren' only removes child objects such as plot data, text objects, etc ...
OuterPosition	[left bottom width height]	Defines the outer boundary of the axes within the figure window. This is useful for providing enough edge margin when plot text labels are defined.
Position	[left bottom width height]	Defines the boundary of the plot axes. Setting this value to [0 0 1 1] using normalized units sets the axes to fill the entire figure window drawing area, this is useful for imaging applications.
Projection	{orthographic} | perspective	Defines the type of projection used when displaying 3D information. 'Perspective' provides depth information of 3D objects when viewed in 2D on the display.
Selected	on | {off}	Determines if current object that is selected will display selection handles on the object
SelectionHighlight	{on} | off	Determines if selected objects will be highlighted when selected
TickDir	{in} | out	Sets the direction of tick marks on the axis lines. 'In' points tick marks toward the center of the plot and 'out' towards the figure window boundary.
TickDirMode	{auto} | manual	MATLAB defaults to auto mode for tick direction, set this to manual if you wish to change the tick dir
TickLength	[2DLength 3DLength]	Sets the length of tick marks, the first element in the vector specifies tick lengths for 2D plots and the second for 3D plots.
Title	handle of text object	Defines the text title of the current axes. In general it is easier to use the *title* command to define the title.
UIContextMenu	handle of a uicontextmenu object	Defines a context menu that should be used for the axes when a right button click occurs.
Units	inches | centimeters | {normalized} | points | pixels | characters	Defines the units that will be used for the axes and is important to define this before setting the 'position' property or other properties that rely on the unit definition.
XAxisLocation	top | {bottom}	Sets the x axis to display on the top or bottom of the plot
YAxisLocation	right | {left}	Sets the y axis to display on the left or right of

		the plot
XColor, YColor, ZColor	ColorSpec	Defines the color of the x, y, and z axis lines of a plot
XDir, YDir, ZDir	{normal} | reverse	Sets the direction of increasing values of the axes. Using the 'reverse' value will flip the plot data that is displayed.
XGrid, YGrid, ZGrid	on | {off}	Enable or disable the grid lines for the x, y, and z axes
XLabel, YLabel, ZLabel	handle of text object	Defines the x, y, and z labels of axes, in general it is easier to use the *xlabel, ylabel, and zlabel* MATLAB commands to define the labels
XLim, YLim, ZLim	[minimum maximum]	Defines the minimum and maximum limits for the x, y, and z axes. This is useful when data covers a large range but only a certain portion is vital to be viewed on the plot. MATLAB defaults to automatic limit mode and scales the axes to cover all data.
XLimMode, YLimMode, ZLimMode	{auto} | manual	Enable or disable manual axes limit mode. When enabled, xlim, ylim, and zlim values are used to define the limits of the axes.
XMinorGrid, YMinorGrid, ZMinorGrid	on | {off}	Enable or disable the display of minor grid lines for the x, y, and z axes.
XScale, YScale, ZScale	{linear} | log	Sets the x, y, and z axes scale to logarithmic or linear.
XTick, YTick, ZTick	vector of data values locating tick marks	Defines the tick marks along the x, y, and z axes. The vector should contain monotonic values covering the desired range of tick mark values.
XTickLabel, YTickLabel, ZTickLabel	string	String values that define the tick mark labels for each axis, the default is numeric values
XTickMode, YTickMode, ZTickMode	{auto} | manual	Enable or disable manual tick mark mode
XTickLabelMode, YTickLabelMode, ZTickLabelMode	{auto} | manual	Enable or disable manual tick mark label mode

2.4.1 Axes Object Settings

Axes Objects contain the largest set of properties among all HG Objects and this provides versatility when defining how data is displayed and represented. **Axes Objects** are a vital part of GUI development since the display of data using plots and images must have one or more **Axes Objects** defined. Often times **Axes Objects** are integrated into the GUI layout design as a central data display element. Therefore, it is important to understand the details of Axes properties to optimize your target application.

Many property settings for **Axes Objects** are especially useful for 3D data plots. If your target application does not require the display of data using 3D plots, then you may not need to worry about camera settings, lighting, etc ... Also, if your application requires the display of image data, it is possible that axis lines, grids, tick marks, etc ... are not relevant to your application. In the following sections we will discuss a few examples that are presented to demonstrate how Axes properties may be used to generate an axes with a particular look and feel for a 2D graphics application, a 3D graphics application, and an imaging application.

2.4.1.1   Axes Properties For 2D Plot Applications

You are likely familiar with the MATLAB plot command and the default Axes produced for a typical 2D data plot. In many GUI applications, the standard default characteristics may not provide the desired look and feel you want the user to experience when viewing or interacting with a 2D plot. Changing the appearance using different color schemes and plot line types can enhance your GUI application. Some properties that affect the appearance of a 2D plot are:

- **Box**
- **Color, ColorOrder**
- **FontAngle, FontName, FontSize, FontWeight**
- **LineStyleOrder, LineWidth, GridLineStyle, MinorGridLineStyle**
- **NextPlot**
- **OuterPosition, Position**
- **TickDir, TickDirMode, TickLength**
- **Title, XLabel, YLabel**
- **XColor, YColor**
- **XGrid, YGrid**

The following exercise demonstrates how to manipulate Axes properties to create specialized 2D **Axes Objects**.

Exercise 2.4: Axes Properties For 2D Graphics Applications

Create an **Axes Object** that will be used to display plot data similar to an oscilloscope display screen. The **Axes Object** should be created with the following parameters:

1. Background color or figure and axes should black

2. Axis and grid lines should be dark green

3. Make sure plot has a boundary box

4. Line plot color should be light green

5. X and Y grid lines should be enabled and displayed as dashed lines

6. Minor X and Y grids should be enabled an use dotted line style

7. Set the NextPlot property to preserve the Axes properties and replace the previous plot data when the plot is updated

8. Set the title as 'Oscilloscope Display', the x-axis as 'Time', and the y-axis as 'Voltage' using the title, xlabel, and ylabel commands respectively.

9. Finally, plot an interesting function to test the output of the new axes style

Exercise 2.4 Solution:

```
% exercise 2.4a - Axes Properties For 2D Graphics Application
function main_fcn

    % initialize colors
    back_color = [0 0 0];
    axis_color = [0 0.6 0];
    plot_data_color = [0.5 1 0.5];

    % create figure
    hFigure = figure;
    % make sure figure is drawn before properties are set
    drawnow

    % set properties of figure and define mouse motion callback function
    set(    hFigure, ...
            'color', back_color, ...
```

```
            'name', 'Oscilloscope Display', ...
            'numbertitle', 'off');


% create an axes object
hAxes = axes;


% set properties of the axes

set(     hAxes, ...
            'box', 'on', ...
            'color', back_color, ...
            'colororder', plot_data_color, ...
            'xcolor', axis_color, ...
            'ycolor', axis_color, ...
            'xgrid', 'on', ...
            'ygrid', 'on', ...
            'xminorgrid', 'on', ...
            'yminorgrid', 'on', ...
            'gridlinestyle', '--', ...
            'minorgridlinestyle', ':', ...
            'nextplot', 'replacechildren');


 % define axes labels
 title('Oscilloscope Output', 'color', axis_color);
 xlabel('Time', 'color', axis_color);
 ylabel('Voltage', 'color', axis_color);


 % plot a Fourier series function approximation for a square wave
 t = 1:0.01:4;
 v = 0.5 + ...
     2/pi.*sin(2*pi.*t) + ...
     2/3/pi.*sin(6*pi.*t) + ...
     2/5/pi.*sin(10*pi.*t) + ...
     2/7/pi.*sin(14*pi.*t);


 plot(hAxes,t,v);
```

The output generated from this example is shown in the figure below:

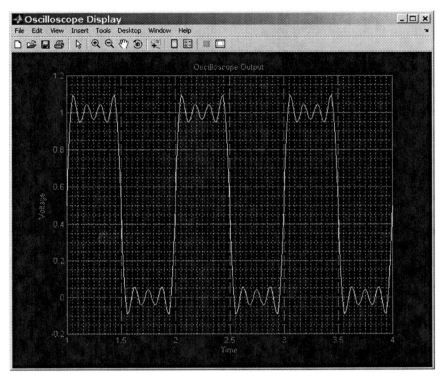

Figure 2.5 - Exercise 2.4 output figure

2.4.1.2   Axes Properties For 3D Plot Applications

As previously mentioned, 3D plot applications generally require a larger set of property controls as compared with 2D applications. Axes properties that are specifically useful for 3D plot applications are listed below:

- **AmbientLightColor**
- **CameraPosition**
- **CameraPositionMode**
- **CameraTarget**
- **CameraTargetMode**
- **CameraUpVector**
- **CameraUpVectorMode**
- **CameraViewAngle**

- **CameraViewAngleMode**
- **Projection**
- **ZColor, ZGrid, ZMinorGrid, etc ...**

The camera properties allow you to define precisely how the user will visualize the 3D data within the plot and may be used to perform complex manipulations of the user viewpoint. These properties are very effective for creating animations that 'fly' the user through the data or rotate the 3D plot over time to circumnavigate surfaces and volumes.

Exercise 2.4b demonstrates the use of the **CameraPosition** property for 3D plot viewpoint manipulation. The camera properties must first be set to manual mode using the respective mode property controls. For example, to enable manual settings for the **CameraPosition** property, you must first set **CameraPositionMode** to 'manual'. Once the mode is set, you can modify the CameraPosition to establish a new viewpoint of the plot scene. Exercise 2.4b changes the **CameraPosition** within a *for* loop along with the *drawnow* command to animate the viewpoint of the plot.

Exercise 2.5: Axes Properties For 3D Plot Applications

Create a figure window and axes with the following properties:

1. Figure background color should be set to black
2. Set the figure colormap to use the *jet* map with 256 shades
3. Set figure name to something like '3D Data Display' and disable the number title
4. Axis line colors should be set to white
5. Set CameraPositionMode to 'manual' and initialize the position to [0 0 0]
6. Use the title, xlabel, ylabel, and zlabel functions to label the axes

Once the figure and axes are created, generate an interesting 2D surface function and plot the surface using the *surf( )* function. Next, change the position of the camera using the **CameraPosition** property within a *for* loop to create an animated view of the 3D plot.

Note, make sure you include the *drawnow* command within the *for* loop to make sure the figure and axes get updated with each iteration.

Exercise 2.5 Solution:

```
% exercise 2.4b - Axes Properties For 3D Graphics Application
function main_fcn

    % initialize colors
    back_color = [0 0 0];
    axis_color = [1 1 1];

    % create figure
    hFigure = figure;
    % make sure figure is drawn before properties are set
    drawnow

    % set properties of figure and define mouse motion callback function
    set(    hFigure, ...
            'color', back_color, ...
            'colormap', colormap(jet(256)), ...
            'name', '3D Data Display', ...
            'numbertitle', 'off');

    % create an axes object
    hAxes = axes;

    % set properties of the axes

    set(    hAxes, ...
            'box', 'on', ...
            'color', back_color, ...
            'xcolor', axis_color, ...
            'ycolor', axis_color, ...
            'cameraposition', [0 0 0], ...
            'camerapositionmode', 'manual', ...
            'nextplot', 'replacechildren');

    % define axes labels
    title('Diffraction Pattern From Rectangular Apertures', 'color',
axis_color);
    xlabel('X', 'color', axis_color);
```

```
ylabel('Y', 'color', axis_color);
ylabel('Z', 'color', axis_color);

% plot of diffraction pattern from 2 rectangular apertures close
% together
x = -3*pi:0.1:3*pi;
y = -3*pi:0.1:3*pi;
d = pi;
c = 0;
[m, n] = size(x)

for j = 1:n
   for i = 1:n

    if x(i) ~= 0
        xt = sin(x(i))^2/x(i)^2 + sin(x(i)+d)^2/(x(i)+d)^2;
    else
        xt = 1;
    end

    if y(j) ~= 0
        yt = sin(y(j))^2/y(j)^2;
    else
        yt = 1;
    end

    f(i,j) = abs(xt * yt);
   end
end

% plot the 2D surface of f(i,j) using surf( )
surf(hAxes, x, y, f, 'Linestyle', 'none');

% animate the cameraposition property to change the view of the 3D
pos_max = 100;

for i = 0:pos_max
        set(hAxes, 'cameraposition', [i i 10-i/20]);
        drawnow
end

for i = pos_max:-2:-pos_max
        set(hAxes, 'cameraposition', [i pos_max 10-pos_max/20]);
```

```
        drawnow
end
```

The images below are snap shots of the display output from the exercise 2.5 example solution above at three points during the animation sequence:

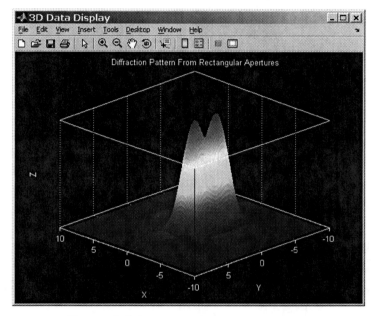

Figure 2.6 Exercise 2.5 output view 1

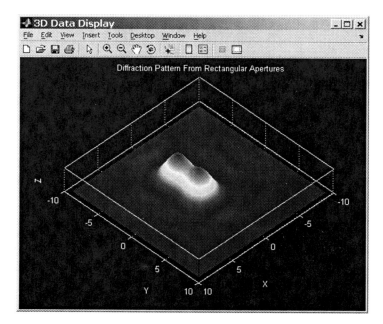

Figure 2.7 - Exercise 2.5 output view 2

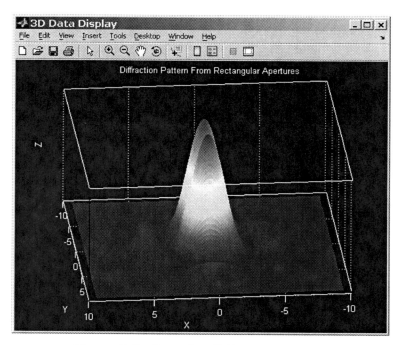

Figure 2.8 - Exercise 2.5 output view 3

2.4.1.3   *Axes Properties For Imaging Applications*

Imaging applications often require special axes formatting based on the intended use of the image information. For example, digital photograph or video display applications may require the removal of axis lines and other 2D plot information that may not be desirable in the imaging figure window. Also, mapping image pixel information to screen pixels is important if you wish avoid scaling artifacts in images when MATLAB automatically formats the current figure and axes sizes. Several axes properties allow you to establish an image output display window that maps image pixels to screen pixels as a one-to-one ratio.

Conversely, imaging applications that use image information for data analysis may benefit greatly by incorporating X and Y position information on the axes as well specifying grid, ticks, and labeling information.

Setting Up A Figure and Axes For Digital Photos or Video

A combination of Figure properties and Axes properties can be used to set the Figure and Axes size equivalent to the image size you wish to display. MATLAB has a built in **Image Object** that is part of the **Core Objects** under the Axes hierarchy and by default MATLAB chooses the format of the Axes when the **Image Object** is called. The following properties should be used to override the default image display format to show the image with the correct aspect ratio and pixel scale on the display:

Figure Properties

   1. Set 'Units' = 'Pixels'

   2. Set 'Position' = [x y N M] , where x and y are the starting pixel position on the display for the figure and N = width and M = height in pixels of the image to display

Axes Properties

   1. Set 'Units' = 'Pixels'

   2. Set 'Position' = [1 1 N M]

   3. Set 'NextPlot' = 'ReplaceChildren' , this property preserves the Axes properties so that the Image command does not force the default settings

4. Set 'XLimMode' = 'Manual' and 'YLimMode' = 'Manual' , this allows you to set the X and Y limits of the axis to fit the image size

5. Set 'XLim' = [1 N] and 'YLim' = [1 M] , these settings force axis size to the image size in pixels

6. Set 'YDir' = 'Reverse' , by default y axes coordinates start in the lower left corner however images generally define the start of the y axis in the top left corner. Reversing the y direction of the axis prevents the image from displaying upside down.

The settings listed above are useful for displaying images that you wish to map one-to-one to the display pixels. You will notice that when you try to maximize or resize the figure window, the image does not scale with the figure size. The background color for the figure fills the area beyond the extent of the image data. You can still zoom in on the image using the toolbar zoom icons, however the image still only displays content defined by the **XLim** and **YLim** constraints.

The **XLim** and **YLim** properties are very useful for controlling the scaling or zooming of images within the figure window. If you set the limits to half the size of the image such that **XLim** = [1 N/2] and **YLim** = [1 M/2], the image will be scaled in the figure such that you will see the top left quadrant of the image at 2x zoom. The combination of the **XLim**, **YLim**, and **Position** properties of the axis and the **Position** property of the figure can be used to scale and zoom images depending on the figure window size or mouse button clicks.

Exercise 2.6: Axes Properties For Imaging: Photos and Video

1. Read an image file using the *imread()* function

2. Get the image size width and height in pixels using the *size()* function

3. Create a figure window that has the same size of the image in pixels

4. Create an axis that has the same size as the image in pixels and set the **XLim** and **YLim** properties to the size of the image

5. Use the **NextPlot** axes property to prevent the *image()* function from resetting the axes properties

6. Display the image by using the *image()* function

Exercise 2.6 Solution:

```matlab
% exercise 2.4c - Axes Properties For Imaging Applications: Digital Photos
and Video
function main_fcn

    % initialize colors
    back_color = [1 1 0];

    % open image file
    img = imread('exer_2.3e_image.jpg', 'jpg');

    % get image width and height information
    % N = width
    % M = height
    % C = 3 for RGB color images
    [M, N, C] = size(img);

    % create figure
    hFigure = figure(1);

    % create an axes object
    hAxes = axes;

    % set figure properties
    set(    hFigure, ...
            'color', back_color, ...
            'name', 'Image Display', ...
            'units', 'pixels', ...
            'position', [100 100 N M], ...
            'numbertitle', 'off');

    % set properties of the axes
    set(    hAxes, ...
            'box', 'off', ...
            'tickdir', 'out', ...
            'units', 'pixels', ...
            'position', [1 1 N M], ...
            'nextplot', 'replacechildren', ...
            'XLimMode', 'manual', ...
            'XLim', [1 N], ...
            'YLimMode', 'manual', ...
            'YLim', [1 M], ...
```

```
        'ydir', 'reverse');


    % place image in hAxes
    hImage = image(img);
```

Figure 2.9 below shows the image figure window from the example solution script. Note that the edges of the image extend to the edges of the figure active region and the aspect ratio is preserved, in this case the image has a portrait orientation.

Figure 2.10 shows the resulting figure window if you use the *image()* function and allow MATLAB to automatically format the axis and figure. In this case, the plot axes are displayed, the image is scaled to fit the default figure size, and the aspect ratio is not correct and causes the image to appear stretched.

Figure 2.9 - Exercise 2.6 output, setting an Axes for images

Figure 2.10 - Image output Axes resulting from *image()* function call

Setting Up Axes For Image Data Analysis

Many imaging applications require image data to show axis information and grid lines to allow the user to analyze the coordinates of the data with ease. Contrary to the requirements for viewing photographs or video, the visual appearance of the image itself may not be as important as the data values at specific locations in the image. By default, MATLAB displays image data within a scaled axes object and you may not need to set additional properties. However, if you wish to display grid lines on the image for more detailed analysis, you need to set the **Layer** property of the axes to *'Top'*. By default this is set to *'Bottom'* and images are drawn on top of tick marks and grid lines. The following example shows image data with the **Layer** property set to *'Top'* :

```
% create an image using the peaks() function
img = peaks(256);


% create figure
```

```
hFigure = figure(1);

% create an axes object
hAxes = axes;

% set figure properties
set(   hFigure, 'name', 'Image Display', 'numbertitle', 'off');

% place image in hAxes
hImage = imagesc(img);

% set properties of the axes
set(   hAxes, 'Layer', 'Top', 'XGrid', 'On', 'YGrid', 'On');
```

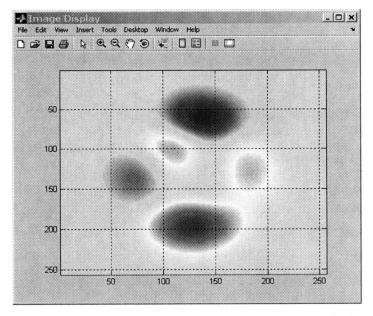

Figure 2.11 - Setting an Axes for image data analysis

2.4.2 Axes Object Callback Functions

The axes callback functions are the same as those defined for all **HG Objects** and are described in section 2.2 and will not be covered here.

2.5 Axes Child Object Properties

As demonstrated in figure 2.1 at the beginning of this chapter, there are many **HG Objects** that are children of **Axes Objects** and they provide all the necessary detailed graphics functionality for an application. For example, the *image()* function introduced in the previous section produces a child object of an axes that contains image data. An **Axes Object** must exist for an **Image Object** to exist. This section briefly introduces you to **Axes Child Objects** and their properties that are useful for GUI applications.

2.5.1 Core Objects

The **Core Child Objects** for axes are as follows:

- Image
- Light
- Line
- Patch
- Rectangle
- Surface
- Text

2.5.1.1 Image Objects

The *image()* and *imagesc()* functions produce **Image Objects** and automatically generate a default Figure and Axes if they do not currently exist. There are several properties of **Image Objects** that are very useful for GUI development that includes **AlphaData**, **AlphaDataMapping**, **CData**, **XData**, and **YData**.

AlphaData and **AlphaDataMapping** allow you to define a transparency mapping for the image data and is useful for image overlay and data fusion. Also, this feature can be used to dynamically fade the image data for interesting visual effects.

CData represents the actual image data, or pixel values, for the image object. This data is an NxMx1 matrix for monochrome image data and NxMx3 RGB matrix if the data represents a color image. If you wish to update an image in a figure and have defined an **Image Object**, you can simply set the new image data of the object with the **CData** property as follows:

```
% initialize image object
hImage = image(image_frame1);


% update image data displayed in figure
set(hImage, 'CData', image_frame2);
```

This method of updating an image display window is very fast since there are no calls to instantiate a figure window, axes, or other image object information. Using the **CData** property is essential for developing real-time video applications where the goal is to achieve a target frame rate. Calling the *image()* function repeatedly is very inefficient and should be avoided.

The **XData** and **YData** properties represent the placement of image data along the x and y axes respectively. These properties are very useful for scaling the size of an image within an **Axes Object**. For example, if you have an image that has a size of 256x256 pixels but only wish to display the image in a 100x100 pixel region of the **Axes Object**, then you can set the **XData** and **YData** properties as follows:

```
% update image xdata and ydata scaling for display
set(hImage, 'XData', [1 100], 'YData', [1 100]);
```

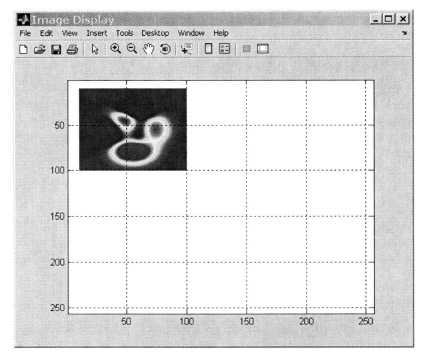

Figure 2.12 - Using XData and YData Axes properties for image scaling

2.5.1.2   Light Objects

Light Objects are generally used for 3D or volumetric plot applications to illuminate surface contours. The most important properties of **Light Objects** are **Color, Position,** and **Style**. You can simply set the color of the light using a 3x1 RGB vector. The **Style** property can either be set to 'infinity' or 'local'. The default **Style** sets the light source at infinity and the illumination is directed toward the position specified using the **Position** property. When **Style** is set to 'local', the **Position** property specifies the location of the light source.

2.5.1.3   Line Objects

Line Objects are mainly used to generate graphical plots for 2D and 3D functions and/or arbitrary line graphics within an axis. A **Line Object** can represent single line segment, a series of lines segments, or a matrix of line segments. The **XData, YData,** and **ZData** properties are used to define the data for a **Line Object**. For 2D lines, only **XData** and **YData** are used with the **ZData** property left as an empty matrix. 3D lines use the **ZData** property for the z-axis data. The following simple example shows how a **Line Object** may be used to generate plots of functions:

```
hLine1 = line(0:0.1:10, sin(0:0.1:10));
hLine2 = line(0:0.01:10, cos((0:0.01:10).^2));
```

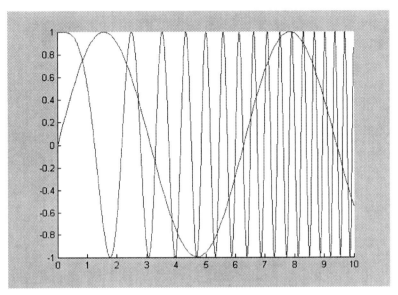

Figure 2.13 - Mulitple line objects using *line()* function

The figure above shows the resulting plot from the two *line()* function calls. Each *line()* function call contains a series of line segments defined by **XData** and **YData**. One difference between creating a 2D plot with the *plot()* function as compared to the *line()* function is that, by default, the *plot()* function will erase the current Axes information and any plot data that is displayed unless the **NextPlot** property has been set to 'Add' or 'ReplaceChildren'.

There are several unique properties available for **Line Objects** that control their appearance: **LineStyle**, **LineWidth**, **Marker**, **MarkerEdgeColor**, **MarkerFaceColor**, and **MarkerSize**. The names of each of these properties give you a sense of their respective function. You are encouraged to investigate these properties further by using the *Handle Graphics Property Browser*.

Several built-in MATLAB functions return **Line Object** handles that may be stored for property manipulation at a later time. For example, the *plot()* function actually returns a handle to a **Line Object**. Therefore, the *plot()* function may be used to initialize a 2D plot while providing an object handle for updating line data or other line properties as necessary. The following code segment demonstrates the use of the *plot()* function to generate a handle to a **Line Object** and manipulate the line's data to animate the plot:

```
% initialize function and plot
 t = 1:0.01:4;
 v = 0.5 + ...
     2/pi.*sin(2*pi.*t) + ...
     2/3/pi.*sin(6*pi.*t) + ...
     2/5/pi.*sin(10*pi.*t) + ...
     2/7/pi.*sin(14*pi.*t);

hLine = plot(t,v);

% generate dynamic function and update line data in plot
for i = 0:0.1:2*pi

    v = 0.5 + ...
        2/pi.*sin(2*pi.*t) + ...
        2/3/pi.*sin(6*pi.*t + i) + ...
        2/5/pi.*sin(10*pi.*t) + ...
        2/7/pi.*sin(14*pi.*t + i);

    % update the Y axis data in hLine handle object
    set( hLine, 'YData', v);

    drawnow; % update figure graphics
end
```

This example alters the phase of two sinusoidal terms in a Fourier series within a *for* loop to create a dynamic function. Only the **YData** property of the *hLine* handle object needs to be updated for the plot to show an animation of the function. This method of updating plot data is much faster than calling the *plot()* function within the *for* loop and is very important for developing real-time GUIs involving dynamic plots.

2.5.1.4 Patch Objects

Patch Objects are low-level graphics primitives that define individual or sets of 2D or 3D polygons. Each polygon object may be defined using a set of vertices and faces. The vertices define the vertex points for a polygon and the face values represent the order of the vertex connection points for a polygon. **Patch Objects** have several properties that control the transparency, or alpha data, color, lighting, and specular appearance of polygons when rendered.

Polygon arrays allow complex rendering of 2D or 3D objects and can also be used to create custom GUI interface objects. The example below demonstrates the use of **Patch Objects** to create a 3D pyramid object that changes height and transparency over time and uses the **FaceColor** property to create smooth, interpolated, color faces:

Example 2.1: Patch Objects

```
clear
clf

% define patch data using vertices and faces
% the vertices and faces define a pyramid object
% vertices
v(:,1) = [-1 -1 0];
v(:,2) = [1 -1 0];
v(:,3) = [1 1 0];
v(:,4) = [-1 1 0];
v(:,5) = [0 0 0];
v = v'

% faces
f(:,1) = [1 2 3 4];
f(:,2) = [1 2 5 1];
f(:,3) = [2 3 5 2];
f(:,4) = [3 4 5 3];
f(:,5) = [4 1 5 4];
f = f'

% faces
fc(:,1) = [0 0 0.5];
fc(:,2) = [0 0.6 0];
fc(:,3) = [0.7 0 0];
fc(:,4) = [0 0.6 0.8];
fc(:,5) = [0 0 0];
fc = fc'

% initial alpha transparency
fa = 1;

% create patch object
```

```matlab
hPatch = patch( 'Vertices', v, ...
                'Faces', f, ...
                'FaceVertexCData', fc, ...
                'FaceVertexAlphaData', fa, ...
                'FaceColor', 'interp', ...
                'FaceAlpha', 'flat');

view(3);  % default to 3D plot view
set(gca, 'ZLim', [0 6]); % set z axis range

 %generate dynamic function and update line data in plot
 for i = 0:0.02:2*pi

    % change face alpha transparency values
    fa = 0.5+0.5*sin(2*i);

    % change pyramid height
    v(5,:) = [0 0 i]';

    % update the hPatch face alpha vales to change transparency
    set( hPatch,     'Vertices', v, ...
                     'FaceVertexAlphaData', fa, ...
                     'FaceAlpha', 'flat');

    drawnow; % update figure graphics
end
```

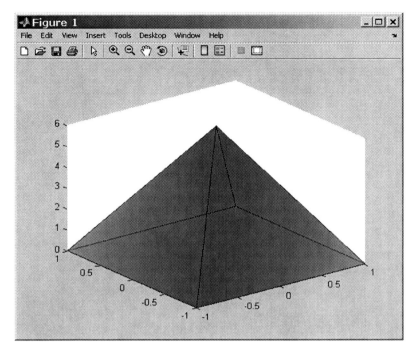

Figure 2.14 - Example 2.1 output, Patch Objects

2.5.1.5 Rectangle Objects

Rectangle Objects are simple graphics primitives that allow you to draw a rectangle within an **Axes Object** specified by the **Position** property. The **Curvature** property allows you to specify both horizontal and vertical curvature values for the corners of the rectangle providing rounded edges. **Rectangle Objects** are useful as 2D bounding boxes for information and can also be used as GUI interface objects as well. The following example demonstrates the **Curvature** property by creating a rectangle that morphs into a circle based on the position of the mouse pointer within the figure:

Example 2.2: Rectangle Objects

```
function main
    global N
    global M


    N=500;
    M=500;


    hFigure = figure(1);
```

```
set(hFigure, 'Units', 'Pixels', ...
            'Position', [100 100 N M]);


handles.hAxes = axes(   'tickdir', 'out', ...
                'units', 'pixels', ...
                'position', [1 1 N M], ...
                'nextplot', 'replacechildren', ...
                'XLimMode', 'manual', ...
                'XLim', [1 N], ...
                'YLimMode', 'manual', ...
                'YLim', [1 M]);



% create rectangle object
handles.hRect = rectangle(  'Position', [100 100 300 300], ...
                            'EdgeColor', [0 0 0], ...
                            'FaceColor', [0.5 0.2 0.2], ...
                            'LineWidth', 2);


set(hFigure, 'WindowButtonMotionFcn', {@hFigure_MotionFcn, handles});

% mouse motion callback function
function hFigure_MotionFcn(hFigure, event_data, handles)
    global N
    global M

    % get position of mouse
        mouse_pos = get(hFigure,'CurrentPoint');

    % set curvature of rectangle object based on mouse position
    set(handles.hRect, ...
        'Curvature', ...
        [1-abs(mouse_pos(1)-N/2)/N*2 1-abs(mouse_pos(2)-M/2)/M*2]);

    drawnow;
```

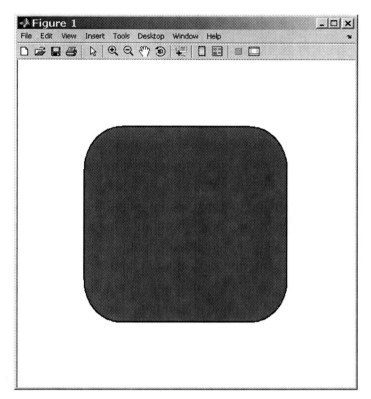

Figure 2.15 - Example 2.2 output, Rectangle Objects

2.5.1.6   Surface Objects

Two-dimensional functions represent surfaces that you can visualize using **Surface Objects**. These objects have very similar appearance, lighting, transparency, and specular properties as compared to **Patch Objects** since they essentially represent a matrix of 3D rectangular patches. The **CData** and **CDataMapping** properties may be used to map image or texture data to **Surface Objects**. The **MeshStyle** property determines if a 2D mesh will be drawn over the surface and may be defined for row or column direction only if desired.

The following example demonstrates a **Surface Object** with a dynamic 2D sinusoidal surface function. The **AlphaData** property is used to render the surface transparency starting from fully transparent for the first iterations of the loop and slowly transitioning to opaque at the end of the loop.

```
function surface_animation

    N=500;
    M=500;

    hFigure = figure(1);
    set(hFigure, 'Units', 'Pixels', ...
                 'Position', [100 100 N M], ...
                 'RendererMode', 'manual', ...
                 'Renderer', 'opengl');

    handles.hAxes = axes;


    % create surface object
    x = -pi:0.1:pi;
    [d xsize] = size(x);

    for y = 1:xsize
        f(:,y) = cos(y/xsize*pi) + sin(x);
    end

    % alpha data
    a = f;            % create matrix same size as function f
    a(:,:) = 0;       % set transparency to 0

    handles.hSurface = surface(  'XData', x, ...
                                 'YData', (1:xsize)./xsize.*6.*pi, ...
                                 'ZData', f, ...
                                 'CData', f, ...
                                 'LineStyle', 'none', ...
                                 'FaceAlpha', 'flat', ...
                                 'AlphaData', a, ...
                                 'AlphaDataMapping', 'none');
    view(3);

    % dynamic function loop
    for j=0:0.3:10

        % update surface function
        for y = 1:xsize
            f(:,y) = cos(y/xsize*pi+j) + sin(x+j);
        end
```

```
        % update transparency matrix
        a(:,:) = j/10;

        % update Zdata and AlphaData of surface
        set(handles.hSurface, 'ZData', f, 'AlphaData', a);

        drawnow;
    end
```

2.5.1.7 Text Objects

Text information is often a key component of GUI interfaces for labeling controls, graphics, and plots, displaying data, and providing feedback to user. Often times you may wish to provide text information within a figure or axis for your GUI applications. **Text Objects** provide you with the ability to display standard text complete with common parameters such as font size and font type within an **Axes Object**. Since **Text Objects** are children of **Axes Objects**, an axis must exist for a **Text Object** to display in a figure.

Properties such as **Color, FontAngle, FontName, FontSize, FontWeight, HorizontalAlignment, VerticalAlignment**, and **Rotation** determine the basic appearance of a **Text Object**. **Text Objects** are contained within a bounding rectangle and this bounding region can be read using the **Extent** property and is useful for aligning several objects or using them as interactive controls. Other properties that control the appearance of the bounding rectangle include: **BackgroundColor, EdgeColor, LineStyle**, and **LineWidth**. The **String** property sets the contents of the text string that will be displayed by the object while the **Position** property defines the location in x, y, z space.

In addition to displaying standard text information, **Text Objects** may also be used to generate TeX or LaTeX format strings for displaying mathematical formulae in symbolic notation. **Text Objects** may also be used interactively as a GUI control objects if desired. Although, as you will see in section 2.6, **UIControl Objects** also provide a **Text Object** that may be more appropriate for displaying text information depending on the application. The following exercise introduces you to the use of **Text Objects** for displaying text and mathematical notation using LaTeX strings and as interactive controls.

Exercise 2.7: Using Text Objects As Interactive Controls

The main goal is to create a figure that will display two text strings that prompt the user to select one of the two text strings to display one of two predetermined functions. Two **Axes Objects** should be used: One as the background of the figure for the **Text Objects** and one to plot functions. The background axes should have a callback function defined for mouse motion to detect if the mouse position is within the **Text Object** boundaries. If the mouse is within either of the **Text Object** regions, then the **Text Object** should change color to indicate the text is currently selected and the appropriate function should be plotted within the second axes.

1. Create a Figure with the dimensions 500 x 500 pixels

2. Create an **Axes Object** with the same dimensions and set the following properties:

    a. Background color should be black

    b. The Axes should fill the entire figure area and not display tick marks

3. Initialize two separate one dimensional functions that will be plotted in the application

4. Create two text objects with the following properties:

    a. Set the position such that the **Text Objects** are located in the top half of the figure window and will not overlap when displayed in the figure

    b. Set the font to Arial, 10 points, and use the Latex interpreter to display each mathematical function in its proper form

    c. Set the string properties to 'Plot Function: ... *Latex string ...*'

    d. Set the color to [0.9 0.8 0.7]

5. Create a second **Axes Object** for plotting the functions. Set the position and size of the second axes to occupy the lower half of the figure window.

6. Create a **WindowButtonMotionFcn** callback function to detect the mouse position and determine if the current position is within the **Text Object** 'Extent' regions. Set the color of the **Text Objects** to [1 1 1] when the mouse is within the region to show selection of the plot function. Update the plot in the second axes if either of the **Text Objects** is selected.

Exercise 2.7 Solution:

```
function interactive_text

    global N
    global M
    global text_select_color
    global text_color

    N=500;
    M=500;
    text_select_color = [1 1 1];
    text_color = [0.9 0.8 0.7];

    % create functions
    handles.w = -4:0.06:4;
    handles.f(:,1) = sin(pi.*handles.w)./(pi.*handles.w);
    handles.f(:,2) = sin(pi.*handles.w).^2./(pi.*handles.w).^2;

    hFigure = figure(1);
    set(hFigure, 'Units', 'Pixels', ...
                 'Position', [100 100 N M]);

    handles.hAxes = axes(    'Color', [0 0 0], ...
                             'tickdir', 'out', ...
                             'units', 'pixels', ...
                             'position', [1 1 N M], ...
                             'nextplot', 'replacechildren', ...
                             'XLimMode', 'manual', ...
                             'XLim', [1 N], ...
                             'YLimMode', 'manual', ...
                             'YLim', [1 M]);

    % create text objects for menu
    handles.text1 = text(    'Position', [100 M-100], ...
                             'BackgroundColor', [0 0 0], ...
                             'Color', text_color, ...
                             'FontName', 'Arial', ...
                             'FontSize', 10, ...
                             'FontUnits', 'pixels', ...
                             'Interpreter', 'Latex', ...
                             'String', 'Plot Function:
$$\frac{sin(\omega\pi)}{(\omega\pi)}$$', ...
```

```
                                   'Units', 'Pixels');


    handles.text2 = text(    'Position', [100 M-150], ...
                             'BackgroundColor', [0 0 0], ...
                             'Color', text_color, ...
                             'FontName', 'Arial', ...
                             'FontSize', 10, ...
                             'FontUnits', 'pixels', ...
                             'Interpreter', 'Latex', ...
                             'String', 'Plot Function:
$$\frac{sin^2(\omega\pi)}{\omega^2\pi^2}$$', ...
                             'Units', 'Pixels');


    handles.hAxes2 = axes(   'units', 'pixels', ...
                             'position', [30 30 N-60 M/2-60], ...
                             'nextplot', 'replacechildren', ...
                             'YLimMode', 'manual', ...
                             'YLim', [-0.2 1], ...
                             'XColor', [1 1 1], ...
                             'YColor', [1 1 1]);


    set(hFigure, 'WindowButtonMotionFcn', {@hFigure_MotionFcn, handles});
    set(hFigure, 'WindowButtonDownFcn', {@hFigure_MotionFcn, handles});


% mouse motion callback function
 function hFigure_MotionFcn(hFigure, event_data, handles)
     global N
     global M
     global text_select_color
     global text_color


    % get position of mouse
        mouse_pos = get(hFigure,'CurrentPoint');


    % check if mouse is within Text Object regions
    text1_region = get(handles.text1, 'Extent');
    text2_region = get(handles.text2, 'Extent');
    %text1_region


    if mouse_pos(1)>=text1_region(1) & ...
        mouse_pos(2)>=text1_region(2) & ...
        mouse_pos(1)<=(text1_region(1)+text1_region(3)) & ...
        mouse_pos(2)<=(text1_region(2)+text1_region(4))
```

```
        set(hFigure, 'CurrentAxes', handles.hAxes);
        set(handles.text1, 'FontWeight', 'Bold', 'Color',
text_select_color);

        % plot function 1
        set(hFigure, 'CurrentAxes', handles.hAxes2);
        plot(handles.w, handles.f(:,1));

    else
        set(hFigure, 'CurrentAxes', handles.hAxes);
        set(handles.text1, 'FontWeight', 'Normal', 'Color', text_color);
    end

    if mouse_pos(1)>=text2_region(1) & ...
        mouse_pos(2)>=text2_region(2) & ...
        mouse_pos(1)<=(text2_region(1)+text2_region(3)) & ...
        mouse_pos(2)<=(text2_region(2)+text2_region(4))

        set(hFigure, 'CurrentAxes', handles.hAxes);
        set(handles.text2, 'FontWeight', 'Bold', 'Color',
text_select_color);

        % plot function 2
        set(hFigure, 'CurrentAxes', handles.hAxes2);
        plot(handles.w, handles.f(:,2));

    else
        set(hFigure, 'CurrentAxes', handles.hAxes);
        set(handles.text2, 'FontWeight', 'Normal', 'Color', text_color);
    end

    drawnow;
```

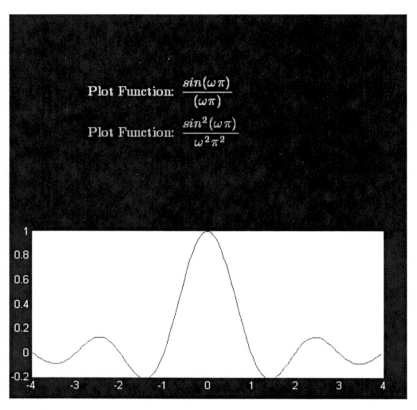

Figure 2.16 - Exercise 2.7 output, Text Objects as Interactive Controls

2.5.2   Plot Objects

MATLAB provides several families of **Plot Objects** that may be used to display data. Each **Plot Object** is categorized into the following series or groups and uses the associated general function calls to generate each type of **Plot Object**:

Table 2.6: Plot Objects

Plot Object Family	Associated Function Calls
AreaSeries	*area()*
BarSeries	*bar()*
ContourGroup	*contour(), contour3(), contourc(), contourf (), contourslice()*
ErrorBarSeries	*errorbar()*
LineSeries	*plot(), plot3(), line(), loglog(), semilogx(), semilogy(), plotyy(), subplot(), stem()*
QuiverGroup	*quiver(), quiver3()*
ScatterGroup	*scatter(), scatter3(), plotmatrix()*
StairSeries	*stairs()*
StemSeries	*stem(), stem3()*
SurfacePlot	*surf(), surfc(), surfl(), surface(), mesh(), meshc(), tetramesh(), trimesh(), trisurf()*

Each **Plot Object** family contains a set of unique properties that may be altered to control plot behavior. For example, **BarSeries** plots have **BarLayout** and **BarWidth** properties to control the appearance of bar objects while **ContourGroup** plots have **ContourMatrix**, **LevelList**, **LevelListMode**, **LevelStep**, and **LevelStepMode** properties that control the behavior of contour lines in plots. You are encouraged to investigate the properties of each **Plot Object** family to familiarize yourself with their capabilities.

The following example code shows you how to generate several **Plot Objects** in a single figure using the *subplot()* function. The MATLAB *peaks()* function is used to create **ContourGroup**, **BarSeries**, **QuiverGroup**, and **ScatterGroup Plot Objects**. Several properties are modified to give you an idea how to generate custom plots.

Example 2.3: Plot Objects

```matlab
% create function
f = peaks(128);


%generate contour plot with text labels at integer intervals
subplot(2,2,1)
contour(f, 'LevelListMode', 'manual', ...
           'LevelList', round(min(f(:))):0.25:round(max(f(:))), ...
           'ShowText', 'on', ...
           'TextListMode', 'manual', ...
           'TextList', round(min(f(:))):1:round(max(f(:))));
title('ContourSeries Example');


%generate bar chart with stacked bars
subplot(2,2,2)
bar(f(1:5:end, 1:5:end), ...
           'BarWidth', 0.5, ...
           'BarLayout', 'stacked');
title('BarSeries Example');


%generate quiver plot without arrowheads
subplot(2,2,3)
[x, y] = meshgrid(1:4:128);
[dx, dy] = gradient(f(1:4:128,1:4:128),0.2,0.2);
quiver(x, y, dx, dy, ...
             'AutoScaleFactor', 3, ...
             'ShowArrowHead', 'off');


set(gca, 'XLim', [1 128], 'YLim', [1 128]);
title('QuiverSeries Example');


%generate scatter plot show the density of the dx and dy gradients
% with position dependent color markers
subplot(2,2,4)
dx_vector = reshape(dx(1:2:end),32^2/2,1);
dy_vector = reshape(dy(1:2:end),32^2/2,1);
norm_dx = (abs(dx_vector) - min(abs(dx_vector)))./(max(abs(dx_vector))-
min(abs(dx_vector))).*0.5;
norm_dy = (abs(dy_vector) - min(abs(dy_vector)))./(max(abs(dy_vector))-
min(abs(dy_vector))).*0.5;


scatter(dx_vector, dy_vector, ...
```

```
            'CData', [sqrt(norm_dx+norm_dy) norm_dx.*0 norm_dx.*0], ...
            'Marker', '*');
title('ScatterSeries Example');
```

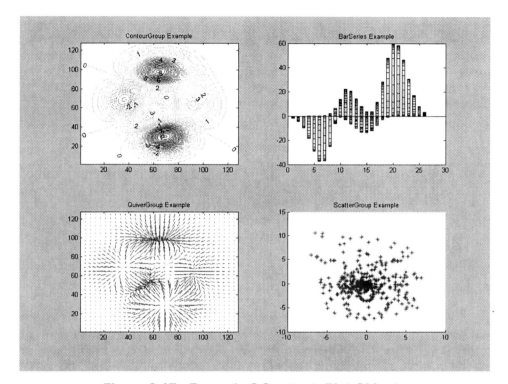

Figure 2.17 - Example 2.3 output, Plot Objects

2.5.3   Group Objects

GUI applications often contain an abundant number of graphic objects within an axis. Hierarchical organization of the graphics objects can simplify GUI programming tasks by using sets of objects to groups. **Group Objects** provide a simple means for you to create object hierarchies that allow standard transformations such as translation, scaling, and rotation. MATLAB provides two types of **Group Objects** for creating object hierarchies:

- **Hggroup** - Creates a group of objects that do not require graphical transformations. This type of **Group Object** allows you to control the visibility or selection properties of the entire group of objects.

- **Hgtransform** - Creates a group of objects that you can manipulate using a transformation matrix. All the properties associated with **Hggroup Objects** also apply to **Hgtransform Objects**.

Hggroup and **Hgtransform Objects** are children of **Axes Objects** and therefore may only exist if an **Axes Object** exists. You cannot group objects to contain a set of axes and their children, only the child objects for a specific **Axes Object**. The following example shows you how to create a group of objects using the *hggroup()* function:

```
% create a group of objects using hggroup
hPlot = plot(0:0.1:10,sin(0:0.1:10));
hGroup = hggroup;
set(hPlot, 'Parent', hGroup);
hText1 = text(2*pi/3,sin(2*pi/3), ...
               '\leftarrowsin(2*\pi/3) = sqrt(3)/2', ...
               'FontSize',12, ...
               'Parent', hGroup);
```

Note that the plot function creates an **Axes Object** and will replace the current axis and children so *hggroup()* is called after the plot command. After the **Hggroup Object** is created, the **Parent** property of the handle to the **Line Object**, *hPlot*, is set to *hGroup*. This makes *hPlot* a child object of *hGroup*. The text command creates an annotation with an arrow that is also a child object to *hGroup*. When both *hPlot* and *hText* are set as children of *hGroup*, you can control the visibility of both objects by setting the **Visible** property of *hGroup* to 'off' as follows:

```
set(hGroup, 'Visible', 'off');
```

You can use this technique to control the display of information on complex plots. You will also notice that when the visibility is enabled, you can select *hPlot* and *hText* as one object. Try selecting the text label and you will notice that both the sinusoidal plot and text label show selection handles.

Defining a group of objects using *hgtransform()* gives you further flexibility for manipulating the objects. Consider the following code that is based on the previous example, however *hGroup* is defined using *hgtransform()*:

```
% create a group of objects using hgtransform
hPlot = plot(0:0.1:10,sin(0:0.1:10));
hGroup = hgtransform;
set(hPlot, 'Parent', hGroup);
hText1 = text(2*pi/3,sin(2*pi/3), ...
              '\leftarrowsin(2*\pi/3) = sqrt(3)/2', ...
              'FontSize',12, ...
              'Parent', hGroup);
```

Now you can use the **Matrix** property of *hGroup* to transform the position, rotation, or scaling of the group. The general form of a transformation matrix, as defined for graphics, is a 4x4 matrix. MATLAB provides a simple function, *makehgtform()*, for creating a 4x4 transform matrix. *Makehgtform()* allows translation, scaling, rotation, and axis rotation and has the follow options:

- **Translation**
  ```
  matrix = makehgtform('translate', [tx ty tz])
  ```

- **Scaling**
  ```
  matrix = makehgtform('scale', [sx sy sz])
  matrix = makehgtform('scale', s)
  ```

- **Rotation**
  ```
  matrix = makehgtform('xrotate', theta_x)
  matrix = makehgtform('yrotate', theta_y)
  matrix = makehgtform('zrotate', theta_z)
  ```

- **Axis Rotation**
  ```
  matrix = makehgtform('axisrotate', [x_axis y_axis z_axis], theta)
  ```

To generate a transformation matrix that contains a combination of transforms, you can simply multiply the matrices in the order that you wish the transform operations to occur. For example:

```
m1 = makehgtform('translate', [tx ty tz])
m2 = makehgtform('scale', s)
m3 = makehgtform('xrotate', theta_x)
matrix = m3*m2*m1
```

The above example will perform the translation, *m1*, first followed by the scaling, *m2*, and finishing with the x rotation, *m3*. Note the order of the matrix multiplication. Now try the following code to rotate the *hGroup* object around the z-axis as an animation using 100 steps:

```
for i=1:100
    % first translate hGroup by x = -3*pi/2
    m1 = makehgtform('translate', [-3*pi/2 0 0]);
    % second, rotate hGroup by theta = 45 degrees around z
    m2 = makehgtform('zrotate', 2*pi/100*i);
    % third, translate hGroup back to original position x = 3*pi/2
    m3 = makehgtform('translate', [3*pi/2 0 0]);

    set(hGroup, 'Matrix', m3*m2*m1);
    set(hText1, 'Rotation', i*360/100);
    drawnow
end
```

Although the previous example of rotating a sinusoidal plot and a text label is not very practical in general, the example introduces you to the power of using *hgtransform()* to control groups of objects. This technique is useful for developing custom GUI controls where you can use groups of objects to represent dial controls, sliders, switches, meters, etc ... and then use *hgtransform()* to manipulate the position or rotation of the control. The figure below shows one frame of the animation generated from the above code when the angle of rotation is 45 degrees.

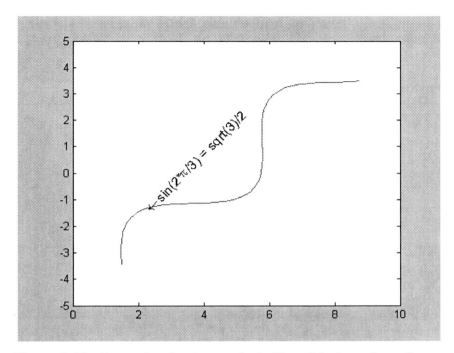

Figure 2.18 - Example of using *makehgtform()* to transform Group Objects

2.5.4   Annotation Objects

Annotation Objects are designed to describe characteristics of a figure's content. **Annotation Objects** differ from other axes children in that they are created within a hidden axes separate from the other axes defined in the target figure. Since **Annotation Objects** are defined within their own axes, you are free to position them within the figure window without concern about the positions of other **Axes Objects**. There are three ways to create **Annotation Objects**:

1. Select VIEW from the figure menu and enable the PLOT EDIT TOOLBAR, this provides a toolbar you can use to create **Annotation Objects**

2. Select the INSERT menu item in a figure and choose to create an **Annotation Object** from a list of object types

3. Use the *annotation()* function to create **Annotation Objects** and set desired properties

There are seven types of **Annotation Objects**, they are listed in the table below:

Table 2.7: Annotation Objects

Annotation Object	Function Syntax
Arrow	annotation('arrow',x,y) begin = x(1), y(1) end = x(2), y(2)
Doublearraow	annotation('doublearrow',x,y) begin = x(1), y(1) end = x(2), y(2)
Textarrow	annotation('textarrow',x,y) begin = x(1), y(1) end = x(2), y(2)
Line	annotation('line',x,y) begin = x(1), y(1) end = x(2), y(2)
Rectangle	annotation('rectangle', [x y w h]) begin = x, y width = w height = h
Ellipse	annotation('ellipse', [x y w h]) begin = x, y width = w height = h
Textbox	annotation('textbox',[x y w h]) begin = x, y width = w height = h

Each **Annotation Object** type has a unique set of properties. For example, **Arrow Objects** allow you to change the arrowhead style, length, and width by defining the **HeadStyle**, **HeadLength**, and **HeadWidth** properties respectively. The following simple example shows you how to use the annotation function:

```
%create annotation objects
hFigure = figure('Position', [100 100 500 500], 'Units', 'pixels');
hArrow = annotation('arrow', [0.2 0.9], [0.1 0.1], ...
                     'HeadStyle', 'cback3', ...
                     'HeadLength', 10);

hTextarrow = annotation('textarrow', [0.3 0.9], [0.2 0.2], ...
                     'HeadStyle', 'cback3', ...
                     'HeadLength', 10, ...
                     'String', 'My TextArrow');

hTextbox = annotation('textbox', [0.3 0.6 0.4 0.2], ...
                     'FontWeight', 'bold', ...
                     'String', 'My text box');
```

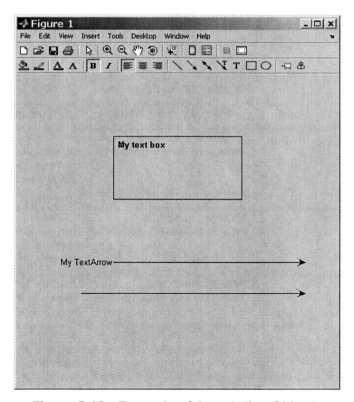

Figure 2.19 - Example of Annotation Objects

Annotation Objects are generally used to mark up plots and graphics and do not have a rich set of properties available for general GUI development. They do not have callback functions or **Parent** properties and cannot be grouped together to form sets of objects. It is not recommended that **Annotation Objects** make up any significant portion of a GUI application framework. However, placing **Annotation Objects** using the annotation toolbar can be an effective way to mark up a GUI application for describing or teaching its functionality.

2.6 UI Object Properties

UI Objects, or **User Interface Objects**, are the second set of figure child objects and are an integral part of developing GUI applications. **UI Objects** include all the essential GUI interface control objects and menu objects that are standard for GUI based operating systems. MATLAB categorizes the integrated interface controls into sub-groups described in the table below:

Table 2.8: UI Objects

UI Object Group	Function Syntax	Short Description
UIControl	handle = uicontrol('Property_Name', value, ...)	Creates GUI interface objects like toggle buttons, push buttons, check boxes, sliders, etc ...
UIContextMenu	handle = uicontrol('Property_Name', value, ...)	Creates a context menu that pops-up when the user right-clicks on an object
UIMenu	handle = uimenu('Property_Name', value, ...)	Creates a complete menu structure in a figure window
UIButtonGroup	handle = uibuttongroup('Property_Name', value, ...)	Groups radio and toggle buttons and manages selection behavior
UIPanel	handle = uipanel('Property_Name', value, ...)	Groups GUI objects within an outlined and entitled region
UIToolbar	handle = uitoolbar('Property_Name', value, ...)	Creates an empty toolbar in a figure window that toolbar objects may be added to

		using UIPushTool and UIToggleTool
UIPushTool	handle = uipushtool('Property_Name', value, ...)	Creates a push button on a toolbar. The parent of a UIPushTool object is a UIToolBar object
UIToggleTool	handle = uitoggletool('Property_Name', value, ...)	Similar to UIPushTool however it creates a toggle button on the toolbar. The parent is also a UIToolbar object

In this section you will learn the basic syntax and properties of **UI Objects** and how they may be created using the function commands defined in the above table. Creating **UI Objects** using function calls is considered a low-level technique for developing GUIs. In general, **UI Objects** are much easier to create and manage using MATLAB's high-level, integrated, GUI Development Environment program named GUIDE. This is especially true for complex GUI programs where the layout of many GUI objects is required. Chapter 3 discusses the details of using GUIDE for GUI development. Although, there are situations where dynamic creation and manipulation of **UI Objects** at the low-level is desirable.

2.6.1   UIControls

UIControl Objects consist of the basic, essential, GUI controls you need to develop an interactive application. You are likely very familiar with these types of controls since they are mainstays of graphical operating systems and are used by most GUI applications. The following list outlines the control styles available for **UIControl Objects**:

Table 2.9: UIControl Styles

UIControl Style	Style Property Name	Graphical Representation
Check Boxes	'checkbox'	☑ Check Box Control
Radio Buttons	'radiobutton'	⊙ Radio Button Control
Edit Text Boxes	'edit'	Edit Box Control
Static Text Labels	'text'	Static Text Label
List Boxes	'listbox'	List box: Item 1 / List Box: Item 2 / List Box: Item 3
Push Buttons	'pushbutton'	Push Button Control
Toggle Buttons	'togglebutton'	Toggle Button Control
Sliders	'slider'	◄ ▌ ►
Pop-up Menus	'popupmenu'	Popup Menu: Item 1 ▼ / Popup Menu: Item 1 / Popup Menu: Item 2 / Popup Menu: Item 3

The **Style** property defines the type of **UIControl Object** that will be invoked from the *uicontrol()* function command. For example, the command *uicontrol('style', 'pushbutton', 'string', 'Plot')* will create a pushbutton control with the string label 'Plot' placed on the button. Since **UIControl Objects** encapsulate several types of controls that have unique functionality, the list of properties defined for the objects covers all control styles. However, properties defined for some control styles are not defined for others. For example, the **Slider Object** is associated with the **SliderStep** property whereas all other **UIControl Objects** that attempt to use this property will simply ignore the request. The table below lists all **UIControl** properties and the associated styles that may use each property:

Table 2.10: UIControl Properties

UIControl Property	Associated UIControl Style(s)	Property Description
BackgroundColor	All styles	Sets the background color of the UIControl
BusyAction	All styles	Defines the behavior of callback functions when other events are invoked
ButtonDownFcn	All styles	Additional callback function that defines an action if the right button is pressed over a UIControl
Callback	All styles except 'text'	Defines the callback function for the control
CData	'pushbutton', 'togglebutton'	Color image data that displays on a button
Children	No styles have children	
Clipping	No styles use clipping	
Enable	All styles	Controls the appearance and state of a control.
Extent	All styles except 'slider'	A read only property provides the size of the UIcontrol character string
FontAngle	All styles except 'slider'	Sets the font angle for text used by the control
FontName	All styles except 'slider'	Sets the font type for text used by the control
FontSize	All styles except 'slider'	Sets the font size for text used by

		the control
FontUnits	All styles except 'slider'	Sets the font units for text used by the control
FontWeight	All styles except 'slider'	Sets the font weight for text used by the control
ForegroundColor	All styles	Sets the foreground color of the UIControl
HandleVisibility	All styles	Defines if the handle to the UIControl is visible to the user or callback functions
HitTest	No styles use HitTest	
HorizontalAlignment	All styles except 'slider'	Sets the justification of text
Interruptible	All styles	Sets the interruption mode of the UIControl callback
KeyPressFcn	All styles except for 'text'	Defines the KeyPressFcn callback, 'text' styles cannot have keyboard focus
ListboxTop	'listbox' only	Defines the top string item for a listbox that is not large enough to display all items
Max	'checkbox', 'edit', 'listbox', 'radiobutton', 'slider', and 'togglebutton'	Maximum value allowed for a UIControl, each control style uses this property in a different manner
Min	'checkbox', 'edit', 'listbox', 'radiobutton', 'slider', and 'togglebutton'	Minimum value allowed for a UIControl, each control style uses

		this property in a different manner
Parent	All styles	Defines the parent object for a UIControl, can be a Figure, UIPanel, or UIButtongroup handle
Position	All styles	Sets the position and size of a UIControl
Selected	All styles	A read only property that indicates the selection state of the UIControl
SelectionHighlight	All styles	Enables or disables selection markers for a UIControl when it is selected
SliderStep	'slider' only	Sets the slider step size for the arrow buttons and trough of the slider.
String	All except for 'slider'	Sets the text string for a UIControl which may be a list for list boxes and pop-up menus
Style	All styles	Selects the style
Tag	All styles	Defines an object tag name that may be used to identify UIControls
TooltipString	All styles	Defines a text string that is displayed when the mouse is moved over a UIControl

Type	All styles	A read only property that returns the string 'uicontrol'
UIContextMenu	All styles	Associates a context menu defined by a UIContextMenu object with a UIControl object
Units	All styles	Defines the units of measurement used when specifying 'position' or 'extent'
UserData	All styles	Defines a user matrix that is associated with a UIControl. Allows you to attach user data to any UIControl.
Value	'checkbox', 'listbox', 'popupmenu', 'radiobutton', 'slider', and 'togglebutton'	Holds the current state or value of a UIControl object such as slider position value or checkbox state
Visible	All styles	Controls the visibility of the UIControl to the user. By setting this value to 'off', the UIControl will not be visible to the user but the object still exists

Understanding the properties of **UIControls** is imperative for creating quality graphical user interfaces. The following sections will discuss each **UIControl Style**, describe key properties, and present examples of how each **UIControl Style** may be programmed to perform GUI tasks.

2.6.1.1 Check Boxes

Check Box controls are generally used to provide the user with the ability to enable and disable individual functions of a GUI program. A set of check boxes often represents an autonomous set of controls such that each check box does not influence the state of other check boxes. Radio button controls, as indicated by their name, are generally used to create mutually exclusive sets of controls whereby the state of one radio button controls the state of the others in the set.

Check boxes use the **Value** property to determine whether the check is enabled or disabled. If the user clicks on a check box when the current state is disabled, the check symbol will appear and the **Value** property will change from '0' to '1'. The **Callback** property is used to define a callback function for the check box. Within the callback function you can use the s*et()* and g*et*() functions to read or write the state of a check box. The example below demonstrates how to instantiate and manage a check box control:

Example 2.4: Check Box Programming

```
function main

    N=500;
    M=300;
    % create a figure
    handles.fig = figure('Units', 'Pixels', ...
                    'Position', [100 100 N M]);


    % create an axes
    handles.axes = axes('Units', 'Pixels', 'Position', [25 25 N-200 M-
50]);


    % create a uicontrol with check box style and string set
    handles.check = uicontrol(  'style', 'checkbox', ...
                            'string', 'Enable Axes Grid Lines', ...
                            'position', [N-150 M/2-25 150 50]);


    % define the callback function to checkbox_callback and pass the
    % handles structure to the function
    set(handles.check, 'Callback', {@checkbox_callback, handles});



  function checkbox_callback(gcf, event_data, handles)
```

```
    % use the get command to retrieve the Value property from the
uicontrol
    % handle 'handles.check'
    val = get(handles.check, 'Value');


    % enable or disable the grid lines on the axes based on the state of
    % the check box
    if val
        grid on;
    else
        grid off;
    end
```

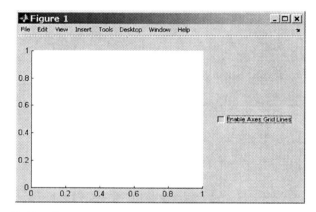

Figure 2.20 - Example 2.4 output, Check Box UIControl 'off'

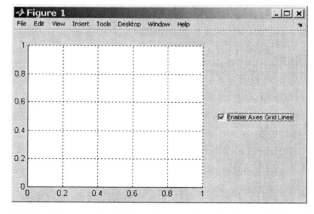

Figure 2.21 - Example 2.4 output, Check Box UIControl 'on'

2.6.1.2   Radio Buttons

Radio buttons behave similarly to check boxes in that their **Value** property defines the current state of the control and the **Callback** property is generally used to define the button action. However, radio buttons are often used in groups to control exclusive behavior for one parameter of a GUI program. For example, if you have a plot and you wish to have a set of radio buttons control the color of the plot line, you want to make sure that the user cannot simultaneously choose two colors or disable all radio buttons and not define any color. Management of radio button controls is usually performed using one of the following methods:

- **UIButtonGroup Objects** - Use **UIButtonGroups** to contain all radio buttons within a group and define a single callback function for the button group.
- **Switch Yard Programming** - Define a single callback function and assign the callback function to each radio button control.
- **Separate Callback Functions** - Define a separate callback function for each radio button and control exclusive behavior within each function.

The first method list above will be discussed in section 2.6.4 when we cover **UIButtonGroup Objects**. Examples of switch yard programming and separate callback function programming will be presented here to give you an idea of the pros and cons of each method.

Switch Yard Programming

The switch yard method defines a single callback function for all radio button objects in an exclusive group. A unique identifier is used as an input parameter to the callback function to allow you to differentiate which radio button produced the call to the function. For example:

```
set(handles.radio1, 'Callback', {@radiobutton_callback, handles, 1});
set(handles.radio2, 'Callback', {@radiobutton_callback, handles, 2});
set(handles.radio3, 'Callback', {@radiobutton_callback, handles, 3});
```

The code above uses the *set()* function to define the callback function *radiobutton_callback()* for three separate radio button objects. The callback function definition passes the handles structure and an additional parameter, in this case 1, 2, or 3, to the callback depending on which radio button object initiates the call.

Within the callback function, the *switch* and *case* commands may be used to define separate actions for each of the radio buttons. In each case in the 'switch yard', the following two essential tasks should be performed:

- Set the **Value** property of the radio button that has just been clicked. This will ensure that at least one radio button is set at all times.

- Clear the **Value** properties of all of the other radio button objects in the group. This ensures that only one radio button is set at any given time.

The following code example uses the switch yard approach with three radio button objects to create a GUI that allows the user to change the plot line color by clicking the radio buttons.

Example 2.5: Switch Yard Method For Radio Buttons

```
function main

    N=500;
    M=300;

    % create a figure
    handles.fig = figure('Units', 'Pixels', ...
                        'Position', [100 100 N M]);

    % create an axes
    handles.axes = axes('Units', 'Pixels', 'Position', [25 25 N-200 M-
50]);

    % create three uicontrols with radiobutton styles and set strings
    handles.radio1 = uicontrol( 'style', 'radiobutton', ...
                                'string', 'Red', ...
                                'position', [N-150 M/2-25 100 50]);

    handles.radio2 = uicontrol( 'style', 'radiobutton', ...
                                'string', 'Green', ...
                                'position', [N-150 M/2-75 100 50]);
```

```
    handles.radio3 = uicontrol( 'style', 'radiobutton', ...
                                'string', 'Blue', ...
                                'position', [N-150 M/2-125 100 50]);


    % generate simple plot
    handles.plot_line = plot(0:0.1:10, sin(0:0.1:10), 'Color', [1 0 0]);


    % define the callback functions to radiobutton_callback and pass the
    % handles structure to the function
    set(handles.radio1, 'Callback', {@radiobutton_callback, handles, 1});
    set(handles.radio2, 'Callback', {@radiobutton_callback, handles, 2});
    set(handles.radio3, 'Callback', {@radiobutton_callback, handles, 3});


    % initialize radio1 Value to '1'
    set(handles.radio1, 'Value', 1);

function radiobutton_callback(gcf, event_data, handles, radio_value)


    switch radio_value


        case 1
            set(handles.radio1, 'Value', 1); % ensure radio1 stays
selected
            set(handles.radio2, 'Value', 0); % set other radio buttons to
0
            set(handles.radio3, 'Value', 0); % set other radio buttons to
0


            set(handles.plot_line, 'Color', [1 0 0]); % set the line color


        case 2
            set(handles.radio2, 'Value', 1); % ensure radio2 stays
selected
            set(handles.radio1, 'Value', 0); % set other radio buttons to
0
            set(handles.radio3, 'Value', 0); % set other radio buttons to
0


            set(handles.plot_line, 'Color', [0 1 0]); % set the line color


        case 3
            set(handles.radio3, 'Value', 1); % ensure radio3 stays
selected
            set(handles.radio1, 'Value', 0); % set other radio buttons to
0
            set(handles.radio2, 'Value', 0); % set other radio buttons to
0
```

```
        set(handles.plot_line, 'Color', [0 0 1]); % set the line color
end
```

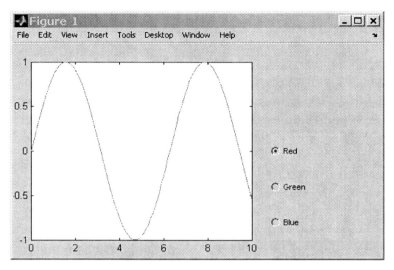

Figure 2.22 - Example 2.5 output, Radiobutton switch yard programming

Separate Callback Functions

Radio button callback functions may also be defined as separate functions for each button in a group. This approach provides you with more control over the callback function definitions. For example, if you wish to pass several variables to the callback defined for the first radio button and several different variables for other radio buttons, then this approach is well suited to accommodate such diverse needs. In practice, using the switch yard programming approach suffices for most applications and minimizes the number of function definitions in your code. When your application contains radio button groups with many buttons per group, using a single callback for each group can help avoid keeping track of countless functions.

However, it is still instructive to demonstrate the separate callback approach since some applications may benefit from this structure. The following example demonstrates this approach to define callback actions that perform the same tasks as shown in the switch yard example above:

Example 2.6: Separate Callbacks Method For Radio Buttons

```
function main

    N=500;
    M=300;

    % create a figure
    handles.fig = figure('Units', 'Pixels', ...
                        'Position', [100 100 N M]);

    % create an axes
    handles.axes = axes('Units', 'Pixels', 'Position', [25 25 N-200 M-
50]);

    % create three uicontrols with radiobutton styles and set strings
    handles.radio1 = uicontrol( 'style', 'radiobutton', ...
                                'string', 'Red', ...
                                'position', [N-150 M/2-25 100 50]);

    handles.radio2 = uicontrol( 'style', 'radiobutton', ...
                                'string', 'Green', ...
                                'position', [N-150 M/2-75 100 50]);

    handles.radio3 = uicontrol( 'style', 'radiobutton', ...
                                'string', 'Blue', ...
                                'position', [N-150 M/2-125 100 50]);

    % generate simple plot
    handles.plot_line = plot(0:0.1:10, sin(0:0.1:10), 'Color', [1 0 0]);

    % define the callback functions and pass the
    % handles structure to the function
    set(handles.radio1, 'Callback', {@radiobutton1_callback, handles});
    set(handles.radio2, 'Callback', {@radiobutton2_callback, handles});
    set(handles.radio3, 'Callback', {@radiobutton3_callback, handles});

    % initialize radio1 Value to '1'
    set(handles.radio1, 'Value', 1);

function radiobutton1_callback(gcf, event_data, handles)
    set(handles.radio1, 'Value', 1); % ensure radio1 stays selected
    set(handles.radio2, 'Value', 0); % set other radio buttons to 0
```

```
    set(handles.radio3, 'Value', 0); % set other radio buttons to 0


    set(handles.plot_line, 'Color', [1 0 0]); % set the line color

function radiobutton2_callback(gcf, event_data, handles)
    set(handles.radio2, 'Value', 1); % ensure radio2 stays selected
    set(handles.radio1, 'Value', 0); % set other radio buttons to 0
    set(handles.radio3, 'Value', 0); % set other radio buttons to 0

    set(handles.plot_line, 'Color', [0 1 0]); % set the line color

function radiobutton3_callback(gcf, event_data, handles)
    set(handles.radio3, 'Value', 1); % ensure radio3 stays selected
    set(handles.radio1, 'Value', 0); % set other radio buttons to 0
    set(handles.radio2, 'Value', 0); % set other radio buttons to 0

    set(handles.plot_line, 'Color', [0 0 1]); % set the line color
```

2.6.1.3 *Edit Text Boxes*

As indicated by the name, edit text boxes are GUI controls that enable the user to input text strings or numerical values in an application. The **String** property of this **UIControl Object** holds the edit text box text string and may be obtained by using the *get()* function. By default the number of input lines an edit box can accept from the user is a single line. You can use the **Min** and **Max** properties to allow multiple line inputs by setting the **Max** minus **Min** values to be greater than one. If **Max** minus **Min** is less than or equal to one then only a single line may be entered. The following example demonstrates how to instantiate an edit text boxes with single and multiple line inputs:

Example 2.7: Edit Text Box Single and Multiple Line Inputs

```
function main

    N=650;
    M=300;

    % create a figure
    handles.fig = figure('Units', 'Pixels', ...
                        'Position', [100 100 N M]);

    % create an axes
    handles.axes = axes('Units', 'Pixels', 'Position', [25 25 N-300 M-
50]);

    % create three uicontrols with edit styles and initialize the strings
    handles.edit_single = uicontrol( 'style', 'edit', ...
                                'string', 'Enter a plot command', ...
                                'HorizontalAlignment', 'left', ...
                                'position', [N-250 M-50 200 25]);

    handles.edit_multiple = uicontrol( 'style', 'edit', ...
                                'string', 'Enter multiple plot commands',
...
                                'max', 2, 'min', 0, ...
                                'HorizontalAlignment', 'left', ...
                                'position', [N-250 M-150 200 100]);

    % define the callback functions
    set(handles.edit_single, 'callback', {@edit_single_callback,
handles});
    set(handles.edit_multiple, 'callback', {@edit_multiple_callback,
handles});


function edit_single_callback(gcf, event_data, handles)
    % get the user input string
    handles.text1 = get(handles.edit_single, 'string');

    % generate plot from edit box input string
    handles.plot_line = eval(handles.text1);

function edit_multiple_callback(gcf, event_data, handles)
    % get the user input string
```

```
handles.text2 = get(handles.edit_multiple, 'string');

% determine number of lines entered in the text box
[num_lines, max_char] = size(handles.text2);

% evaluate all the code lines in the text box
for i = 1:num_lines
    eval(handles.text2(i,:))
end
```

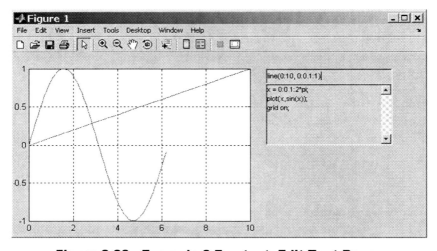

Figure 2.23 - Example 2.7 output, Edit Text Boxes

Note that multiple line input edit boxes return a two dimensional character array where the first index corresponds to the number of lines entered in the text box and the second index corresponds to the number characters required to store the longest string. A new line is formed in the text box when you press enter and the callback function executes when you remove focus from the **UIControl** by pressing on a new control or by pressing the right mouse button after a new line is entered.

Since the **String** property returns character strings, the string must be converted to the appropriate numerical format for controls that require numerical input. You can use the *str2double()* or *str2num()* functions to convert the input string to a number. For example, within the callback function you can place the *get()* function within the *str2double()* function to return the numerical representation of the input string:

```
function edit_single_callback(gcf, event_data, handles)
    % get the user input string and convert to numerical double
```

```
handles.num = str2double(get(handles.edit_single, 'string'));
```

2.6.1.4   *Static Text Labels*

The simplest **UIControl** is the static text label and is generally used to label other **UIControl Objects** in a GUI application. Static text controls are really not controls in the sense that their callback function may not be invoked. Static text labels are similar to edit boxes in that the **String** property controls the text contents and properties such as **HorizontalAlignment**, **FontSize**, **FontName**, etc ... control the visual appearance. The following example demonstrates the use of static text for creating labels. Consider the previous example demonstrating the use of edit text boxes and modify the code to insert static text labels:

Example 2.8: Static Text Labels

```
% create static text controls
uicontrol( 'style', 'text', ...
           'string', 'Single Line Input Edit Box', ...
           'HorizontalAlignment', 'left', ...
           'fontname', 'arial', ...
           'fontweight', 'bold', ...
           'position', [N-250 M-45 200 20]);


uicontrol( 'style', 'text', ...
           'string', 'Multiple Line Input Edit Box', ...
           'max', 2, 'min', 0, ...
           'HorizontalAlignment', 'left', ...
           'fontname', 'arial', ...
           'fontweight', 'bold', ...
           'position', [N-250 M-125 200 20]);
```

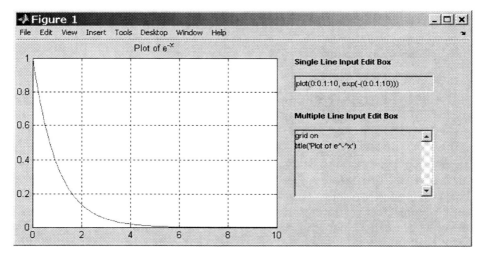

Figure 2.24: Example 2.8 output, Static Text Labels

2.6.1.5   List Boxes

List box controls are generally used to present the user with a set of items that may be selected to perform an action or actions. By default, list box controls allow only a single line item to be selected at any given time. However, by setting the **Min** and **Max** properties in a similar fashion as edit boxes, you can allow multiple line items to be selected when the user holds the shift or control keys and clicks on several different lines. The list of items is stored in the **String** property as a two-dimensional character array. The first dimension represents the item line number as it appears in the list while the second dimension represents the number of characters in the longest string in the list. The **Value** property holds the index to the current item that is selected in the list. For multiple item selections, the **Value** property contains a vector of indices that reference each line item.

The following example shows you how to create a list box control that can accept multiple input selections. The input selections represent mathematical functions that are multiplied together when multiple items are selected. The resulting function is plotted in a separate figure window. If only a single line item is selected, then only that function is plotted without any multiplication of the other functions.

Example 2.9: Multiple Input List Box

```
function main

    N = 300;
    M = 300;

    % create a figure for the list box
    handles.fig = figure('Units', 'Pixels', ...
                    'Position', [100 100 N M]);



    % create a list box control with multiple input capabilities
    handles.list_box = uicontrol(handles.fig, ...
                        'style', 'listbox', ...
                        'string', ...
                        'f(x) = sin(x) |f(x) = e^x: |f(x) = x^2', ...
                        'HorizontalAlignment', 'left', ...
                        'min', 0, 'max', 2, ...
                        'position', [0 0 N M]);

    % create a separate figure for the plot output
    handles.fig2 = figure('Units', 'Pixels', ...
                    'Position', [400 100 N M]);



    % create an axes for plotting
    handles.axes = axes;

    % define list item plot functions
    handles.n = -2*pi:0.01:2*pi;
    handles.func(1,:) = sin(handles.n);
    handles.func(2,:) = exp(handles.n);
    handles.func(3,:) = handles.n.^2;

    % define the callback functions
    set(handles.list_box, 'callback', {@list_box_callback, handles});


function list_box_callback(gcf, event_data, handles)
    % get the Value property indices for the selected item(s)
    handles.list_index = get(handles.list_box, 'value');
```

```
[d, num_selected] = size(handles.list_index);

% create an output function as a multiplication of all items selected
f = 1;
for i = 1:num_selected
    f =    handles.func(handles.list_index(i),:) .* f;
end

% plot the output function
plot(handles.axes, handles.n, f)
```

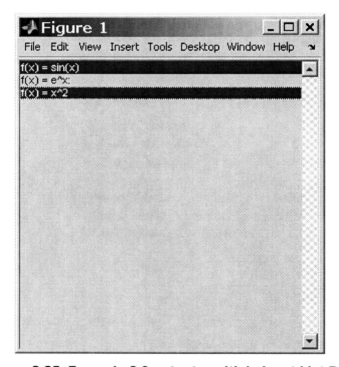

Figure 2.25: Example 2.9 output, multiple input List Box

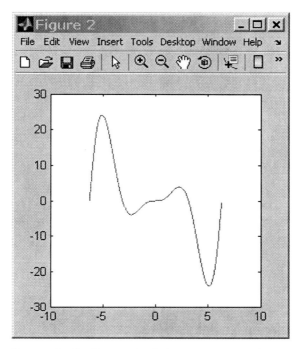

Figure 2.26: Example 2.9 output, plot figure

The above example uses the size command to determine how many items are simultaneously selected from the list box and stores the result in the *num_selected* variable. The *for* loop steps through *num_selected* iterations and multiplies each function selected by the previous result. The final product of functions is then plotted in the second figure window. This example does not use the contents of the item strings directly, only the indices.

The list box items are created using a single string with vertical slash characters, '|', as separators between items. Also, note that there are no spaces after the vertical slashes. If spaces are used after the slashes, the list box strings will be shifted when displayed. You can also define the list box item strings using a cell array of strings or a padded character matrix. The following example demonstrates the use of cell arrays to define the list box items and how you can retrieve the item strings for use in the callback:

Example 2.10: List Box Control Using Cell Arrays

```
function main

    N = 300;
    M = 300;

    % create a figure for the list box
    handles.fig = figure('Units', 'Pixels', ...
                         'Position', [100 100 N M]);

    % cell array of strings for list box items
    list_items(1) = cellstr('sphere');
    list_items(2) = cellstr('peaks');
    list_items(3) = cellstr('cylinder');

    % create a list box control
    handles.list_box = uicontrol(handles.fig, ...
                                 'style', 'listbox', ...
                                 'string', ...
                                 list_items, ...
                                 'HorizontalAlignment', 'left', ...
                                 'position', [0 0 N M]);


    % define the callback functions
    set(handles.list_box, 'callback', {@list_box_callback, handles});


function list_box_callback(gcf, event_data, handles)
    % get the Value property indices for the selected item(s)
    handles.list_index = get(handles.list_box, 'value');
    handles.list_items = get(handles.list_box, 'string');

    % evaulate the string currently selected from the list
    figure(2)
    eval([handles.list_items{handles.list_index} ';']);
```

The above example uses the *cellstr()* function to create a cell array for the list box items. In this case, each text string represents a MATLAB command and the *eval()* function is used to execute the current string item received from the **String** property in the list box callback function. Note that the **Min** and **Max** properties were not set so that only a single item may be selected from the list.

2.6.1.6 Push Buttons

Pushbutton controls are a simple click button that initiates an action and does not hold its state. Common examples of pushbutton controls are OK and cancel buttons that appear in popup dialog boxes in many GUI applications. Configuring these controls is very simple:

1. Create a **UIControl Object** with the **Style** property set as 'Pushbutton'

2. Create a callback function that will be associated with the pushbutton control

3. Place the actions that you wish to execute within the callback function

The following example code demonstrates how to create pushbutton controls and program their respective callback functions. This example uses three pushbutton controls named Run, Play Audio, and Reset. The Run button, when pressed, creates a sinusoidal signal with varying frequency based on the frequency modifier number that you enter into the edit text box. Each time you press Run, the callback function appends an additional sinusoidal signal to the previous signal and plots the result. When you press the Play Audio button, the resulting signal is played through your computer system's audio output, assuming you have an audio output defined on your system. The Reset button simply resets the signal to zero so you can start over in creating a new audio sequence.

Example 2.11: Push Button Controls

```
function main

    global step
    global f
    global A
    N = 300;
    M = 200;
    step = 1;
    f = 1;
    A = 1;


    % create a figure for the list box
    handles.fig = figure('Units', 'Pixels', ...
                         'Position', [100 100 N M]);


    % create pushbutton controls
    handles.pushbutton1 = uicontrol(handles.fig, ...
                             'style', 'pushbutton', ...
                             'string', 'Play Audio', ...
                             'position', [N/2-75 60 150 30]);


    handles.pushbutton2 = uicontrol(handles.fig, ...
                             'style', 'pushbutton', ...
                             'string', 'Run', ...
                             'position', [N/2-75 90 150 30]);


    handles.pushbutton3 = uicontrol(handles.fig, ...
                             'style', 'pushbutton', ...
                             'string', 'Reset', ...
                             'position', [N/2-75 30 150 30]);


    % create edit text and static text controls
    handles.edit_text = uicontrol(handles.fig, ...
                             'style', 'edit', ...
                             'string', '1', ...
                             'position', [N/2-75 120 150 30]);


    uicontrol(handles.fig,        'style', 'text', ...
                             'string', 'Enter Frequency Modifier (0 to
1000)', ...
                             'position', [N/2-100 150 200 30]);
```

```
    % create a separate figure for the plot output
    handles.fig2 = figure('Units', 'Pixels', ...
                        'Position', [N+100 M 400 300]);



    % create an axes for plotting
    handles.axes = axes;


    % define the callback functions
    set(handles.pushbutton1, 'callback', {@pushbutton1_callback,
handles});
    set(handles.pushbutton2, 'callback', {@pushbutton2_callback,
handles});
    set(handles.pushbutton3, 'callback', {@pushbutton3_callback,
handles});
    set(handles.edit_text, 'callback', {@edit_callback, handles});

% pushbutton callback for play audio button
function pushbutton1_callback(gcf, event_data, handles)
    global f
    soundsc(f, 1000);


% pushbutton callback for RUN button
function pushbutton2_callback(gcf, event_data, handles)
    global step
    global f
    global A

    for i = 1:300
     f(step+1) = sin(step^1.2*A);
     step = step + 1;
    end
    stairs(handles.axes, f);

% pushbutton callback for RESET button
function pushbutton3_callback(gcf, event_data, handles)
    global step
    global f
    f = 1;
    step = 1;
    stairs(handles.axes, f);

% callback for edit text box
```

```
function edit_callback(gcf, event_data, handles)
    global A
    A = str2num(get(handles.edit_text, 'String'));
```

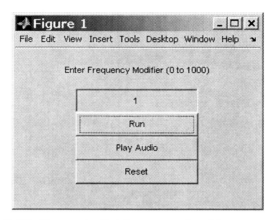

Figure 2.27: Example 2.11 output, Pushbutton controls

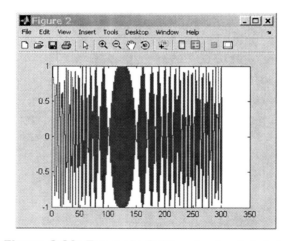

Figure 2.28: Example 2.11 output, plot data

The **String** property is used to label the button and by default the text is center justified on the button surface. The **CData** property is an array that may be set to place an image on the button surface. This is useful for creating buttons with a graphical image icon to represent the function of the control. The **CData** property must be a true color RGB array such as a JPEG color image. An easy way to create **CData** arrays for button icons is to create the graphic and save it as a common RGB image format such as JPEG or Bitmap and then use the *imread()* function to load the image into the **CData** array.

Another useful property of pushbuttons is the **ToolTipString** property. This string property defines the text that will be displayed while the mouse pointer is over the button. **ToolTipString** is especially useful for buttons with graphical icons since it provides the user with a text description of the button's function. The following example shows you how to use both **CData** and **ToopTipString** to create graphical icon buttons. This example assumes you have created button graphics and saved them to JPEG files.

Example 2.12: Pushbuttons With Graphical Icons Using CData

```
function main

    N = 300;
    M = 200;

    % create a figure
    handles.fig = figure('Units', 'Pixels', ...
                        'Position', [100 100 N M]);



    % load button icon images
    stop_icon = imread('stop.jpg','jpg');
    play_icon = imread('play.jpg','jpg');
    pause_icon = imread('pause.jpg','jpg');
    forward_icon = imread('forward.jpg','jpg');
    back_icon = imread('back.jpg','jpg');
    button_color = [1 1 1];

    % create pushbutton controls with CData icons and ToolTipStrings
    handles.stop_button = uicontrol(handles.fig, ...
                            'style', 'pushbutton', ...
                            'backgroundcolor', button_color, ...
                            'position', [N/2-15 60 30 30], ...
                            'cdata', stop_icon, ...
                            'tooltipstring', 'STOP');

    handles.play_button = uicontrol(handles.fig, ...
                            'style', 'pushbutton', ...
                            'backgroundcolor', button_color, ...
                            'position', [N/2-45 60 30 30], ...
                            'cdata', play_icon, ...
                            'tooltipstring', 'PLAY');
```

```
handles.pause_button = uicontrol(handles.fig, ...
                          'style', 'pushbutton', ...
                          'backgroundcolor', button_color, ...
                          'position', [N/2+15 60 30 30], ...
                          'cdata', pause_icon, ...
                          'tooltipstring', 'PAUSE');

handles.forward_button = uicontrol(handles.fig, ...
                          'style', 'pushbutton', ...
                          'backgroundcolor', button_color, ...
                          'position', [N/2+45 60 30 30], ...
                          'cdata', forward_icon, ...
                          'tooltipstring', 'FORWARD');

handles.back_button = uicontrol(handles.fig, ...
                          'style', 'pushbutton', ...
                          'backgroundcolor', button_color, ...
                          'position', [N/2-75 60 30 30], ...
                          'cdata', back_icon, ...
                          'tooltipstring', 'BACK');
```

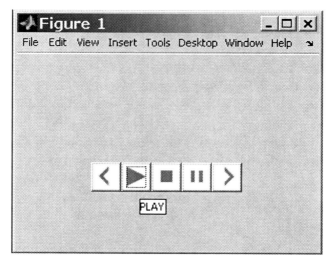

Figure 2.29: Example 2.12 output, Pushbuttons with graphical icons

2.6.1.7   Toggle Buttons

Toggle buttons have very similar properties as compared to pushbutton controls, however toggle buttons hold their state of ON or OFF when pressed or depressed. The **Value** property holds the toggle button state such that a ON corresponds to '1' and OFF to '0'. You can use a simple *if* statement to determine the current state of the button within the callback function. For example:

```
function toggle_button_callback(hObject, event_data, handles)
        if get(handles.toggle_button, 'Value')
                %button is pressed
        else
                %button is depressed
        end
```

Another useful property for both push and toggle button controls is the **Enable** property. This controls the accessibility of the button to the user such that the button will appear grayed-out when the **Enable** property is set to 'off' and will not respond when set to 'inactive' and remain in its current state. The example below is taken from example 2.6.1.6 although the Play and Pause buttons are replaced with toggle buttons. Also, the Forward and Back buttons' **Enable** properties are set to 'off' while the Play button is down and the Pause and Stop buttons are set to 'inactive' when the Play button is not pressed. Once the Play button is pressed, its **Enable** property is set to 'inactive' to hold the pressed state until the Stop button is pressed.

Example 2.13: Toggle Buttons

```
function main

    N = 300;
    M = 200;
    % create a figure
    handles.fig = figure('Units', 'Pixels', ...
                        'Position', [100 100 N M]);

    % load button icon images
    stop_icon = imread('stop.jpg','jpg');
    play_icon = imread('play.jpg','jpg');
    pause_icon = imread('pause.jpg','jpg');
    forward_icon = imread('forward.jpg','jpg');
    back_icon = imread('back.jpg','jpg');
```

```
button_color = [1 1 1];

% create pushbutton controls with CData icons and ToolTipStrings
handles.stop_button = uicontrol(handles.fig, ...
                        'style', 'pushbutton', ...
                        'backgroundcolor', button_color, ...
                        'position', [N/2-15 60 30 30], ...
                        'cdata', stop_icon, ...
                        'tooltipstring', 'STOP', ...
                        'enable', 'off');

handles.play_button = uicontrol(handles.fig, ...
                        'style', 'togglebutton', ...
                        'backgroundcolor', button_color, ...
                        'position', [N/2-45 60 30 30], ...
                        'cdata', play_icon, ...
                        'tooltipstring', 'PLAY');

handles.pause_button = uicontrol(handles.fig, ...
                        'style', 'togglebutton', ...
                        'backgroundcolor', button_color, ...
                        'position', [N/2+15 60 30 30], ...
                        'cdata', pause_icon, ...
                        'tooltipstring', 'PAUSE', ...
                        'enable', 'off');

handles.forward_button = uicontrol(handles.fig, ...
                        'style', 'pushbutton', ...
                        'backgroundcolor', button_color, ...
                        'position', [N/2+45 60 30 30], ...
                        'cdata', forward_icon, ...
                        'tooltipstring', 'FORWARD');

handles.back_button = uicontrol(handles.fig, ...
                        'style', 'pushbutton', ...
                        'backgroundcolor', button_color, ...
                        'position', [N/2-75 60 30 30], ...
                        'cdata', back_icon, ...
                        'tooltipstring', 'BACK');

% define the callback functions
set(handles.stop_button, 'callback', {@stop_button_callback, handles});
```

```
    set(handles.play_button, 'callback', {@play_button_callback,
handles});
    set(handles.pause_button, 'callback', {@pause_button_callback,
handles});
    set(handles.forward_button, 'callback', {@forward_button_callback,
handles});
    set(handles.back_button, 'callback', {@back_button_callback,
handles});

function stop_button_callback(gcf, event_data, handles)
    set(handles.play_button, 'Enable', 'On', 'Value', 0);
    set(handles.stop_button, 'Enable', 'Off');
    set(handles.pause_button, 'Enable', 'Off', 'Value', 0);

function play_button_callback(gcf, event_data, handles)
    set(handles.play_button, 'Enable', 'Inactive');
    set(handles.stop_button, 'Enable', 'On');
    set(handles.pause_button, 'Enable', 'On');

function pause_button_callback(gcf, event_data, handles)
function forward_button_callback(gcf, event_data, handles)
function back_button_callback(gcf, event_data, handles)
```

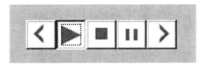

Figure 2.30: Example 2.13, togglebuttons stop and pause grayed-out

Figure 2.31: Example 2.13, togglebutton play 'on'

Figure 2.32: Example 2.13, togglebutton pause and play 'on'

2.6.1.8 Sliders

Slider controls provide a quick and easy way to dynamically change parameters or variables in a GUI application. Some examples of scenarios where you may want to use sliders include: Zooming plot axes, increasing or decreasing variables in an equation, or changing the brightness of an image. There are four key properties that require initialization to control the behavior of a slider bar:

- **Min** - Controls the minimum value returned from the slider control
- **Max** - Controls the maximum value returned from the slider control
- **SliderStep** - The is a two value vector that determines the step size for the slider when the arrow buttons or trough of the slider is clicked. The vector is defined as followed:

  [slider_arrow_step slider_trough_step]

  These values must be between 0 and 1.
- **Value** - This property holds the current slider value and may be set to initialize the position of the slider.

The **SliderStep** property values correspond to the step sizes in the range of 0 to 1. For example, if **SliderStep** is set to [0.1 0.01], then 10 steps total will occur for the arrow button while 100 steps total will occur as the trough is clicked. If the **Min** and **Max** property values are set to 0 and 100 respectively and the **SliderStep** is set to [0.1 0.01], then each up or down arrow button click will increase or decrease the **Value** property by 10 and trough clicks will increase or decrease **Value** by 1.

The following example demonstrates how you can setup a slider control that has both positive and negative values and how to initialize the slider bar position to zero. Also, static text controls are added to display the min, max, and current values of the slider:

```
handles.fig = figure(   'Units', 'Pixels', ...
                        'Position', [25 50 200 100]);


handles.slider = uicontrol( 'style', 'slider', ...
                            'position', [25 25 150 25], ...
                            'min', -100, 'max', 100, ...
                            'sliderstep', [0.1 0.1], ...
                            'value', 0);
```

```
uicontrol('style', 'text', 'string', '-100', 'position', [25 55 25 25]);
uicontrol('style', 'text', 'string', '100', 'position', [150 55 25 25]);
```

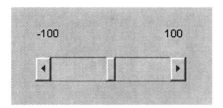

Figure 2.33: Simple slider control

The next example demonstrates how to use slider controls to create an interactive GUI application. Two sliders are created to control the scale and position of the x-axis of a plot. The callback functions for each slider update the axis scale and position. Also, the **BackgroundColor** property is changed based on the position of the slider. As the value gets closer to the **Max** value, the trough color becomes whiter.

Example 2.14: Slider Controls

```
function main
    global xscale
    global xpos

    N=500;
    M=300;
    xscale = 1;
    xpos = 0;

    % create a figure
    handles.fig = figure('Units', 'Pixels', ...
                        'Position', [100 100 N M]);

    % create an axes
    handles.axes = axes('Units', 'Pixels', 'Position', [25 150 N-50 M-
175]);

    % create two slider controls
    handles.slider1 = uicontrol( 'style', 'slider', ...
                                'position', [25 20 N-50 20], ...
                                'min', 1, 'max', 99, ...
                                'sliderstep', [0.01 0.1], ...
                                'value', xscale, ...
                                'backgroundcolor', [xscale/100 xscale/100
xscale/100]);

    handles.slider2 = uicontrol( 'style', 'slider', ...
                                'position', [25 60 N-50 20], ...
                                'min', 0, 'max', 100, ...
                                'sliderstep', [0.01 0.1], ...
                                'value', xpos, ...
                                'backgroundcolor', [xpos/100 xpos/100
xpos/100]);

    uicontrol( 'style', 'text', 'string', 'X-axis Scale', ...
                                'position', [25 40 100 20]);
    uicontrol( 'style', 'text', 'string', 'X-axis Position', ...
                                'position', [25 80 100 20]);

    % generate simple plot
    handles.plot_line = plot(0:0.1:100, sin((0:0.1:100).^1.5));
```

```
% define the callback functions
set(handles.slider1, 'Callback', {@slider1_callback, handles});
set(handles.slider2, 'Callback', {@slider2_callback, handles});


function slider1_callback(hObject, event_data, handles)
    global xscale
    global xpos
    xscale = get(handles.slider1, 'value');
    set(handles.axes,'xlim', [xpos xpos+100-xscale]);
    set(handles.slider1, 'backgroundcolor', [xscale/100 xscale/100
xscale/100]);
    drawnow


function slider2_callback(hObject, event_data, handles)
    global xscale
    global xpos
    xpos = get(handles.slider2, 'value');
    set(handles.axes, 'xlim', [xpos xpos+100-xscale]);
    set(handles.slider2, 'backgroundcolor', [xpos/100 xpos/100 xpos/100]);
    drawnow
```

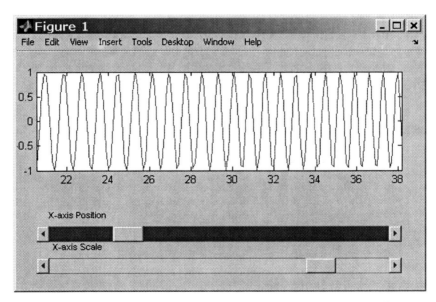

Figure 2.34: Example 2.14 output, dual slider controls

2.6.1.9   Popup Menus

Popup menus generally provide the user with a short list of selectable options that may be clicked to perform actions. Only one item from the list may be selected at any given time. Popup menus are also compact GUI controls in terms of window area real estate and may only require the space of a single line of text string. You should limit the number of options such that the popup list does not expand beyond the limits of the screen area. The following example shows a typical callback function for a popup menu control:

```
function popup_menu_callback(gcf, event_data, handles)
    switch get(handles.popup_menu, 'Value')
        case 1
            % Item 1 actions
        case 2
            % Item 2 actions
        case 3
            % Item 3 actions
        .
        .
        .

    end
```

Note that the **Value** property may be used to determine which popup item has been selected and a *switch/case* statement may be used to channel the item actions. The following example uses a popup menu control to set the 3D style of a surface plot.

Example 2.15: Popup Menus

```
function main

    N = 500;
    M = 500;

    % create a figure
    handles.fig = figure('Units', 'Pixels', ...
                    'Position', [100 100 N M]);

    % create an axes
    handles.axes = axes('Units', 'Pixels', 'Position', [25 100 N-50 M-
125]);
```

```matlab
% create pushbutton controls with CData icons and ToolTipStrings
handles.popup_menu = uicontrol(handles.fig, ...
                            'style', 'popupmenu', ...
                            'string', 'Mesh |Surface |Surface Without
Lines |Surface With Lighting', ...
                            'position', [25 50 200 25]);


% plot of diffraction pattern from 2 rectangular apertures close
% together
handles.x = -3*pi:0.3:3*pi;
handles.y = -3*pi:0.3:3*pi;
d = pi;
c = 0;
[m, n] = size(handles.x);


for j = 1:n
    for i = 1:n

        if handles.x(i) ~= 0
            xt = sin(handles.x(i))^2/handles.x(i)^2 +
sin(handles.x(i)+d)^2/(handles.x(i)+d)^2;
        else
            xt = 1;
        end


        if handles.y(j) ~= 0
            yt = sin(handles.y(j))^2/handles.y(j)^2;
        else
            yt = 1;
        end


        handles.f(i,j) = abs(xt * yt);
    end
  end


% Create mesh plot
mesh(handles.axes, handles.x, handles.y, handles.f);


% define the callback function
set(handles.popup_menu, 'callback', {@popup_menu_callback, handles});


function popup_menu_callback(gcf, event_data, handles)


    switch get(handles.popup_menu, 'Value')
```

```
case 1
    % Create mesh plot
    mesh(handles.axes, handles.x, handles.y, handles.f);
case 2
    % Create surface plot
    surf(handles.axes, handles.x, handles.y, handles.f);
case 3
    % Create surface plot without lines
    surf(handles.axes, handles.x, handles.y, handles.f,
'Linestyle', 'none');
case 4
    % Create surface plot without lines and add lighting
    surf(handles.axes, handles.x, handles.y, handles.f,
'Linestyle', 'none');
    light('Position',[0 -1 0],'Style','infinite');
end
```

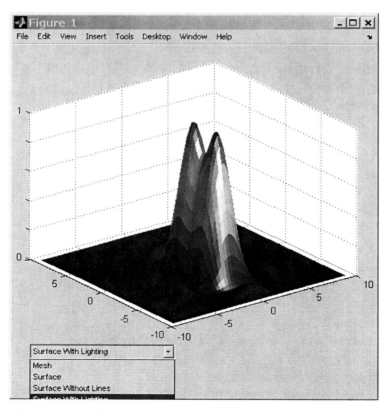

Figure 2.35: Example 2.15 output, popup menu control

2.6.2   UIMenu

Menu bars located at the top of a GUI application generally form the main control center for a program. **UIMenu Objects** allow you to create and manage GUI menu bars for your application. The default main menu items for a figure include File, Edit, View, Help, etc ... and each of these menu items contains a list of sub-menu items. You can create sub-menus by first instantiating a **UIMenu** object as a parent object and then assign a second **UIMenu** object as a child object to the first **UIMenu**. The following steps may be used to create a menu with sub-menu items:

1. First, create a **Figure Object** and disable the **Menubar** property to hide the default menu for the figure. If you do not disable the menu bar, the *uimenu()* function will simply add menu items to the default menu:

    ```
    fig = figure('Menubar', 'none');
    ```

2. Next, create a main menu item using the *uimenu()* function and **Label** property:

    ```
    main_menu1 = uimenu('Label', 'Menu 1');
    ```

3. Then add items to the main menu by invoking the *uimenu()* function and assign the **Parent** property to the main menu object. Also, use the **Callback** property to define the function called when the menu item is selected:

    ```
    uimenu('Parent', main_menu1, ...
           'Label', 'Item1', ...
           'Callback', {@menu_item1_callback, handles});
    uimenu('Parent', main_menu1, ...
           'Label', 'Item2', ...
           'Callback', {@menu_item2_callback, handles});
    ```

4. If you wish to add a sub-menu, simply define an object variable to the sub-menu item and use this as a **Parent** object for the next level of the hierarchy:

    ```
    sub_menu1 = uimenu('Parent', main_menu1, ...
    ```

```
                      'Label', 'Sub-Menu 1'}
           uimenu('Parent', sub_menu1, ...
                  'Label', 'Sub Menu Item1', ...
                  'Callback', {@sub_menu_item1_callback, handles});
```

Additional properties that affect the behavior and appearance of **UIMenu** objects include the following:

- **Accelerator** - This property sets the shortcut key you wish to associate with the menu item. The shortcut key may be invoked by pressing CTRL + shortcut key (for PCs).

- **Checked** - Setting this property to 'on' places a check mark next to the menu item to indicate the item has been selected.

- **ForegroundColor** - Sets the color of the menu item text.

- **Position** - Defines the position of the menu item within the menu bar or menu item list. Setting this property to 1 places the item first on the menu bar or first in the menu item list.

- **Separator** - Setting this property to 'on' places a separator line above the menu item.

Exercise 2.8: UIMenu Programming

Create a GUI figure that has two menu items located on the menu bar named Plot View and Rotate. The Plot View menu should have the following menu items: Mesh, Surface, and Surface + Contour. The Mesh item should be checked when the GUI is initialized and each item should be checked when selected by the user. The Rotate menu should have the following menu items with separators placed where the | characters are denoted: Animate x-axis rotation | Animate y-axis rotation | Animate z-axis rotation.

Create a two-dimensional surface function when the GUI is initialized and place the data in the handles structure. Plot the function using the *mesh*() function upon startup. Define the callback functions for Mesh, Surface, and Surface + Contour such that the two dimensional function is plotted using the *mesh*(), *surface*(), and *surfacec*() functions respectively. Next, define the Rotate menu item callback functions such that the camera position rotates around the X, Y, or Z axis of the 3D plot. Also, add accelerator keys for the X, Y, and Z rotation menu items.

Exercise 2.8 Solution:

```
function main

    N = 500;
    M = 500;

    % create a figure
    handles.fig = figure('Units', 'Pixels', ...
                        'Position', [100 100 N M], ...
                        'Menubar', 'none', ...
                        'Color', [1 1 1]);

    % create an axes object with manual cameraposition mode
    handles.axes = axes('box', 'on', ...
                        'cameraposition', [0 0 0], ...
                        'camerapositionmode', 'manual', ...
                        'cameraupvector', [0 0 1], ...
                        'cameraupvectormode', 'manual', ...
                        'nextplot', 'replacechildren');

    % create a 2D surface function
    i=1; j=1;
    for x = -10:0.5:10
        for y = -10:0.5:10
            if x ==0 | y==0
                handles.plot_data(i,j) = 0;
            else
                handles.plot_data(i,j) = x*y*(x^2-y^2)/(x^2+y^2);
            end
            j = j + 1;
        end
        j = 1;
        i = i + 1;
    end
    mesh(handles.axes, -10:0.5:10,-10:0.5:10,handles.plot_data);

    handles.camera_position = [1 1 1];

    % create a the View menu
    handles.menu1 = uimenu('Label', 'Plot View');
    handles.menu1_item1 = uimenu(handles.menu1, ...
```

```
                             'Label', 'Mesh', ...
                             'Checked', 'on');
    handles.menu1_item2 = uimenu(handles.menu1, ...
                             'Label', 'Surface');
    handles.menu1_item3 = uimenu(handles.menu1, ...
                             'Label', 'Surface + Contour');


    set(handles.menu1_item1, 'Callback', {@menu_item1_callback, handles});
    set(handles.menu1_item2, 'Callback', {@menu_item2_callback, handles});
    set(handles.menu1_item3, 'Callback', {@menu_item3_callback, handles});


    % create the Rotate menu
    handles.menu2 = uimenu('Label', 'Rotate');
                    uimenu(handles.menu2, ...
                             'Label', 'Animate x-axis rotation', ...
                             'Accelerator', 'x', ...
                             'Callback', {@menu_animx_callback, handles});
                    uimenu(handles.menu2, ...
                             'Label', 'Animate y-axis rotation', ...
                             'Accelerator', 'y', ...
                             'Separator', 'on', ...
                             'Callback', {@menu_animy_callback, handles});
                    uimenu(handles.menu2, ...
                             'Label', 'Animate z-axis rotation', ...
                             'Accelerator', 'z', ...
                             'Separator', 'on', ...
                             'Callback', {@menu_animz_callback, handles});


% callback function for View menu items
function menu_item1_callback(hObject, event_data, handles)
    mesh(handles.axes, -10:0.5:10, -10:0.5:10, handles.plot_data);
    if ~strcmp(get(handles.menu1_item1, 'Checked'), 'on')
        set(handles.menu1_item1, 'Checked', 'on');
        set(handles.menu1_item2, 'Checked', 'off');
        set(handles.menu1_item3, 'Checked', 'off');
    end


function menu_item2_callback(hObject, event_data, handles)
    surf(handles.axes, -10:0.5:10, -10:0.5:10, handles.plot_data);
    if ~strcmp(get(handles.menu1_item2, 'Checked'), 'on')
        set(handles.menu1_item2, 'Checked', 'on');
        set(handles.menu1_item1, 'Checked', 'off');
        set(handles.menu1_item3, 'Checked', 'off');
```

```
        end

function menu_item3_callback(gcf, event_data, handles)
    surfc(handles.axes, -10:0.5:10, -10:0.5:10, handles.plot_data);
    if ~strcmp(get(handles.menu1_item3, 'Checked'), 'on')
        set(handles.menu1_item3, 'Checked', 'on');
        set(handles.menu1_item1, 'Checked', 'off');
        set(handles.menu1_item2, 'Checked', 'off');
    end


% callback function for Rotate menu items
function menu_animx_callback(hObject, event_data, handles)
    set(handles.axes, 'cameraupvector', [1 0 0]);
    for i = 0:100
        set(handles.axes, 'cameraposition', [20 20*sin(4/3*pi*i/100)
20*cos(4/3*pi*i/100)]);
        drawnow
    end


function menu_animy_callback(hObject, event_data, handles)
    set(handles.axes, 'cameraupvector', [0 1 0]);
    for i = 0:100
        set(handles.axes, 'cameraposition', [20*sin(2*pi*i/100) 20
20*cos(2*pi*i/100)]);
        drawnow
    end


function menu_animz_callback(hObject, event_data, handles)
    set(handles.axes, 'cameraupvector', [0 0 1]);
    for i = 0:100
        set(handles.axes, 'cameraposition', [20*sin(4/3*pi*i/100)
20*cos(4/3*pi*i/100) 20]);
        drawnow
    end
```

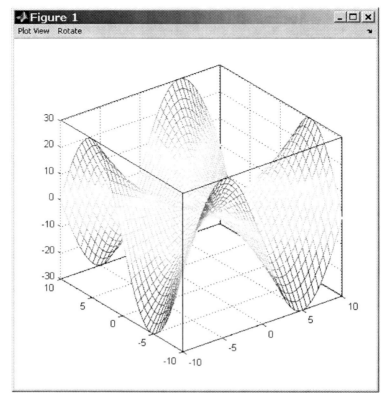

Figure 2.36: Exercise 2.8 output, UIMenu programming example

2.6.3   UIContextMenu

Context menus are designed for defining menu action lists for specific graphics objects. You can define context menus for figures, axes, lines, UIControls such as buttons, or any handle graphics object that has a **UIContextMenu** property designator. The *uicontextmenu()* function is used to create a context menu object. Several steps are required to initialize a context menu:

1. Define the graphics object you wish to have a context menu associated with such as *handles.object*

2. Create a context menu object by calling the *uicontextmenu()* function:

```
handles.context_menu = uicontextmenu;
```

3. Create the individual menu items for the context menu by using the *uimenu()* function. The **Label** property of *uimenu()* defines the string text that appears for the menu item:

```
handles.item1 = uimenu(handles.context_menu, 'Label', 'Item1');
handles.item2 = uimenu(handles.context_menu, 'Label', 'Item2');
    .
    .
```

4. Next, associate the context menu with the graphics object by using the set function and the graphics object's **UIContextMenu** property:

```
set(handles.object, 'UIContextMenu', handles.context_menu)
```

5. Define the callback functions for each *uimenu* item:

```
set(handles.object, 'Callback', {@context1_callback, handles});
set(handles.object, 'Callback', {@context2_callback, handles});
    .
    .

function context1_callback(hObject, event_data, handles)
    % actions
function context2_callback(hObject, event_data, handles)
    % actions
    .
    .
```

Since context menus are created using **UIMenu Objects**, properties such as **Accelerator, Checked**, and **Separator** may be used to tailor the menu's functionality. Also, sub-menus may be developed to form complex menu hierarchies.

The example below demonstrates how to define context menus for a **Figure** and **Axes Object**. Two separate context menus are defined, one for the axes and one for the figure. The figure context menu will only appear when you right click outside of the axes area but within the active figure window area while the axes context only appears when you right click over the axes area. The **Checked** property is used to control the state of the axes context menu items. When selected, each item is checked or not checked depending on the previous state.

Example 2.16: Context Menus

```
function main

    N = 500;
    M = 500;

    % create a figure
    handles.fig = figure('Units', 'Pixels', ...
                         'Position', [100 100 N M]);

    % create a uicontextmenu associated with the figure
    handles.fig_context = uicontextmenu;
    handles.fig_cm1 = uimenu(handles.fig_context, ...
                            'Label', 'Black Background');
    handles.fig_cm2 = uimenu(handles.fig_context, ...
                            'Label', 'White Background');
    handles.fig_cm3 = uimenu(handles.fig_context, ...
                            'Label', 'Dark Green Background');

    set(handles.fig, 'uicontextmenu', handles.fig_context)
    set(handles.fig_cm1, 'Callback', {@fig_context1_callback, handles});
    set(handles.fig_cm2, 'Callback', {@fig_context2_callback, handles});
    set(handles.fig_cm3, 'Callback', {@fig_context3_callback, handles});

    % create an axes
    handles.axes = axes('Units', 'Pixels', ...
                        'Position', [25 100 N-50 M-125], ...
                        'Box', 'on', ...
                        'Color', 'none', ...
                        'XColor', [0.5 0.2 0.2], ...
                        'YColor', [0.5 0.2 0.2]);

    % create two functions
        handles.f1 = line(0:0.05:10, sin(0:0.05:10), 'Visible', 'off');
        handles.f2 = line(0:0.05:10, cos(0:0.05:10), 'Visible', 'off');

    % create a uicontextmenu associated with the axes
    handles.axes_context = uicontextmenu;
    handles.axes_cm1 = uimenu(handles.axes_context, ...
                            'Label', 'Show Plot 1');
    handles.axes_cm2 = uimenu(handles.axes_context, ...
```

```
                               'Label', 'Show Plot 2');
    handles.axes_cm3 = uimenu(handles.axes_context, ...
                               'Label', 'Grid On');


    set(handles.axes, 'uicontextmenu', handles.axes_context);

    % set callback functions for all menu items
    set(handles.axes_cm1, 'Callback', {@axes_context1_callback, handles});
    set(handles.axes_cm2, 'Callback', {@axes_context2_callback, handles});
    set(handles.axes_cm3, 'Callback', {@axes_context3_callback, handles});



% callback function for figure context menu
function fig_context1_callback(gcf, event_data, handles)
    set(handles.fig, 'Color', [0 0 0]);


function fig_context2_callback(gcf, event_data, handles)
    set(handles.fig, 'Color', [1 1 1]);


function fig_context3_callback(gcf, event_data, handles)
    set(handles.fig, 'Color', [0 0.2 0]);



% callback function for axes context menu
function axes_context1_callback(gcf, event_data, handles)
    if strcmp(get(handles.axes_cm1, 'Checked'),'on')
        set(handles.axes_cm1, 'Checked', 'off');
        set(handles.f1, 'Visible', 'off');
    else
        set(handles.axes_cm1, 'Checked', 'on');
        set(handles.f1, 'Visible', 'on');
    end

function axes_context2_callback(gcf, event_data, handles)
    if strcmp(get(handles.axes_cm2, 'Checked'),'on')
        set(handles.axes_cm2, 'Checked', 'off');
        set(handles.f2, 'Visible', 'off');
    else
        set(handles.axes_cm2, 'Checked', 'on');
        set(handles.f2, 'Visible', 'on');
    end
```

```
function axes_context3_callback(gcf, event_data, handles)
    if strcmp(get(handles.axes_cm3, 'Checked'),'on')
        set(handles.axes_cm3, 'Checked', 'off');
        grid off;
    else
        set(handles.axes_cm3, 'Checked', 'on');
        grid on;
    end
```

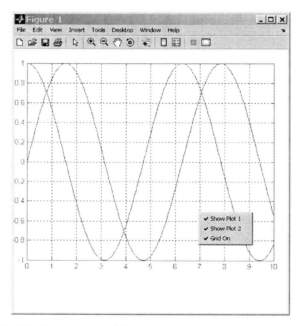

Figure 2.37: Example 2.16 output, UIContextMenu for Axes

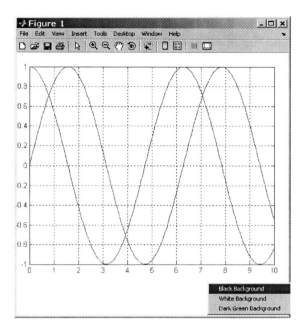

Figure 2.38: Example 2.16 output, UIContextMenu for Figure

2.6.4   UIButtonGroup

Button groups such as radio buttons and toggle buttons often require management of exclusive behavior such that only one button may be selected at a time while others in the group become unselected. The **UIButtonGroup Object** is designed to provide a container for groups of radio buttons and toggle buttons. **UIButtonGroup** objects provide the following functions for a GUI:

- Contain radio and toggle button controls by acting as a parent object for the group and provides a rectangular region on screen with a title to show the extent of the group area

- Provides a single callback function named **SelectionChangeFcn** to manage button actions

- Provides a property named **SelectedObject** that allows you to determine which button has been selected

UIButtonGroup objects are not limited to containing radio and toggle buttons, **Axes**, **UIControl**, **UIPanel**, and other **UIButtonGroup** objects may be set as children also. The following example demonstrates the syntax and callback functionality of a **UIButtonGroup** object and uses radiobuttons as children:

Example 2.17: UIButtonGroup Objects

```
function main

   N = 500;
   M = 500;

   % create a figure
   handles.fig = figure('Units', 'Pixels', ...
                        'Position', [100 100 N M], ...
                        'Color', [1 1 1]);
   handles.axes = axes('Units', 'Pixels', ...
                        'Position', [0 63 375 375]);
   colormap(hot(256));

   handles.buttongroup = uibuttongroup(  'Units', 'pixels', ...
                                         'Position', [375 0 125 M], ...
                                         'Title', 'Button Group');
      uicontrol( 'Style','Radio', ...
                 'String','One Sphere',...
                 'Position',[20 3*M/4 100 30], ...
                 'Parent', handles.buttongroup, ...
                 'HandleVisibility','off');
      uicontrol( 'Style','Radio', ...
                 'String','Two Spheres',...
                 'Position',[20 M/2 100 30], ...
                 'Parent', handles.buttongroup, ...
                 'HandleVisibility','on');
      uicontrol( 'Style','Radio', ...
                 'String','Three Spheres',...
                 'Position',[20 M/4 100 30], ...
                 'Parent', handles.buttongroup, ...
                 'HandleVisibility','on');

   set(handles.buttongroup, ...
       'SelectionChangeFcn',{@selection_callback, handles});
   drawnow

   [x, y, z] = sphere(30);
```

```
    surf(x/2, y/2, z/2);
    axis([-1 1 -1 1 -1 1]);
    axis off;

function selection_callback(hObject, eventdata, handles)

    [x, y, z] = sphere(30);
    switch get(get(hObject,'SelectedObject'),'String')
        case 'One Sphere'
            surf(x/2, y/2, z/2);
            axis([-1 1 -1 1 -1 1]);
            axis off;
        case 'Two Spheres'
            surf(x/2, y/2, z/2+1);
            hold on;
            surf(x/2, y/2, z/2);
            axis([-1 1 -1 1 -1 1]);
            axis off;
            hold off;
        case 'Three Spheres'
            surf(x/2, y/2, z/2+1);
            hold on;
            surf(x/2, y/2, z/2-1);
            surf(x/2, y/2, z/2);
            axis([-1 1 -1 1 -1 1]);
            axis off;
            hold off;
    end
```

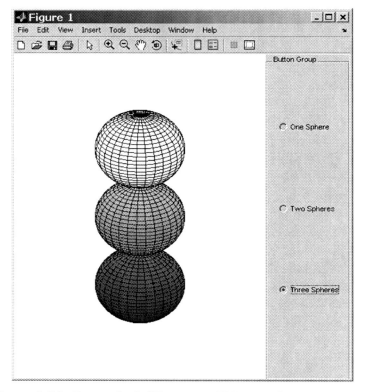

Figure 2.39: Example 2.17 output, UIButtonGroup example

2.6.5 UIPanel

UIPanel Objects are GUI elements that encapsulate and organize groups of GUI controls and **Axes Objects**. **UIPanels** perform the following fundamental roles for a GUI interface:

- Define a parent object with **Axes**, **UIControl**, **UIButtongroup**, and **UIPanel** objects as children
- Child objects inherit properties of a **UIPanel Object** and this allows groups of objects to be manipulated simultaneously with single **UIPanel** property commands
- Provide a rectangular encapsulated area within the GUI figure with a text label that clearly shows the hierarchical division of child objects

The **Parent** property of child objects may be used to define a **UIPanel** as the parent object or the **Children** property of the **UIPanel** may be used to define the child objects. This versatility allows child objects to be instantiated before or after the **UIPanel** is instantiated. The example below demonstrates using both methods for creating a **UIPanel** with child objects:

```
% create a the main UIPanel and define child objects
handles.panel1 = uipanel('Units', 'pixels', ...
                    'Title', 'UIPanel Object', ...
                    'Position', [100 100 N-200 M-200]);


% create a the child buttons for panel
handles.buttons(1) = uicontrol('Parent', handles.panel1, ...
                        'Units', 'pixels', ...
                        'Position', [100 50 100 40], ...
                        'String', 'Child Button 1', ...
                        'Style', 'togglebutton');


handles.buttons(2) = uicontrol('Parent', handles.panel1, ...
                        'Units', 'pixels', ...
                        'Position', [100 90 100 40], ...
                        'String', 'Child Button 2', ...
                        'Style', 'togglebutton');
```

UIPanels have several properties for defining the appearance of the panel that include: **BackgroundColor**, **BorderType**, **BorderWidth**, **FontAngle**, **FontName**, **FontSize**, **FontUnits**, **FontWeight**, **ForegroundColor**, **HighlightColor**, **ShadowColor**, **Title**, and **TitlePosition**. You can also define **ButtonDownFcn** and **ResizeFcn** callback functions for panels and create a **UIContextMenu** as well.

The following example shows how you can use a **UIPanel** to contain a group of GUI objects, hide the GUI objects, and move the panel of objects by manipulating the properties of the **UIPanel** parent object:

Example 2.18: UIPanel Object Group Manipulation

```
function main

    N = 500;
    M = 500;

    % create a figure
    handles.fig = figure('Units', 'Pixels', ...
                        'Position', [100 100 N M], ...
                        'Menubar', 'none', ...
                        'Color', [1 1 1]);

    handles.button1 = uicontrol('Units', 'pixels', ...
                            'Position', [100 425 125 40], ...
                            'String', 'Hide Panel Controls', ...
                            'Style', 'togglebutton');

    handles.button2 = uicontrol('Units', 'pixels', ...
                            'Position', [250 425 125 40], ...
                            'String', 'Move Panel', ...
                            'Style', 'togglebutton');

    % create a the main UIPanel
    handles.panel1 = uipanel('Units', 'pixels', ...
                            'Backgroundcolor', [1 1 1], ...
                            'Foregroundcolor', [0 0 0], ...
                            'Title', 'UIPanel Object', ...
                            'Position', [100 100 N-200 M-200]);

    % define push button objects with panel1 as the parent
    handles.pbutton1 = uicontrol('Parent', handles.panel1, ...
```

```
                              'Units', 'pixels', ...
                              'Position', [100 10 100 40], ...
                              'String', 'Panel Button 1', ...
                              'Style', 'pushbutton');


    handles.axes = axes('Parent', handles.panel1, ...
                        'Units', 'pixels', ...
                        'Position', [50 100 N-300 M-350]);
    plot(handles.axes, 1:100, sin((1:100).^2));


    % define callback for button1 and button2
    set(handles.button1, 'callback', {@hide_panel_callback, handles});
    set(handles.button2, 'callback', {@move_panel_callback, handles});


function hide_panel_callback(hObject, event_data, handles)

    if get(handles.button1, 'value')
        set(handles.panel1, 'Visible', 'off');
    else
        set(handles.panel1, 'Visible', 'on');
    end


function move_panel_callback(hObject, event_data, handles)
    N = 500;
    M = 500;

    if get(handles.button2, 'value')
        for i = 0:1:23
            set(handles.panel1, 'Position', [100+i^2 100 N-200 M-200]);
            drawnow
        end
    else
        for i = 23:-1:0
            set(handles.panel1, 'Position', [100+i^2 100 N-200 M-200]);
            drawnow
        end
    end
```

2.6.6   UIToolbar, UIPushTool, and UIToggleTool

Toolbars allow you to create efficient shortcuts for commonly used functions such as file saving, creating new figures, selecting modes of a program, etc ... Most GUI applications use toolbars to augment functions that are defined within the menu hierarchy. MATLAB provides two interactive button styles for **UIToolbar Objects** that include a pushbutton and togglebutton. These buttons operate similarly to the pushbutton and togglebutton **UIControl** styles. The **UIPushTool** and **UIToggleTool Objects** are children of a toolbar object instantiated using **UIToolbar**.

UIPushTool and **UIToggleTool** buttons use a 20x20 pixel image icon on the button surface to indicate to the user the button's action or function. The **CData** property of each button type may be used to define the image icon that will appear on the surface of the button. The following example shows how to create a simple toolbar:

```
tbar = uitoolbar;
uitoggletool(tbar, 'CData', button_icon1, ...
                   'OnCallback', {@button_down_fucntion}, ...
                   'OffCallback', {@button_up_function});
uipushtool(tbar, 'CData', button_icon2, ...
                   'ClickedCallback', {@clicked_function});
```

Note that the **UIToggleTool** has three main callback function properties named **ClickedCallback**, **OnCallback**, and **OffCallback** while **UIPushTool** only has **ClickedCallback**. The **TooltipString** property is useful for providing text descriptions of the toolbar button functions.

Exercise 2.9: Using UIToolbars

Use the **UIToolbar**, **UIPushTool**, and **UIToggleTool Objects** to create a simple plot viewer application. Create a figure and add a toolbar while leaving the default menu and toolbar intact. Generate four functions to use for plotting in the application. Create a toggle tool button and two push tool buttons:

- The toggle tool button should allow the user to control the plot view such that in the up position the view is a single plot in the figure while the down position corresponds to a 2x2 subplot view of the plots.

- The two push tool buttons should correspond to forward and back button controls to allow the user to click through and view each plot.

- The two push tool buttons should be disabled when the toggle tool button is pressed down when the GUI is in sub-plot view mode.

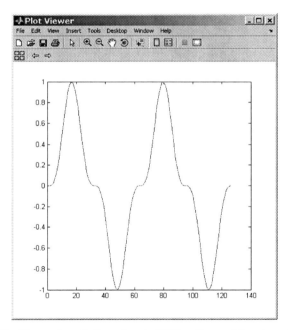

Figure 2.40: Exercise 2.9 output, UIToolbar object not selected

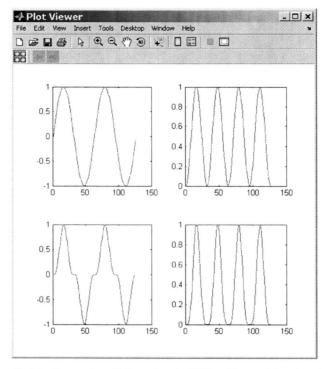

Figure 2.41: Exercise 2.9 output, UIToolbar object selected

Exercise 2.9 Solution

```
function main

    global current_plot
    N = 500;
    M = 500;

    current_plot = 1;

    % create a figure
    handles.fig = figure('Units', 'Pixels', ...
                        'Position', [100 100 N M], ...
                        'Color', [1 1 1], ...
                        'Name', 'Plot Viewer', ...
                        'NumberTitle', 'off');

    % generate plots
    x = 0:0.1:4*pi;
    for i = 1:4
```

```
        handles.plot(:,i) = sin(x).^i;
    end

    handles.toolbar = uitoolbar(handles.fig);

    % load uitoolbar icon images
    cdat_subplot = imread('subplot.jpg', 'jpg');
    cdat_back = imread('back.jpg', 'jpg');
    cdat_forward = imread('forward.jpg', 'jpg');

    uitoggletool(handles.toolbar, ...
                'CData',cdat_subplot, ...
                'TooltipString','Sub-Plot Layout View', ...
                'OnCallback', {@subplot_view_callback, handles}, ...
                'OffCallback', {@plot_view_callback, handles});

    uipushtool(handles.toolbar, ...
                'CData',cdat_back, ...
                'TooltipString','Previous Plot', ...
                'ClickedCallback', {@back_callback, handles},...
                'Separator', 'on');

    uipushtool(handles.toolbar, ...
                'CData',cdat_forward, ...
                'TooltipString','Next Plot', ...
                'ClickedCallback', {@forward_callback, handles});

function subplot_view_callback(hObject, event_data, handles)
    global current_plot
    current_plot = 1;
    buttons = get(handles.toolbar, 'Children');
    set(buttons(1:2), 'Enable', 'off');
    for i=1:4
        subplot(2,2,i); plot(handles.plot(:,i));
    end

function plot_view_callback(hObject, event_data, handles)
    global current_plot
    buttons = get(handles.toolbar, 'Children');
    set(buttons(1:2), 'Enable', 'on');
    subplot(1,1,1);
    plot(handles.plot(:,current_plot));
```

```
function back_callback(hObject, event_data, handles)
    global current_plot
    if current_plot == 1
        current_plot = 4;
    else
        current_plot = current_plot - 1;
    end
    plot(handles.plot(:,current_plot));


function forward_callback(hObject, event_data, handles)
    global current_plot
    if current_plot == 4
        current_plot = 1;
    else
        current_plot = current_plot + 1;
    end
    plot(handles.plot(:,current_plot));
```

Chapter 3
MATLAB GUIDE
GUI Development Environment

3.1 Introduction To GUIDE, Graphical User Interface Development Environment

Development of GUI programs may be accomplished using two separate methodologies in MATLAB: Low-level M-file code or high-level graphical layout. In the previous chapter you learned how to use low-level commands to generate GUI objects and controls. This chapter explains how to develop GUIs at a high-level by using GUIDE, the integrated tool MATLAB provides for GUI development. GUIDE provides user access to all the built-in GUI functions that are included in MATLAB and is designed similar to other GUI development environments that makes it a breeze to learn if you have designed GUIs using other languages. However, even if you do not have experience with GUI development, GUIDE is a simple tool that makes complex graphical user interface code design a simple task.

Main Features of GUIDE:

- **Component Palette:** Graphical button interface for creating GUI objects

- **Graphical GUI Figure Layout:** Provides a click-and-drag method of placing and positioning component objects on the GUI figure

- **Menu Editor:** Provides simple method of creating menu structure for you GUI

- **Property Inspector:** Provides easy access to all GUI object properties that control appearance and behavior of each object

- **Object Browser:** Displays hierarchical view of all GUI component objects

- **M-file Editor:** Shortcut button to the M-file code of the GUI project for easy editing

- **GUI Options Selector:** Popup window that provides selection of options for the style and behavior of the GUI design

- **Run Button:** Allows activation of current GUI design to evaluate performance throughout development

3.1.1   Advantages of Using GUIDE

As mentioned above, it is possible to develop GUIs in MATLAB using only **UIControl** and **UIMenu Objects**. These handle objects provide the user with the capability of instantiating any type of GUI component available in MATLAB from M-file code alone. This technique is referred to as low-level GUI development since it does not rely on any additional tools such as GUIDE to create a GUI program. This method was the only option available for early versions of MATLAB before GUIDE was developed and provided as an integrated tool.

Although developing GUIs using low-level UI object calls can be effective for generating backward compatible GUI projects or working with versions of MATLAB that do not have GUIDE available, complex GUI development becomes a daunting task, especially for multiple figure GUIs. Also, low-level graphical layout of each GUI component requires you to specify the coordinates and maintain the layout in numerical form in the M-file code. Overall, the amount of work required to develop a complex interface becomes much greater without the advantage of a graphical tool such as GUIDE.

Automatic code generation is another compelling reason to develop at a high-level. Each object creation in GUIDE allows M-file code generation automatically with control of the naming of functions and objects. Code generation saves you from typing or copying code sections for every GUI object definition and associated callback functions.

Key features of GUIDE provide additional advantages that assist you in speedy development. The *Property Inspector* and *Object Browser* provide a visual, interactive interface for each component object in your design. This allows you to quickly access and initialize all the properties of your GUI components. Also, each type of GUI component has different properties for controlling appearance and behavior. The *Property Inspector* eases the task of determining what is available for each GUI component.

Summary of GUIDE Advantages:

- **Simplicity of Layout:** Graphical layout is intuitive for GUI development and provides a well organized structure for complex designs

- **Automatic Code Generation:** GUIDE will generate callback function code and main GUI code allowing you to focus on details of the GUI design

- **Object Property Control:** The *Property Inspector* and object browser provide a complete view of available properties and hierarchy allowing you to modify GUI component behavior efficiently

Note that using GUIDE for high-level development does not eliminate the possibility of using low-level **UIControl** and **UIMenu** functions within your code. There are instances, such as dynamic GUIs that require GUI component changes based on dynamic content, where using **UIControls** and **UIMenus** may be very useful. In general, you should decide based on the type of GUI application if you may need to mix low and high-level approaches.

3.1.2   Getting Started With GUIDE

Starting GUIDE may be accomplished by simply typing *guide* at the MATLAB command prompt or by clicking the GUIDE button on the toolbar of the main MATLAB window. If the toolbar is not visible, then right click over the menu bar or shortcut bar and select toolbar. The toolbar should appear with a set of icon buttons. The GUIDE button is shown with an arrow and red text in the figure below:

Figure 3.1: Starting GUIDE from MATLAB session toolbar

Starting GUIDE by clicking this button will popup a window entitled GUIDE Quick Start. This window allows you to start a new GUI project and choose predefined templates, or you can click the Open Existing GUI tab and open an existing project. The following figure shows the GUIDE Quick Start window:

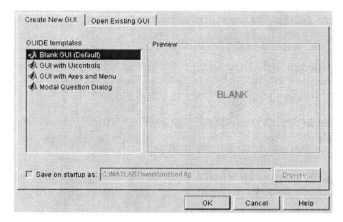

Figure 3.2: GUIDE Quick Start window

You can also specify a project name upon startup to skip the Quick Start window. This method can save a step when you are working with the same project.

```
>> guide gui_name
```

Another way to provide shortcuts to GUI projects is to use the shortcut bar in the MATLAB main window if it is available in the version you are working with. Creating shortcuts is especially advantageous when your GUI design project contains multiple GUI figure windows that must be defined in separate *.fig files. You can add a shortcut by right clicking the mouse over the shortcut bar and the following menu will appear:

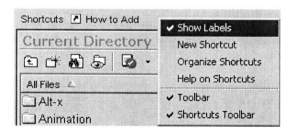

Figure 3.3: Context menu for MATLAB toolbar

You can create a shortcut by clicking on the "New Shortcut" menu item that will popup the "Shortcut Editor" window. In the example below, the 'Label' is set to 'Main GUI' and the 'Callback', or MATLAB command, is *guide main_gui*. After you click save, a new shortcut button will appear in the shortcut bar with the name Main GUI. You can follow this procedure to create multiple shortcuts, each starting an instance of GUIDE with a different figure name. The figure below shows an example of three shortcuts that have been added with the labels: Main GUI, Plot Figure GUI, and Image Figure GUI.

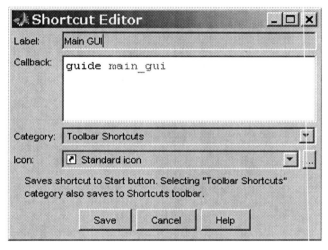

Figure 3.4: Shortcut Editor

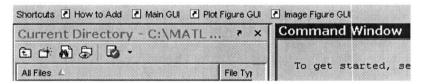

Figure 3.5: Shortcut added to toolbar

In general, when the GUIDE Quick Start window prompts you to select a new project template, the blank default template should be chosen unless the predefined templates match your desired layout closely. Another option in the Quick Start window is a "Save On Startup As" option that allows you to enter the project name you would like to use and GUIDE will save the new project with this name upon startup. This is useful since you will not need to make sure you perform a "Save As" operation after you have started the layout.

3.2   GUIDE Options and Setup

Once you create a new project by starting GUIDE, the main GUIDE window will appear with a blank figure GUI area and a set of icons on the left side of the window that is called the Component Palette. The default display of the GUI component tool shows small icons without names. You can change the default preferences by selecting "File" from the menu and then selecting "Preferences …". Select "GUIDE" from the list of preferences and click "Show names in component palette" to enable component names:

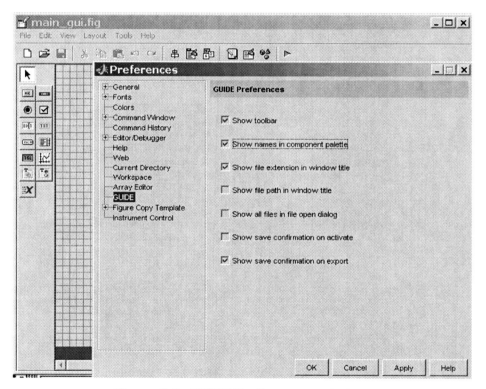

Figure 3.6: GUIDE Preferences window

You may find the component palette easier to use with the full names enabled if you are not familiar with the icons. The following figure shows the GUIDE window after the component names are enabled:

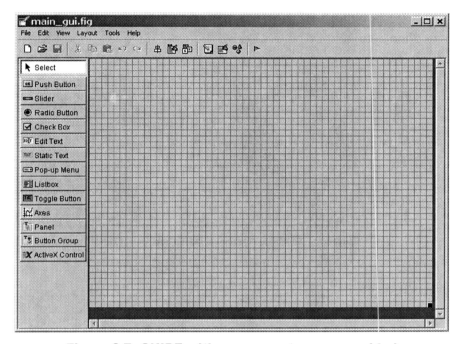

Figure 3.7: GUIDE with component names enabled

3.2.1   GUI Options

Before you begin defining the layout of the your design, it is important to prepare the main GUI figure to meet the specifications for your application. For example:

- What size should the figure be upon startup?
- Should the figure be resizable by the user?
- What color scheme do you want?
- Will the application allow multiple instances of the GUI to run simultaneously?

The options listed above may be defined by selecting the 'GUI Options ... ' menu item on the 'Tools' menu found on the menu bar. After selecting this item you will see the GUI Options window appear as is shown in the following figure:

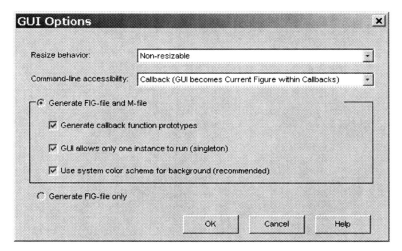

Figure 3.8: GUI Options window in GUIDE

Resize Behavior

- **Non-resizable:** This option restricts the window size to the user defined size of the figure when designed in GUIDE. This is generally used for most GUI designs since you do not need to design code to correctly control the layout of component objects for resize actions. For all examples in this text we will use the non-resizable option.

- **Proportional:** This option allows the user to change the size of the GUI figure and scale all component objects in the GUI such that they remain proportional to the original layout. For some applications this may be useful although GUI objects can become unreadable when resized to small windows or appear awkward when resized to large windows.

- **Other (Use ResizeFcn):** The third option allows you to define how the GUI objects should scale when a resize event occurs. Upon a resize event, the **ResizeFcn** callback function will be called to process your scaling code.

Command-line Accessibility

- **Callback (GUI Becomes Current Figure within Callbacks):** This option allows the GUI figure to become the current figure only within callback functions and is most commonly used.

- **Off (GUI Never Becomes Current Figure):** This option is preferable for multiple GUI figure applications such that function calls that output data to figures will not mistake the GUI figure as a generic figure for plotting, etc … The examples in this text will use this option to avoid errors with the GUI figures.

- **On (GUI May Become Figure From Command Line):** This option allows you to use the GUI figure as the current figure for command line expressions that may require a figure for data output. This option may lead to your GUI figure becoming overwritten by data generated from the command line. Caution should be used with this option as well.

- **Other (Use Settings From *Property Inspector*):** GUI figures contain a property called "HandleVisibility" that controls if the figure's handle may be observed as the current figure. The options for the "HandleVisibility" are: On, Off, and Callback, the same three options listed above.

Generate FIG-file and M-file : This option directs GUIDE to automatically generate M-file code along with the figure file. Three sub options are also available:

- **Generate Callback Function Prototypes:** This option will instruct GUIDE to generate callback function code in the M-file for each GUI component placed in the layout. This option should be enabled for automatic code generation for ease of development.

- **GUI Allows Only One Instance To Run (Singleton):** This option restricts the number of concurrent instances of the GUI application during a MATLAB session. In general, restricting this to singleton, or only allowing a single instance, is preferable. If you have a special need to run multiple instances you can disable this restriction.

- **Use System Color Scheme For Background:** This option is enabled by default and restricts the background color property of the GUI figure to use the system defined colors. There are many applications where you may want to disable this feature so that you can modify the colors. For example, if you wish to change the **Color** property of the figure to change the background color, then you need to disable this option.

Generate FIG-file Only : This option restricts GUIDE from generating an M-file for the GUI application. This option should only be used if you have experience writing GUI application code and have a specific need to control the code generation.

3.2.2   Grids and Rulers

Organizing and aligning the layout of GUI components can be somewhat tedious if you have a large number of components. One way to simplify the layout task is to enable grids and rulers by selecting the 'Grids and Rulers ...' menu item from the 'Tools' menu. This window allows you select the grid size and enable rulers and snap-grid options. These are very useful features to speed up your layout.

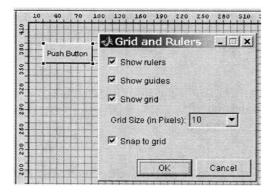

Figure 3.9: Grids and Rulers setup window

3.2.3   GUI Figure Size

Setting the default size of your GUI figure is very important since it will affect the user's ability to efficiently work with the application as well as determine the number of GUI components that may be placed in the figure. In general, you should be aware of the target user audience and available common display resolutions for your users if possible. Common display resolutions are in the range of 1024x768 pixels to 1920x1200 pixels with some computers containing multiple displays. Try not to create default figure sizes that are close to the maximum resolution of the target user's display, this can become cumbersome. Conversely, you do not want to restrict the size so small that all the GUI components are cramped and confusing in the GUI figure.

Once you have established the target size of your GUI figure, you can set the size in two ways: Using the Property Inspector or select and drag the edge of the figure in GUIDE. If you use the Property Inspector to change the size, first find the **Units** property and select 'pixels' as the units. Next, find the **Position** property and change the 'width' and 'height' to the desired GUI figure size. Working with pixel units for sizes provides a one-to-one reference to the display resolution in pixels.

Exercise 3.1: Creating A GUI Project

Create a GUI project named *main_gui* with the following properties:

- Non-resizable, 480x320 pixels
- Command Line Accessibility: Off
- Instruct GUIDE to generate both the FIG-file and M-file
- Enable grids and rulers

3.3   Property Inspector and Object Browser

In the previous section you learned how to utilize the Property Inspector to change the component object size properties of the main GUI figure. This section covers in detail how to use both the Property Inspector and Object Browser tools to efficiently develop your GUI applications.

3.3.1   Property Inspector

The Property Inspector may be launched in the following ways:

- Double click a GUI object (quickest)
- Right click over a GUI object and select "Property Inspector" from the item list

- Click the "Property Inspector" icon on the shortcut toolbar in GUIDE

Only one instance of the Property Inspector is launched. If you click on a different GUI object while the Property Inspector is open, then the properties for the current selected object will appear in the window. This is very useful for quickly browsing and editing properties for any of the objects in your GUI figure. Simply click an object and all the information about that object appears in an organized list that you can view and edit.

3.3.2   Object Browser

The *Object Browser* is another convenient tool that provides a hierarchical list of all GUI objects present in your design. The *Object Browser* may be invoked in using the following methods:

- Right click over a GUI object and select "Object Browser" from the item list
- Click the "Object Browser" icon on the shortcut toolbar in *GUIDE*

Exercise 3.2: Property Inspector and Object Browser Tools

Place the following GUI objects on the *main_gui* figure area:

a. Axes object

b. Static text object

c. Edit text object

d. Push button object

e. Radio button object

Do not attempt to place the objects in a particular order on the figure, use the Property Inspector and Object Browser to edit the properties of each object as follows:

1. Set **Units** property for all objects to 'pixels' by selecting all objects in the Object Browser and then change the **Units** property. This is an efficient way to change multiple object properties at once.

2. Next, click on the **Axes Object** in the Object Browser and find the **Position** property, expand the property, and change the values of x, y, width, and height to 160, 20, 300, 200 respectively.

3. Repeat modifying the position and size of each object with the following parameters:

   a. Static Text = [20 190 100 30]

   b. Edit Text Box = [20 240 440 20]

   c. Push Button = [20 190 100 30]

   d. Radio Button = [20 150 100 20]

When these properties have been successfully modified you should have a figure window with the following object layout:

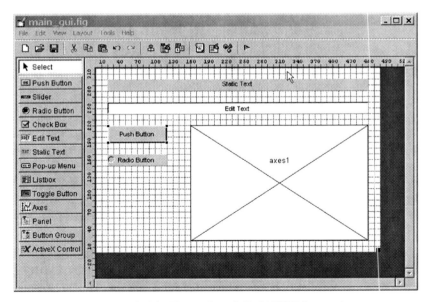

Figure 3.10: Exercise 3.2 GUIDE layout

Make sure to save the project as *main_gui* and try running the GUI by clicking 'Run' button on the GUIDE shortcut toolbar.

3.4   Generating Callback Functions

An easy way to display the available callback functions for an object and create callbacks in the GUI M-file is to right click over an object, click on the 'View Callbacks' item, and select the desired callback you wish to implement. When you click on the callback item from the list, you will notice that the **Callback** property will contain an auto-generated callback function name and the M-file is automatically updated with the basic function code definition. For example, if you create the Callback function for the push button in *main_gui*, the following code will be generated and added to *main_gui.m*:

```
% --- Executes on button press in pushbutton1.
function pushbutton1_Callback(hObject, eventdata, handles)
% hObject    handle to pushbutton1 (see GCBO)
% eventdata  reserved - to be defined in a future version of MATLAB
% handles    structure with handles and user data (see GUIDATA)
```

Notice that the name of the callback function that is generated is defined from the **Tag** property. Modifying the **Tag** property is an efficient way of defining the names of each callback function for your GUI.

3.4.1   Callback Naming Conventions

Adhering to a naming convention for your callback functions will simplify the detailed programming of your GUI after the functional structure is defined. Keeping track of GUI objects with auto-generated names will lead to code that may be hard to follow since your push button objects will be named *pushbutton1*, *pushbutton2*, etc ... Also, GUIDE generates the names based on each instance you place an object so that numerical increments may not represent a particular order in terms of location in the GUI.

To avoid this type of confusion you should develop a naming convention that will provide more description for each object. The convention that will be used throughout this text is as follows:

GUI Object **Tag** Property = *ObjectTypeName_ActionDescription*

Where the *ObjectTypeName* is *pushbutton*, *radiobutton*, *listbox*, etc ... and the *ActionDescription* indicates the callback action that will be associated with the callback such as *update_plot* or *calc_matrix*. The combined **Tag** name should appear as follows:

> **Tag** = *pushbutton_update_plot*
>
> or
>
> **Tag** = *radiobutton_calc_matrix*

Exercise 3.3: Callback Function Naming Using The Tag Property

Try setting up the following callback functions for the *main_gui* project with the listed action descriptions using the naming conventions defined above. Also, you will need to set the **String** or **Name** properties of the objects to display the text to the user that represents the function of the GUI object action. The String Name column in the table defines the text that should be displayed to the user.

Table 3.1: Exercise 3.3 HG Object definitions

Graphic Object	Callback Functions	Action Description	String Name
Push button	Callback, CreateFcn	update_plot	*String* = Update Plot
Radio button	Callback, CreateFcn	display_text	*String* = Display Text
Edit box	Callback, CreateFcn	user_plot_input	*String* = Enter Plot Command
Static text	none	title	*String* = Interactive Plot GUI
Axes	CreateFcn	plot	none
Figure	none	main_gui	*Name* = Main GUI

Each time you create a callback function, GUIDE will automatically generate the function code in the *main_gui.m* file. After you create all necessary callback functions and set the object string names, run the GUI to verify the results. The figure below shows how the GUI should look when run from GUIDE:

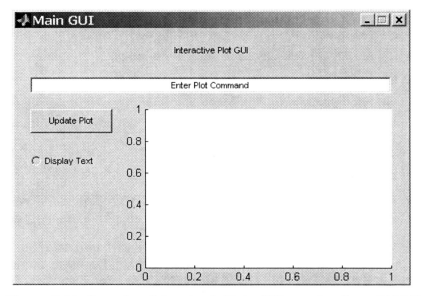

Figure 3.11: Exercise 3.3 output, Main GUI running from GUIDE

3.5 Creating User Interface Menus

Another important aspect of GUI development is the creation of User Interface Menus. GUIDE has an integrated tool called Menu Editor that allows you to create complete hierarchical menu interfaces with callback functions. The Menu Editor may be launched by clicking the 'Tools' menu option in GUIDE and then clicking on the 'Menu Editor ...' item. The following window should appear:

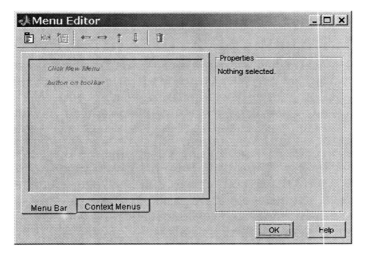

Figure 3.12: Menu Editor window

There are two tabs labeled Menu Bar and Context Menus in the main window that allow you to create each type of menu.

3.5.1   Menu Bars

The Menu Editor provides a very simple interface for developing Menu Bars. To create a Menu Bar, simply click on the New Menu shortcut toolbar icon and a single menu item labeled *Untitled1* should appear in the window. If you click this item, a list of UIMenu Properties should appear on the right side of the window. The **Label** property defines the text that will appear on the menu. The **Tag** property is the similar to other graphic object **Tag** properties in that it provides a tag for the menu object and is used in the automatic generation of the Callback function name. There are additional features such as the *Accelerator* option that allows you to define a Ctrl+Hot Key shortcut that will call the menu item callback function.

Clicking the *New Menu* icon again will create a second menu for the *Menu Bar*. Menu items may be added by clicking on the menu name and then clicking the *New Menu Item* icon on the shortcut bar. Each time you create a new menu item make sure you edit the **Label** and **Tag** property before viewing the **Callback** function. Once the **Labels** and **Tags** are defined you can view the M-file code by clicking the *View Button.* Clicking this button will instruct GUIDE to automatically generate all menu item callback functions.

3.5.2   Context Menus

Each graphic object has a property called **UIContextMenu** that allows you to select a *Context Menu* from a list of context menus developed using the Menu Editor. This structure allows you to create a few commonly used *Context Menus* and assign these to individual GUI objects.

You can create a context menu by opening the Menu Editor and clicking the *Context Menus* tab at the bottom of the window. The steps involved are similar to creating Menu Bars. Once you have created a new *Context Menu* you can assign this to any GUI object **UIContextMenu** property. The figure below shows how to assign the *Context Menu* using Property Inspector:

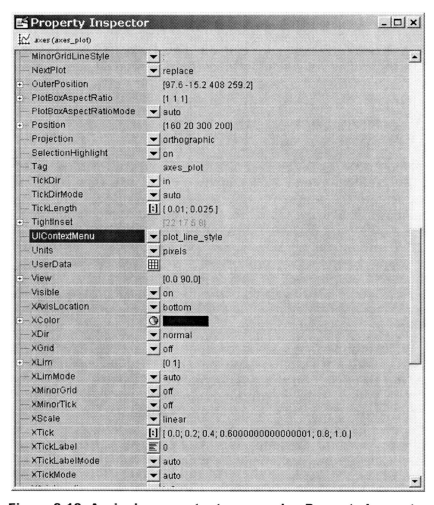

Figure 3.13: Assigning a context menu using Property Inspector

Exercise 3.4: Creating Menu Bars and Context Menus

Create a menu bar for the *main_gui* project with the following items and hierarchy:

File

  Load Workspace ...

  Save Workspace ...

Help

  Using Interactive Plot GUI

  About

In the menu editor you should have the following menu layout:

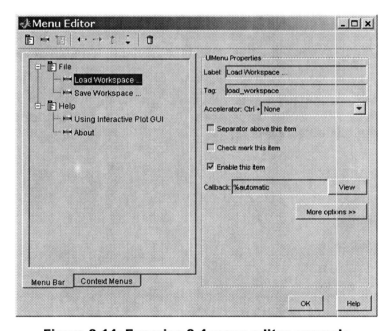

Figure 3.14: Exercise 3.4 menu editor example

Try running *main_gui* once the menu bar is complete, you should **have** the following figure:

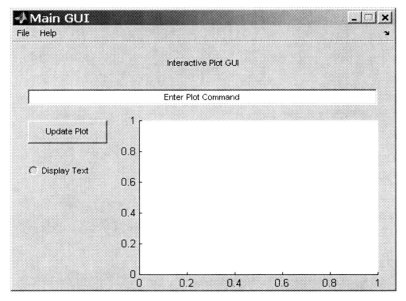

Figure 3.15: Exercise 3.4, Main GUI example with Menus added

Next, create a context menu called *plot_line_styles* with the following menu items and assign this context menu to the **UIContextMenu** property of the **Axes Object**:

plot_line_styles

      Solid

      Dotted

      Dashed

When completed, run the GUI and perform a right click over the Axes area, the context menu should appear.

3.6   Automatic M-file Code Generation and Structure

This section describes the details of the structure of auto-generated M-file code from GUIDE and provides tips for maintaining code structure and naming conventions when working with auto-generated code.

3.6.1   Auto-generated M-file Structure

The list below summarizes the structure of the M-file code that is generated from GUIDE. Some parameters will vary based on the options for the GUI such as if the figure will be singleton, etc ...

- Main Function
- Main Function Initialization
- Opening Function
- Output Function
- Callback Functions

3.6.2   Main Function

GUIDE creates an M-file with a main function that has the same name as the M-file and figure file names. The main function has default input and output variables defined as *varargin* and *varargout* respectively. These variable argument parameters are useful for passing data to the GUI upon startup or creating output data when the GUI is terminated. For example, if you wish to launch a child window GUI from a parent GUI you can pass data to the child when launched and back to the parent when the child is closed. The code listed below is the main function for the *main_gui* project:

```
function varargout = main_gui(varargin)
% MAIN_GUI M-file for main_gui.fig
%       MAIN_GUI, by itself, creates a new MAIN_GUI or raises the existing
%       singleton*.
%
%       H = MAIN_GUI returns the handle to a new MAIN_GUI or the handle to
%       the existing singleton*.
%
%       MAIN_GUI('CALLBACK',hObject,eventData,handles,...) calls the local
```

```
%       function named CALLBACK in MAIN_GUI.M with the given input
arguments.
%
%       MAIN_GUI('Property','Value',...) creates a new MAIN_GUI or raises
the
%       existing singleton*.  Starting from the left, property value pairs
are
%       applied to the GUI before main_gui_OpeningFunction gets called.  An
%       unrecognized property name or invalid value makes property
application
%       stop.  All inputs are passed to main_gui_OpeningFcn via varargin.
%
%       *See GUI Options on GUIDE's Tools menu.  Choose "GUI allows only
one
%       instance to run (singleton)".
```

GUIDE does an excellent job of commenting the M-file to show you what options are available for invoking the main function. For example, you can start the GUI by calling the main function including property values that you want to use to initialize the figure.

By default, the first *varargout* output argument is set to the handle of the GUI figure object, *hObject*. You can define additional output arguments using the following syntax:

```
varargout{1} = hObject;
varargout{2} = user_data_2;
...
varargout{n} = user_data_n;
```

Similarly, you can use the *varargin* argument to read in data to the GUI with the following syntax:

```
user_data_in1 = varargin{1};
user_data_in2 = varargin{2};
...
user_data_n = varargin{n};
```

The *varargin* argument assignments should be placed in the *OpeningFcn()*. Note that the definitions of the *varargin* and *varargout* arguments will not be altered by GUIDE when it updates the code automatically.

3.6.3   Main Function Initialization

The initialization section of the main function is clearly marked with Begin and End labels and 'DO NOT EDIT' is emphasized in the comments. This section is automatically generated based on options from GUIDE so it is good practice to avoid editing this section. The code listed below shows the output from GUIDE for the *main_gui* project:

```
% Begin initialization code - DO NOT EDIT
gui_Singleton = 1;
gui_State = struct('gui_Name',       mfilename, ...
                   'gui_Singleton',  gui_Singleton, ...
                   'gui_OpeningFcn', @main_gui_OpeningFcn, ...
                   'gui_OutputFcn',  @main_gui_OutputFcn, ...
                   'gui_LayoutFcn',  [] , ...
                   'gui_Callback',   []);
if nargin && ischar(varargin{1})
    gui_State.gui_Callback = str2func(varargin{1});
end

if nargout
    [varargout{1:nargout}] = gui_mainfcn(gui_State, varargin{:});
else
    gui_mainfcn(gui_State, varargin{:});
end
% End initialization code - DO NOT EDIT
```

Note that the *gui_Singleton* variable defines if multiple instances of the GUI may be instantiated, for the current project the value is set to allow only a single instance to run. The *gui_State* structure contains information that is passed to the *gui_mainfcn* that starts the actual GUI figure.

3.6.4   Renaming GUI Projects

If you have selected to allow GUIDE to automatically generate the main M-file, it is important to understand how to rename project files without corrupting any information that will result in errors for your GUI code. Note that the name of the M-file is also the name of the main function for the GUI and this name is used by GUIDE in the creation of GUI callback function names. If you change the name of the M-file and FIG-file directly using a file browser for example, then your M-file will still contain references to the previous name of the M-file. GUIDE does not recognize that the M-file name is different and does not automatically update the names of functions with your new name.

The best way to rename your project files and avoid errors is to simply save the project with a new name from within GUIDE using the 'Save As ...' option. Saving your project using this method instructs GUIDE to update all the name references within the M-file to the new name you provide for the project.

3.6.5   Removing GUI Objects and Associated Callback Functions

Another important aspect of maintaining automatically generated code when using GUIDE is removal of GUI objects and associated code. In general, GUIDE does not remove callback function code after it has been created for a GUI object. For example, if you place a radiobutton in your design and then generate a callback function, you will see the callback function code shell in the M-file. Now, if you decide you no longer want the radiobutton and delete it from the layout in GUIDE, the function code remains in the M-file. You need to delete the function code by hand from the M-file. This is good practice so that you do not end up with many functions in your code that are not associated with any object and will never be called.

Chapter 4
Structure of MATLAB GUIs

4.1   GUI Design Style, Layout, and Program Flow

Chapter 2 introduced you to low-level GUI programming using the **HG Object** hierarchy while chapter 3 introduced GUIDE as a high-level programming tool for generating GUI layouts and automating baseline code creation. This chapter expands on these previous chapters by introducing you to a system level architecture approach to GUI application development including the definition of the design style appropriate for the intended user audience, creating user friendly data structures, working with dialog boxes and advanced user controls, and clearly establishing program flow.

4.1.1   Defining The GUI

Often times a GUI application design begins with a set of specifications and parameters that serve as baseline requirements that the program must accomplish to meet the needs of the user. Establishing a basic specification is a powerful tool that can help you design the correct structure a priory and avoid needing to completely restructure the application midstream.

Defining the GUI requires planning out the application goals and design style based on the specification for the application. Below is a list of example questions that should be considered when planning a GUI application:

Application Goals:
- What is the target application?
- What are the specifications and parameters required for the GUI?
- Who is the target user and how many users will utilize the GUI?
- How will the GUI assist users in achieving solutions to their problems?

Design Style:

- Should the GUI be menu centric, UIControl centric, or a combination?

- Does the application require a single figure or multiple figure design?

- Will the GUI require plot or image figures and how will the user need to interact with these objects?

- Does the design require custom controls such as image based click tabs, radial dials, or dynamic UIControls?

For simple applications you may not need to perform a rigorous analysis when defining the GUI however complex GUI designs tend to benefit from this approach.

4.1.2 GUI Design Styles and Layout

The GUI design style is important for assuring smooth usability for the application. For example, if you have only five control parameters that the user will interact with in the GUI, a design style that is UIControl centric may be best to allow the user to see the controls and quickly interact with them. However, if the application is more complex and has several operating modes and many parameters, then it may be better to provide a comprehensive Menu Bar structure so that the GUI does not become cluttered with UIControls and require a very large GUI window. Planning the design style up front based on the application needs can help you generate a GUI that is user friendly.

Another aspect of usability that is important in the planning phase is the general layout of the GUI. Drawing or sketching out the graphical layout of each figure window and the general menu hierarchies can help you optimize the usability of the GUI.

4.1.3 Program Flow

Defining the program flow is another important exercise in the planning phase that can help you realize the overall architecture of the GUI and determine what types of controls and interfaces may be necessary or most useful. The program flow is often a set of flow charts that describes the interaction between GUI controls, callback functions, and HG objects. Again, for simple applications this type of planning may not be necessary but for complex GUIs this can provide a good architectural reference.

4.1.4   Example of Defining A GUI: FigView

Example 4.1: Example of Defining A GUI: Figview

An example GUI application project will be considered in this chapter to familiarize you with the process of MATLAB GUI development. The example project specification is presented below and will be followed in each subsequent section:

Project Name:	FigView
Project File Names:	figview.m, figview.fig

Basic Description:

MATLAB plot creation GUI that allows you to create a list of plot commands and select plots for viewing in separate figures.

Application Goals:

Design a GUI that allows the user to enter plot commands and plot names to create plot objects. Each plot object the user creates should be displayed using an axes object and should be added to a list displayed in a listbox. The GUI should include a context menu that pops up when the user right clicks over the axes or the listbox to allow the user to delete all plots or launch the current plot in a separate figure window for editing and saving.

Design Style:

A combination of a menu bar and UIControl objects will be used in the GUI layout. An axes object will be used to display the current plot that is selected. UIpanel objects will be used for separate UIControl sections for Plot Creation and Select Current Plot.

Graphical Layout:

The GUI layout sketch for the FigView interface is shown below:

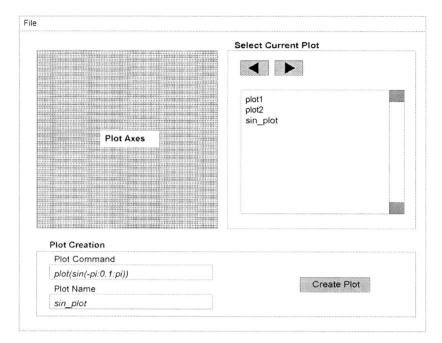

Figure 4.1: Example 4.1 conceptual drawing of FigView GUI layout

Menus:

The menu bar and context menus hierarchies are shown below:

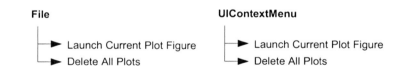

The 'Launch Current Plot Figure' sub-item should pop up a new figure window and display the current plot. The File Menu and UIContextMenu have the same functions. The 'Delete All Plots' sub-item should launch a question dialog box that asks the user: "Are you sure you want to delete all plots?"

4.2   Handles Data Structure Organization

MATLAB GUIs generated from GUIDE use an object data structure referred to as the *handles* data structure. In chapter 2, many of the examples also use a handles object data structure mainly to familiarize you with the conventions used in MATLAB. This section describes how the handles data structure may be used to hold information about GUI objects and how to pass information between callback functions. Also, the concept of using the **Tag** property of objects is introduced along with some basic naming conventions that can help when developing complex GUIs.

4.2.1   Handles Data Structures

When you design a GUI and generate code using GUIDE you will notice that each callback function has a common format, for example:

```
% --- Executes on selection change in listbox1.
function listbox1_Callback(hObject, eventdata, handles)
```

The auto-generated code for a new listbox control has three input arguments that include the following:

- **hObject** : Handle to the current active object callback or figure
- **eventdata** : Event data passed to the callback function such as the last key pressed (this is not used for GUIs developed using GUIDE)
- **handles** : Handles data structure containing GUI object and user information

As discussed in Chapter 3, the **Tag** property is used to identify a handle to a particular GUI object. For example *handles.listbox1* is the handle to the listbox object shown above when the **Tag** property is set to *listbox1* and may be used to set or get property information for the listbox.

    If you wish to expand the accessibility of any user-defined variable throughout the GUI code, you can add them to the *handles* structure that is passed to every function and holds all the object information for the GUI. This is an effective and efficient way of storing all the information in one structure. For example, if you wish to generate data within a callback function such as storing the state of the **Value** property of the listbox, you can add the user variable to the handles structure as follows:

```
handles.listbox_value = get(handles.listbox1, 'Value');
```

Now the *handles* structure contains the field *listbox_value*, however the accessibility of this field is still only local to the current callback function. Since the *handles* structure contains application data for the current GUI figure application, it needs to be updated for the entire application to gain access to the *listbox_value* field. You can update the *handles* structure by adding the *guidata()* function code shown below:

```
% --- Executes on selection change in listbox1.
function listbox1_Callback(hObject, eventdata, handles)
        handles.listbox_value = get(handles.listbox1, 'Value');
        guidata(hObject, handles);
```

The *guidata()* function allows you to store *handles* to the GUI application figure object. The *guidata()* function in conjunction with the *guihandles()* function may also be used to retrieve the *handles* structure from a figure, this is particularly useful when you need to define a separate figure window for plotting data and you wish to obtain information about the figure.

In general, you will need to use *guidata()* any time you change a field value or add a field to the *handles* structure. To avoid errors it is good practice to place a *guidata()* function call at the end of each callback function.

Following the FigView example GUI project defined in section 4.1.4, we develop a *handles* data structure for the GUI that uses the **Tag** properties of each object and a sub-structure for user data. The diagram shown below demonstrates a typical *handles* structure that follows the naming convention described in chapter 3:

Handles Data Structure

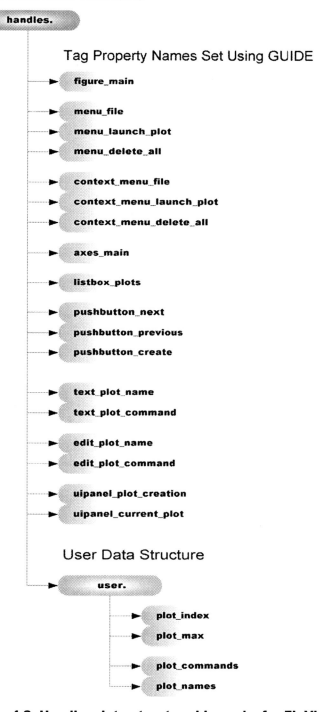

Figure 4.2: Handles data structure hierarchy for FigView

Each GUI control and object **Tag** use labels to clearly identify the style or type of control and the basic function that it performs. Although these **Tag** definitions may produce long variable names for the *handles* structure, the names are easy to remember and generate very readable code for editing.

A sub-structure named *user* was added here to hold user variables and data for sharing across callback functions and throughout FigView. The creation of a separate sub-structure for user data has two main advantages:

- *handles.user* always denotes user data and will not be confused with GUI controls and objects

- *handles.user* may be passed to functions as a pointer exclusively to user data without passing GUI parameters

4.2.2   Initializing GUI Properties and Variables

The *OpeningFcn()* function of a GUI figure is often used to initialize GUI properties and other user variables since this function is called just prior to when the GUI becomes visible. All GUI object properties are available during the execution of *OpeningFcn()*. Initializing GUI properties and variables that affect the initial display of your GUI program and the initial state of UI objects is generally required for proper operation. Examples of properties that are often initialized are:

- String text in edit boxes
- Values of radiobuttons and check boxes
- Values of listboxes
- Axes properties such as type of plot, grid lines, colors
- Slider ranges and initial slider values

There are two ways to initialize object properties: using the Property Inspector in GUIDE or using the *set()* function. The *OpeningFcn()* for FigView is shown below and uses the *set()* function to initialize UI objects:

figview_OpeningFcn

```
% --- Executes just before figview is made visible.
function figview_OpeningFcn(hObject, eventdata, handles, varargin)

    % Choose default command line output for figview
    handles.output = hObject;

    % initialize handles data structure
    handles.user.plot_index = 1;        % plot number index
    handles.user.plot_max = 1;          % total number of plots created

    % initialize GUI controls, disable until the first plot is created
    set(handles.pushbutton_previous, 'Enable', 'off');
    set(handles.pushbutton_next, 'Enable', 'off');
    set(handles.listbox_plots, 'Enable', 'off');
    set(handles.menu_launch_plot, 'Enable', 'off');

    % Update handles structure
    guidata(hObject, handles);
```

GUIDE automatically places a *guidata()* function in the *OpeningFcn()* that will update *hObject* with all initialization changes you make to the *handles* structure. Make sure you place your initialization code before the *guidata()* call. Two user variables are added to the structure and initialized and four properties are initialized. The listbox, pushbuttons, and *launch_plot* menu items are disabled upon startup so that they are not accessible to the user until a plot is created.

Exercise 4.1: FigView Layout and Handles Structure Creation

Use GUIDE to layout FigView based on the design sketch shown in 4.1.4 and use the Property Inspector to set the **Tag** properties following the *handles* data structure diagram shown in section 4.2.1. Make sure you set the option in GUIDE to automatically generate the baseline M-file code. When complete you should have a GUI shell with each callback function generated by GUIDE and the following layout:

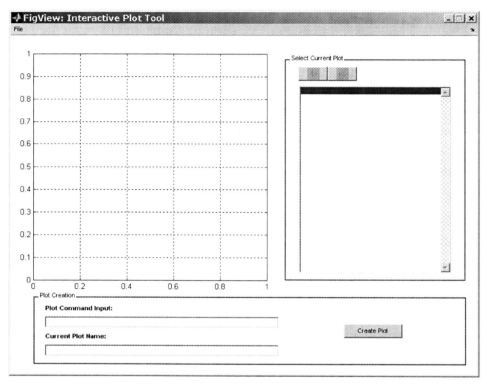

Figure 4.3: FigView layout

4.2.3   Handles and Callback Function Examples

Chapter 2 introduced you to passing handles to callback functions to allow object manipulation. This section describes more details of how the *handles* structure may be used with callback functions and user defined functions by demonstrating examples for the FigView GUI application.

FigView uses two edit box controls to allow the user to enter a MATLAB plot command and a plot name. The string text entered for each edit box is automatically stored in the **String** property of each edit box object when the user presses enter. In this application, we only need to read the edit box strings when the Create Plot pushbutton is pressed so the edit box callback functions do not need further code:

```
% --- Executes during object creation, after setting all properties.
function edit_plot_command_CreateFcn(hObject, eventdata, handles)


% --- Executes during object creation, after setting all properties.
function edit_plot_name_Callback(hObject, eventdata, handles)
```

The *pushbutton_create_Callback* should perform the following tasks:

1. Enable the pushbuttons, listbox, and launch_plot menu items the first plot is created upon pressing the Create Plot button

2. The *handles.user.plot_index* variable should be set to *plot_max* to ensure the newly created plot is set to an index higher than the previously created plot

3. The *plot_commands* and *plot_names* lists should be updated with the new string entered from the edit boxes

4. The new plot command should be evaluated using a user function named *update_plot()*

5. The listbox **String** property should be updated with the new plot name

6. Finally, the *plot_index* and *plot_max* variables should be incremented for the next plot command

The following code accomplishes the requirements listed above:

pushbutton_create_Callback

```
function pushbutton_create_Callback(hObject, eventdata, handles)


    set(handles.pushbutton_previous, 'Enable', 'on');
    set(handles.pushbutton_next, 'Enable', 'on');
    set(handles.listbox_plots, 'Enable', 'on');
    set(handles.menu_launch_plot, 'Enable', 'on');


    handles.user.plot_index = handles.user.plot_max;


    handles.user.plot_commands(handles.user.plot_index)=
{get(handles.edit_plot_command, 'String')};
    handles.user.plot_names(handles.user.plot_index)=
{get(handles.edit_plot_name, 'String')};


    % update plot axes with current plot command selected
    handles = update_plot(handles);
```

```
% update listbox text with the list of plot names created
set(handles.listbox_plots,   'String', handles.user.plot_names, ...
                        'Value', handles.user.plot_index );


handles.user.plot_max = handles.user.plot_max + 1;


% Update handles structure
guidata(hObject, handles);
```

Notice that the plot commands and plot names are saved to the *handles* structure as cell types to allow variable length text strings to exist in the same vector. The user defined *update_plot()* function passes the *handles* structure as input and output arguments to ensure it may be used in the function and changes to *handles* are returned to the main program. Also, note that the listbox_plot object **String** and **Value** properties are updated with the new plot information and plot index.

It should be clear from this example how a callback function can easily read or manipulate other GUI objects and user data by using the *handles* data structure that is passed as an input argument. The following code sections from the complete FigView application further demonstrate how to use the handles structure:

menu_file_Callback

```
% no actions
```

menu_launch_plot_Callback

```
function menu_launch_plot_Callback(hObject, eventdata, handles)
% hObject     handle to menu_launch_plot (see GCBO)
% eventdata   reserved - to be defined in a future version of MATLAB
% handles     structure with handles and user data (see GUIDATA)
    % launch new figure
    figure


    % evaluate plot string and plot in new figure
    eval(handles.user.plot_commands{handles.user.plot_index});
```

menu_delete_all_Callback

```
function menu_delete_all_Callback(hObject, eventdata, handles)
% hObject     handle to delete_all (see GCBO)
```

```
% eventdata   reserved - to be defined in a future version of MATLAB
% handles     structure with handles and user data (see GUIDATA)
    handles.user.plot_index = 1;

    handles.user.plot_max = 1;

    handles.user.plot_commands = {};

    handles.user.plot_names = {};


    % update listbox text with the list of plot names created
    set(handles.listbox_plots, 'String', '', 'Value', 1);


    % disable current plot controls
    set(handles.pushbutton_previous, 'Enable', 'off');

    set(handles.pushbutton_next, 'Enable', 'off');

    set(handles.listbox_plots, 'Enable', 'off');


    % reset axes
    plot(1);

    set(handles.axes_main, 'XGrid', 'on', 'YGrid', 'on');


    % Update handles structure
    guidata(hObject, handles);
```

context_menu_file_Callback

```
% no actions defined
```

context_menu_launch_plot_Callback

```
function context_menu_launch_plot_Callback(hObject, eventdata, handles)
% hObject     handle to context_menu_launch_plot (see GCBO)
% eventdata   reserved - to be defined in a future version of MATLAB
% handles     structure with handles and user data (see GUIDATA)
        menu_launch_plot_Callback(hObject, [], handles);
```

Since the menu bar and context menus have the same functionality, you can simply call the *menu_launch_plot_Callback()* function within the context menu callback in order to avoid repetitious code. This also demonstrates how callback function execution is not limited to GUI object calls. Another way to define the same action for multiple GUI objects is to simply define the callback function with the same name for all objects that share the callback.

context_menu_delete_all_Callback

```
function context_menu_delete_all_Callback(hObject, eventdata, handles)
% hObject     handle to context_menu_delete_all (see GCBO)
% eventdata   reserved - to be defined in a future version of MATLAB
% handles     structure with handles and user data (see GUIDATA)
      menu_delete_all_Callback(hObject, [], handles);
```

axes_main

```
% no callbacks defined
```

listbox_plot_Callback

```
function listbox_plots_Callback(hObject, eventdata, handles)
    handles.user.plot_index = get(handles.listbox_plots,'Value');
    handles = update_plot(handles);


    % Update handles structure
    guidata(hObject, handles);
```

update_plot (user defined)

```
% update the plot with the current plot selected
function handles = update_plot(handles)

    % make sure GUI figure is current figure
    figure(handles.figure_main);

    % set plot command and name fields for current plot selected
    set(handles.edit_plot_command, 'String', ...
        handles.user.plot_commands{handles.user.plot_index});
    set(handles.edit_plot_name, 'String', ...
        handles.user.plot_names{handles.user.plot_index});

    % evaluate plot string
    eval(handles.user.plot_commands{handles.user.plot_index});
```

pushbutton_next_Callback

```
function pushbutton_next_Callback(hObject, eventdata, handles)
% hObject     handle to pushbutton_next (see GCBO)
% eventdata   reserved - to be defined in a future version of MATLAB
% handles     structure with handles and user data (see GUIDATA)

    % check if plot index is max, otherwise increase by 1
    if handles.user.plot_index >= handles.user.plot_max-1
```

```
        handles.user.plot_index = 1;
else
        handles.user.plot_index = handles.user.plot_index + 1;
end


set(handles.listbox_plots, 'Value', handles.user.plot_index);


% update plot axes with current plot command selected
handles = update_plot(handles);


% Update handles structure
guidata(hObject, handles);
```

pushbutton_next_CreateFcn

```
function pushbutton_next_CreateFcn(hObject, eventdata, handles)
% hObject    handle to pushbutton_next (see GCBO)
% eventdata  reserved - to be defined in a future version of MATLAB
% handles    empty - handles not created until after all CreateFcns called
        % read next button image icon and place on pushbutton
        set(hObject, 'CData', imread('forward2.jpg', 'jpg'));
```

pushbutton_previous_Callback

```
function pushbutton_previous_Callback(hObject, eventdata, handles)
% hObject    handle to pushbutton_previous (see GCBO)
% eventdata  reserved - to be defined in a future version of MATLAB
% handles    structure with handles and user data (see GUIDATA)

    % check if plot index is 1, otherwise decrease by 1
    if handles.user.plot_index <= 1
        handles.user.plot_index = handles.user.plot_max-1;
    else
        handles.user.plot_index = handles.user.plot_index - 1;
    end


    set(handles.listbox_plots, 'Value', handles.user.plot_index);


    % update plot axes with current plot command selected
    handles = update_plot(handles);


    % Update handles structure
    guidata(hObject, handles);
```

pushbutton_previous_CreateFcn

```
function pushbutton_previous_CreateFcn(hObject, eventdata, handles)
% hObject    handle to pushbutton_previous (see GCBO)
% eventdata  reserved - to be defined in a future version of MATLAB
% handles    empty - handles not created until after all CreateFcns called
        % read next button image icon and place on pushbutton
        set(hObject, 'CData', imread('back2.jpg', 'jpg'));
```

text_plot_name

```
% no callbacks defined
```

text_plot_command

```
% no callbacks defined
```

edit_plot_name_Callback

```
% no actions defined
```

edit_plot_command_Callback

```
% no actions defined
```

uipanel_plot_creation

```
% no callbacks defined
```

uipanel_current_plot

```
% no callbacks defined
```

When all of the above functions are implemented, FigView is then ready to run and plot functions. Try running FigView and create a plot using input functions such as the *sphere()* or *peaks()*. You will notice that each plot you create will appear in the listbox and all plots created are saved to this list. Now you can select each plot and the axes will display your selection. The context menus also allow you to launch the current plot in a separate, new figure. The image below shows a screen shot of the FigView in action:

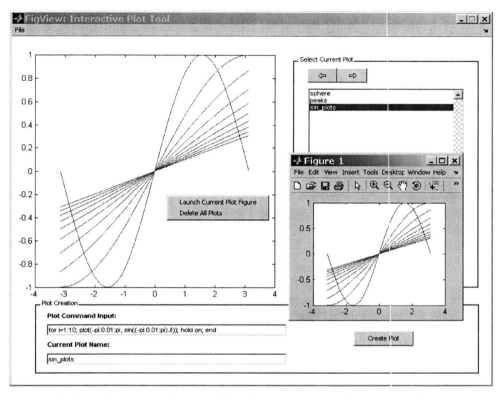

Figure 4.4: FigView running after functional programming

4.2.4   Limitations of Handles

Although the *handles* data structure is a powerful instrument for designing GUI applications, there are a few limitations that prevent it from working well with real-time operations such as animation loops. Since the *handles* structure only updates after the *guidata()* function call AND completion of the function call, i.e. exiting the function, a loop within a callback function cannot receive input from other callback functions to instruct the loop to stop. This issue may be addressed by using global variable structures or timer objects. Chapter 5 discusses this in more detail when describing MATLAB GUI architecture for real-time operation and how to address this issue.

Another limitation is the inability to create **Tags** with sub-structure definitions. For example, if you try to set the **Tag** property of a GUI object to *listbox.plots*, then an error will occur. You can imagine that it may be useful to have a more clearly defined structure hierarchy where GUI objects with similar characteristics can be grouped. However, you can only have *handles.listbox_plots* as opposed to *handles.listbox.plots*.

4.3   Event Handling

GUI applications often have multiple input and output events that must be handled to function correctly. Events may be user actions such as clicking on a pushbutton or slider control as well as updating a figure's drawing surface with all graphic objects. MATLAB uses an event queue method of handling events that is similar to any typical GUI application. This section discusses the details of the MATLAB event queue and different types of events important for developing interactive GUIs.

4.3.1   The Event Queue

The event queue is a stream of event calls that are stored based on the time the event was invoked. The queue is a first-in, first-out architecture that makes sure the oldest events have priority and are processed first. The figure below shows an example diagram of the event queue including the event source and event processing callback function that handles the event:

Event Source	Event Queue	Event Processing
	Oldest event	
Mouse moved	Mouse Motion Event	WindowButtonMotionFcn
Mouse button pressed	Mouse Button Click Event	WindowButtonDownFcn
Mouse moved	Mouse Motion Event	WindowButtonMotionFcn
Mouse moved	Mouse Motion Event	WindowButtonMotionFcn
Slider control action	Slider Event	Slider_CallbackFcn
Slider control action	Slider Event	Slider_CallbackFcn
Key pressed on keyboard	Key Press Event	KeypressFcn
Mouse moved	Mouse Motion Event	WindowButtonMotionFcn
Surface command called	Draw Surface Object Event	Processed when Callback finishes or an event processing command is called such as *drawnow*
Line command called	Draw Line Object Event	Processed when Callback finishes or an event processing command is called such as *drawnow*
Drawnow command called	Figure Draw Update Event	Redraw figure graphics and flush event queue
Mouse moved	Mouse Motion Event	WindowButtonMotionFcn
	Newest event	

New Events
Entering Queue

Figure 4.5: MATLAB event queue and processing diagram

Incoming events that cannot be processed immediately are placed in the event queue only if the **BusyAction** property of the object is set to 'queue'. By default, HG objects have the **BusyAction** property set to 'queue'. If the **BusyAction** property is set to 'cancel' and another callback is being processed, then the new event is discarded and not placed in the queue.

You can also use the **Interruptible** property to control the priority of processing events. By default, all objects have their **Interruptible** property enabled so that new events can interrupt the currently executing callback to handle new incoming events. You can set this property to 'off' for an object to ensure that its callback functions have top priority and must finish executing before new events are handled.

As you have seen in previous examples, the *drawnow* command may be used to force the current figure to redraw all graphics objects. This command processes all graphic object event calls pending in the queue and then redraws the figure to display all new graphic content. This command is especially useful when you need to update graphic objects within a loop inside a callback function. If you place the *drawnow* command in the loop after the graphic object calls, the figure graphics will be updated immediately.

MATLAB has several other commands that halt callback execution and process all events in the queue. These commands are listed below:

Table 4.1: Commands That Cause Flushing of The Event Queue

Command	Description
drawnow	Suspends current callback execution and processes all graphic object events in the queue and returns execution to the callback function
figure	Opens a new figure or raises the current figure and processes all graphic events for the figure
getframe	Processes all pending graphic object event calls and captures an image frame of the entire axes or figure area
pause	Temporarily pauses program execution and flushes the event queue
waitfor	Halts callback execution until the specified condition is met such as a specific object property condition

The following example code demonstrates the use of the *waitfor* command for controlling callback execution. In this example, the pushbutton callback function opens a warning dialog box informing the user that they have enabled mouse tracking. By placing a *waitfor* command after the dialog box command halts the execution of the *pushbutton_Callback()* function until the dialog box is closed. In this case, when the user clicks the OK button on the dialog box it closes and the callback function proceeds. The *handles.mouse_track* variable is set and mouse tracking is then enabled in the *figure1_WindowButtonMotionFcn()* callback function.

Example 4.2: Event Processing

pushbutton_Callback

```
function pushbutton_Callback(hObject, eventdata, handles)


    handles.warning = warndlg('You have enabled mouse tracking!',
'Warning');

    waitfor(handles.warning)

    handles.mouse_track = 1;

    guidata(hObject, handles);
```

figure1_WindowButtonMotionFcn

```
function figure1_WindowButtonMotionFcn(hObject, eventdata, handles)


    if handles.mouse_track
        pos = get(handles.figure1, 'CurrentPoint');
        set(handles.text, ...
            'String', [num2str(pos(1)) ', ' num2str(pos(2))]);
    end

    guidata(hObject, handles);
```

MATLAB provides additional functions to control program execution that are similar to the *waitfor* command, they are:

Table 4.2: *uiwait()* and *uiresume()* Functions

Function	Description
uiwait(h, timeout)	Halt program execution until *uiresume()* is called, h object is deleted, or the timeout condition (in seconds) elapses
uiresume(h)	Resumes program execution that was halted by a *uiwait()* function

4.3.2   Mouse Events

You have seen several examples in previous sections that demonstrate basic implementations of mouse event callback functions such as *WindowButtonMotionFcn()*. This sections delves further into the details of mouse events and callback functions and how to detect and process common mouse events such as double clicks and holding down a mouse button. We begin by reviewing the available callback functions and HG Object properties related to mouse events, these functions and properties are listed below:

Table 4.3: Mouse Event Callback Functions

Mouse Event Callback Function	Associated HG Objects	Basic Description
WindowButtonDownFcn	Figure	Callback function that executes when mouse button is pressed within a figure window
WindowButtonUpFcn	Figure	Callback function that executes when mouse button is depressed within a figure window
WindowButtonMotionFcn	Figure	Callback function that executes when mouse moves within a figure window
ButtonDownFcn	All objects except for Root	Callback function that executes whenever either a left or right mouse button is pressed over an object.

Table 4.4: HG Objects and Associated Mouse Event Properties

HG Object	Associated Property	Basic Description
Axes	CurrentPoint, [x y z]	Mouse coordinate location in current Axes units at the position of the most recent mouse button click
Figure	CurrentPoint, [x y]	Mouse coordinate location in current Figure units at the position of the most recent mouse button click
	SelectionType	Holds information regarding the most recent mouse button event type that occurred in a figure window.
Root	PointerLocation, [x, y]	Mouse coordinate location from the bottom left of the display screen

There are several mouse event controls that are standard to most GUI operating systems that are important for creating rich GUI applications. The **SelectionType** property in combination with the mouse event callback functions allows you to use most of the common features of mouse input events. The **SelectionType** property is used to determine which button on the mouse was pressed in a figure window. The following list shows the return values of the **SelectionType** property based on mouse input events:

'normal'   = left mouse button clicked

'alt'   = right mouse button or Control+left button

                clicked

'extend'   = both mouse buttons or Shift+left button clicked

'open'   = double click any mouse button

For example, if you wish to track mouse button down events and control program execution based on which mouse button was pressed in a figure you can use the following code:

```
function  figure_WindowButtonDownFcn(hObject, event_data, handles)

       switch get(handles.figure, 'SelectionType')
              case 'normal'
                      'Left Mouse Button Pressed Down'
              case 'alt'
                      'Right Mouse Button Pressed Down'
              case 'extend'
                      'Both Mouse Buttons Pressed Down'
              case 'open'
                      'Mouse Button Double Click'
       end
```

Although the ability to detect a double click is very useful for many applications, it can also cause some confusion when you wish to detect left and right clicks at all click speeds. For example, if you want to use the left and right mouse clicks to zoom in and out of a plot, the 'open' condition will be returned if either mouse button is clicked repetitively at a rate equal to or greater than the double click rate setting of your GUI operating system.

The 'open' value is returned for both the left and right mouse button double clicks so you must somehow distinguish double clicks as originating from either the left or right button. Fortunately, this may be accomplished by tracking the left and right button clicks using the 'normal' and 'alt' **SelectionType** values. The first click from a left or right click sequence, regardless of the clicking rate, returns either a 'normal' or 'alt' value. This allows you to track the first click and use this value to differentiate the button clicks when the 'open' value is returned during fast click repetitions. The example code below demonstrates this technique:

```
switch get(handles.figure_main, 'SelectionType')
    case 'normal'
        % left click when single click occurs
        % track last click as left or right
        handles.last_click = 'left';

    case 'alt'
        % right click when single click occurs
        % track last click as left or right
        handles.last_click = 'right';

    case 'open'
        switch handles.last_click
            case 'left'
            % left click when double click occurs
                handles.last_click = 'left';

            case 'right'
            % right click when double click occurs
                handles.last_click = 'right';

        end
end
```

Now that you have been introduced to programming mouse event callback functions, you can add custom GUI functionality that can considerably improve the usability and interface of your applications. In the following exercise you will learn how to use mouse events to create a custom plot zooming function and display the current plot axes coordinates as the mouse moves within the axes object. These functions will be added to the current FigView application you have developed throughout this chapter.

Exercise 4.2: Mouse Event Programming, FigView

Open the FigView project and add a View menu with an 'Enable Zoom' item on the menu. Next, use the *WindowButtonDownFcn()* callback along with the figure's **SelectionType** property to allow the user to zoom into the current plot axes with a left button click and zoom out using a right button click. The status of the 'Enable Zoom' menu item should determine if the zoom functionality is active. When enabled, the menu item should be check marked. In order for the right button click to work properly, you should disable the **UIContextMenu** property for the *axes_main* object.

Also, use the *WindowButtonMotionFcn()* callback to detect mouse motion within the current axes area by using the axes **Position** property. Capture the current axes coordinates of the mouse and display them above the axes at the top of the figure. You can get the coordinates by using the **CurrentPoint** axes property.

The center of the zoom region should be located at the current mouse position in the axes. The formulae below provide a hint as to how to scale the axes coordinates to create a zooming effect:

z = zoom factor (0.5 scale corresponds to 2x zoom)

x = current mouse position X cordinate

y = current mouse position Y cordinate

xmax = current X axis maximum from XLim property

xmin = current X axis minimum from XLim property

ymax = current Y axis maximum from YLim property

ymin = current Y axis minimum from YLim property

Zooming In

xmax' = (xmax - x) * z + x

xmin' = (xmax - x) * z + x

ymax' = (ymax - y) * z + y

ymin' = (ymax - y) * z + y

Zooming Out

xmax' = (xmax - x) / z + x

$$xmin' = (xmax - x) / z + x$$

$$ymax' = (ymax - y) / z + y$$

$$ymin' = (ymax - y) / z + y$$

Exercise 4.2 Solution (Functions Added to FigView):

figview_OpeningFcn

```
function figview_OpeningFcn(hObject, eventdata, handles, varargin)

    % Choose default command line output for figview
    handles.output = hObject;

    % initialize handles data structure
    handles.user.plot_index = 1;  % plot number index
    handles.user.plot_max = 1;    % total number of plots created

    handles.enable_zoom = 1;      % enable zoom upon start
    handles.zoom_in = 0.5;        % zoom scale, 2x
    handles.in_axes = 0;          % assume mouse is not in axes at start

    % initialize GUI controls, disable until the first plot is created
    set(handles.pushbutton_previous, 'Enable', 'off');
    set(handles.pushbutton_next, 'Enable', 'off');
    set(handles.listbox_plots, 'Enable', 'off');
    set(handles.menu_launch_plot, 'Enable', 'off');
    set(handles.menu_enable_zoom, 'Checked', 'on');

    % Update handles structure
    guidata(hObject, handles);
```

menu_enable_zoom_Callback

```
function menu_enable_zoom_Callback(hObject, eventdata, handles)

    if handles.enable_zoom
        handles.enable_zoom = 0;
        set(handles.menu_enable_zoom, 'Checked', 'off');
    else
        handles.enable_zoom = 1;
        set(handles.menu_enable_zoom, 'Checked', 'on');
    end
```

```
guidata(hObject, handles);
```

figure_main_WindowButtonMotionFcn

```
function figure_main_WindowButtonMotionFcn(hObject, eventdata, handles)

    % determine if mouse is within axes_main area in the figure
    handles.mouse_pos_fig = get(handles.figure_main, 'CurrentPoint');
    axes_area = get(handles.axes_main, 'Position');

    if (handles.mouse_pos_fig(1) < ...
        (axes_area(1) + axes_area(3))) & ...
        (handles.mouse_pos_fig(1) > ...
        (axes_area(1))) & ...
        (handles.mouse_pos_fig(2) < ...
        (axes_area(2) + axes_area(4))) & ...
        (handles.mouse_pos_fig(2) > ...
        (axes_area(2)))

        handles.in_axes = 1;

        % update axes mouse position text
        handles.mouse_pos = get(handles.axes_main, 'CurrentPoint');
        set(handles.text_pos, 'String', ...
            ['x = ' num2str(handles.mouse_pos(1,1)) ...
            ' , y = ' num2str(handles.mouse_pos(1,2))]);
    else
        handles.in_axes = 0;
    end

    guidata(hObject, handles);
```

figure_main_WindowButtonDownFcn

```
function figure_main_WindowButtonDownFcn(hObject, eventdata, handles)

    if handles.enable_zoom
        switch get(handles.figure_main, 'SelectionType')
            case 'normal'
                    handles = zoom_axes(handles, handles.zoom_in);
                    handles.last_click = 'left';

            case 'alt'
```

```
                      handles = zoom_axes(handles, 1/handles.zoom_in);
                      handles.last_click = 'right';

            case 'open'
                switch handles.last_click
                    case 'left'
                        handles = zoom_axes(handles, handles.zoom_in);
                        handles.last_click = 'left';

                    case 'right'
                        handles = zoom_axes(handles, 1/handles.zoom_in);
                        handles.last_click = 'right';
                end

        end
        drawnow
    end

    guidata(hObject, handles);
```

zoom_axes

```
function handles = zoom_axes(handles, zoom_scale)

    xlim = get(handles.axes_main, 'XLim');
    xmax = xlim(2);
    xmin = xlim(1);
    x = handles.mouse_pos(1,1);


    ylim = get(handles.axes_main, 'YLim');
    ymax = ylim(2);
    ymin = ylim(1);
    y = handles.mouse_pos(1,2);


    sx_zoom = zoom_scale;
    xmax_zoom = (xmax - x )*sx_zoom + x;
    xmin_zoom = (xmin - x)*sx_zoom + x;
    set(handles.axes_main, 'XLim', [xmin_zoom xmax_zoom]);


    sy_zoom = zoom_scale;
    ymax_zoom = (ymax - y)*sy_zoom + y;
    ymin_zoom = (ymin - y)*sy_zoom + y;
    set(handles.axes_main, 'YLim', [ymin_zoom ymax_zoom]);
```

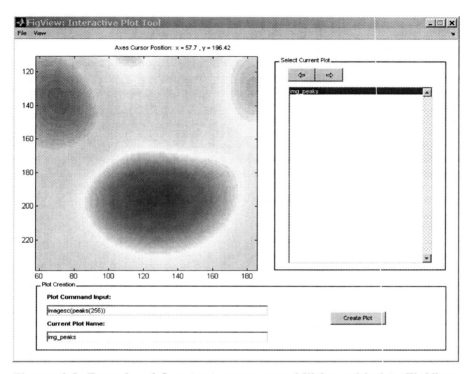

Figure 4.6: Exercise 4.2 output, zoom capabilities added to FigView

4.3.3   Key Press Events

Controlling GUI execution using only mouse events does not always provide the most efficient interactive interface. Most GUI applications include shortcut keyboard commands that may be used to mirror functions that are available through the menu bar or tool bar. For example, you may want to use the 'i' and 'o' keys to allow the user to zoom in and out of a plot or press 'CTRL+s' to popup a save file dialog box to save a figure file. These types of keyboard events may be captured and processed using the *KeyPressFcn()* that is associated with many HG Objects. The list of HG Objects that have an associated *KeyPressFcn()* callback function is shown below:

- Figure
- UIControls
    - o   Push Button
    - o   Slider
    - o   Radio Button
    - o   Check Box
    - o   Edit Box
    - o   Pop-up Menu
    - o   Listbox
    - o   Toggle Button

Key press events for figures are processed when the figure window has focus and UIControl key press events are processed when the control has focus (when the control shows a dotted line boundary around the object). When a UIControl object has focus, the figure's *KeyPressFcn()* callback does not get processed, only the UIControl's *KeyPressFcn()* is processed. The following simple example shows how to detect and process key press events within a callback:

```
figure_KeyPressFcn(hObject, eventdata, handles)
        % get the current key press character
        % keypress will contain the string character of the key pressed
        keypress = get(handles.figure, 'CurrentCharacter');


        switch keypress
                case 'a'
                        ' "a" key pressed'
                case 'b'
                        ' "b" key pressed'
        end
```

Processing key press events using string character representation only works for certain characters. For example, if you wish to use the arrow keys to control behavior of your application, you will notice that you cannot simply represent these as characters in a *switch/case* tree. You can however use the numerical key codes for each key or combination of keystrokes. The following example demonstrates how you can convert the values returned from the **CurrentCharacter** property to key codes to detect and process a wider range of keystroke combinations:

```
figure_KeyPressFcn(hObject, eventdata, handles)
        % get the current key press character and convert to code
        keycode = double(get(handles.figure, 'CurrentCharacter'));


        switch keycode
                case 97
                        ' "a" key pressed'
                case 98
                        ' "b" key pressed'
                case 1
                        ' "CTRL + a" keys pressed'
                case 2
                        ' "CTRL + b" keys pressed'
        end
```

Keystroke combinations that require SHIFT or CONTROL have different codes associated as shown in the above example. The PC key code for 'a' is 97 while the key code for 'CTRL + a' is 1. The tables below provide you with the key code values associated with individual and combination keystrokes for PC keyboards:

Table 4.5: PC Alphabetical Key Stroke Codes

Key Stroke	Code	Key Stroke	Code	Key Stroke	Code
A	97	SHIFT + A	65	CTRL + A	1
B	98	SHIFT + B	66	CTRL + B	2
C	99	SHIFT + C	67	CTRL + C	3
D	100	SHIFT + D	68	CTRL + D	4
E	101	SHIFT + E	69	CTRL + E	5
F	102	SHIFT + F	70	CTRL + F	6
G	103	SHIFT + G	71	CTRL + G	7
H	104	SHIFT + H	72	CTRL + H	8
I	105	SHIFT + I	73	CTRL + I	9
J	106	SHIFT + J	74	**CTRL + J**	**13**
K	107	SHIFT + K	75	CTRL + K	11
L	108	SHIFT + L	76	CTRL + L	12
M	109	SHIFT + M	77	**CTRL + M**	**13**
N	110	SHIFT + N	78	CTRL + N	14
O	111	SHIFT + O	79	CTRL + O	15
P	112	SHIFT + P	80	CTRL + P	16
Q	113	SHIFT + Q	81	CTRL + Q	17
R	114	SHIFT + R	82	CTRL + R	18
S	115	SHIFT + S	83	CTRL + S	19
T	116	SHIFT + T	84	CTRL + T	20
U	117	SHIFT + U	85	CTRL + U	21
V	118	SHIFT + V	86	CTRL + V	22
W	119	SHIFT + W	87	CTRL + W	23
X	120	SHIFT + X	88	CTRL + X	24
Y	121	SHIFT + Y	89	CTRL + Y	25
Z	122	SHIFT + Z	90	CTRL + Z	26

Table 4.6: PC Numeric and Special Key Stroke Codes

Key Stroke	Code	Key Stroke	Code	Key Stroke	Code
1	49	SHIFT + 1	33	ESC	27
2	50	SHIFT + 2	64	LEFT Arrow	28
3	51	SHIFT + 3	35	RIGHT Arrow	29
4	52	SHIFT + 4	36	UP Arrow	30
5	53	SHIFT + 5	37	DOWN Arrow	31
6	54	SHIFT + 6	94	Space Bar	32
7	55	SHIFT + 7	38	**Enter**	**13**
8	56	SHIFT + 8	42	Backspace	8
9	57	SHIFT + 9	40	Delete	127
0	48	SHIFT + 0	41		
-	45	SHIFT + -	95		
=	61	SHIFT + =	43		
`	96	SHIFT + `	126		
[	91	SHIFT + [	123		
]	93	SHIFT +]	125		
\	92	SHIFT + \	124		
;	59	SHIFT + ;	58		
'	39	SHIFT + '	34		
,	44	SHIFT + ,	60		
.	46	SHIFT + .	62		
/	47	SHIFT + /	63		

Each single keystroke or combination of keystrokes provides a unique code identifier except for the 'Enter' key, 'CTRL+J', and 'CTRL+M' which all return the value 13. If you do wish to use these key press events, then you should be aware that they would all be processed using the value 13.

Another important point to note concerning the use of the CONTROL and SHIFT modifier keys is that when held down they will generate a key press event at the rate defined by your operating system's key repeat rate. Both the CONTROL and SHIFT keys alone do not return a key code when you retrieve the **CurrentCharacter** property. Instead they return an empty matrix that can cause errors in your *switch/case* tree if you do not filter events that return empty matrix values. The example below shows how you can filter keystrokes that do not return codes by using the *isempty()* function:

```
function figure_KeyPressFcn(hObject, eventdata, handles)

    keycode = double(get(handles.figure_main, 'CurrentCharacter'));

    if ~isempty(keycode)
        switch keycode
            % i key press
            case double('i')
                '"i" key pressed'
            % o key press
            case double('o')
                '"i" key pressed'
            % up arrow key
            case 30
                'UP Arrow key pressed'
            % down arrow key
            case 31
                'DOWN Arrow key pressed'
            % CTRL+Z keys
            case 26
                '"CTRL+Z" pressed'
        end
    end
```

Lastly, if you are using menu bars that utilize short cut key combinations using the CONTROL and SHIFT key modifiers, make sure these do not conflict with a separate functionality defined in the *KeyPressFcn()* callback function.

Example 4.3: Key Press Event Processing

The following example code may be added to FigView to provide an additional method of zooming in and out of the axes using the 'i' and 'o' keys. Also, the arrow keys are processed to translate the axes limits to effectively scroll around a plot.

figure_main_WindowButtonDownFcn

```
function figure_main_KeyPressFcn(hObject, eventdata, handles)
    keycode = double(get(handles.figure_main, 'CurrentCharacter'));

    % get current axes limits
    xlim = get(handles.axes_main, 'XLim');
    ylim = get(handles.axes_main, 'YLim');
    x_scale = (xlim(2)-xlim(1))/20;
    y_scale = (ylim(2)-ylim(1))/20;

    if handles.enable_zoom & handles.in_axes & ~isempty(keycode)
        switch keycode
            % zoom in using 'i' key
            case double('i')
                handles = zoom_axes(handles, 0.95);
            % zoom out using 'o' key
            case double('o')
                handles = zoom_axes(handles, 1/0.95);
            % up arrow key
            case 30
                set(handles.axes_main, 'YLim', [ylim(1)-y_scale ylim(2)-
y_scale]);
            % down arrow key
            case 31
                set(handles.axes_main, 'YLim', [ylim(1)+y_scale
ylim(2)+y_scale]);

            % left arrow key
            case 28
                set(handles.axes_main, 'XLim', [xlim(1)-x_scale xlim(2)-
x_scale]);
            % right arrow key
            case 29
                set(handles.axes_main, 'XLim', [xlim(1)+x_scale
xlim(2)+x_scale]);
        end
```

```
end
guidata(hObject, handles);
```

4.3.4   Timer Events

An additional event object that is useful for developing interactive and dynamic GUI applications is the **Timer** object. **Timer** objects provide a powerful mechanism for scheduling events that occur at specific time intervals and utilize their own callback functions for event processing. You can set up as many **Timer** objects as you wish and associate separate callback functions to each object. This versatility allows you to create complex and synchronized periodic event scenarios without using program loops. **Timer** objects are created using the *timer()* function and the following table describes the properties associated with timers:

Table 4.7: Timer Object Properties

Property Name	Values	Description
AveragePeriod	double	Holds the average time between each *TimerFcn()* call since the timer started
BusyMode	{'drop'} | 'error' | 'queue'	Determines the action of a timer when the *TimerFcn()* is called before the previous call is finished
ErrorFcn	callback function	Callback function that executes when an error occurs for the timer
ExecutionMode	{'singleShot'} | 'fixedDelay' | 'fixedRate' | 'fixedSpacing'	Determines the method in which the timer executes events
InstantPeriod	double	Time interval between the previous two executions of the *TimerFcn()*
Name	text string | {timer-*i*}	Defines the name of the timer object
ObjectVisibility	{'on'} | 'off'	Sets the visibility of the

		timer objects such that they may not be queried using the *timerfind()* function
Period	double {1.0}, must be > 0.001	Defines the timer period in seconds between each consecutive *TimerFcn()* call
Running	{'off'} | 'on'	Returns a value indicating if the timer is currently running
StartDelay	double { 0.0 }	Delay in seconds from the start of the timer object and execution of the first *TimerFcn()* call
StartFcn	callback function	Function that is called when the timer is started
StopFcn	callback function	Function that is called when timer is stopped
Tag	text string	User defined label
TasksToExecute	double {Inf}	Defines the number of iterations the *TimerFcn()* should execute
TasksExecuted	double	Holds the number of iterations that have executed
TimerFcn	callback function	Timer callback function that executes at every Period
Type	text string	Always set to 'timer'
UserData	user defined	User defined data

As mentioned above, the *timer()* function is used to instantiate a **Timer** object. For example, if you wish to create a timer that has a periodic interval of 0.1 seconds and operates for 1000 iterations, then you can use the following syntax:

```
handles.timer = timer('Period', 0.1, ...
```

```
                       'TasksToExecute', 1000, ...
                       'ExecutionMode', 'fixedRate');
```

There are additional functions that **Timer** objects use to control the starting and stopping of the timer as well as deleting the **Timer** object when you are finished. The *start()*, *stop()*, and *delete()* functions may be used to accomplish these actions. The following example demonstrates the use of a **Timer** object:

```
function figure_OpeningFcn(hObject, event, handles)
        handles.timer = timer('StartDelay', 2, ...
                        'Period', 1, ...
                        'ExecutionMode', 'fixedRate', ...
                        'TimerFcn', {@TimerFcn_Callback, hObject});
        start(handles.timer);
        guidata(hObject, handles);


function TimerFcn_Callback(timer_object, event, hObject)
        % provides access to the figure's handles structure
        handles = guidata(hObject);


        'Timer Fired'


function figure_DeleteFcn(hObject, event, handles)
        stop(handles.timer);
        delete(handles.timer);
```

The above example uses the *OpeningFcn()* of a GUI application to instantiate and start the timer with a two second delay and defines the *TimerFcn_Callback()* function for the timer's callback. Once the timer is started, the *TimerFcn_Callback()* will be executed once every second until the **Timer** object is stopped in the *DeleteFcn()* function of the figure using the *stop()* function. It is important to delete the **Timer** object from memory otherwise it will remain in memory even if the application is closed.

Also, notice that the example above uses the *guidata(hObject)* function call to obtain the current figure's *handles* structure. This needs to be performed since the *TimerFcn_Callback()* function is not part of the GUI callback functions generated in GUIDE. If you simply pass the *handles* structure to the timer callback function, then only the current *handles* data will be passed to the function. Any changes will not be passed to the function automatically and causes difficulty with accessing dynamic data. By passing the figure handle, in this case *hObject*, to the timer function, you can use the *guidata()* function to retrieve the most current handles structure.

Timer objects are very useful for real-time animations and GUI applications that require periodic object updating. One application of timers is to create dynamic UIControls such as blinking text or animated control buttons. You can simply set up a timer that updates a text or button property. Other examples of practical uses of **Timer** objects include the following:

- Updating plots, images, or graphics periodically and automatically
- Creating real-time animation loops that still allow the user to interact with GUI controls smoothly
- Creating dynamic UIControls and graphics objects
- Measure real-time events and processing time

One major advantage of using **Timer** objects as opposed to using while-loops or similar programming techniques is that **Timer** objects is that they are part of the event queue. If you force the GUI application to enter a while-loop within a callback function, the *handles* data structure does not get updated outside of the callback and this may cause problems. Also, the loop can consume processing time and prevent the event queue from being processed quickly for UIControls that can cause dropped commands and choppy GUI behavior. More details on how to use timers for animation loops and other dynamic controls will be covered in Chapter 5.

Example 4.4: Timer Events

The following example demonstrates the use of a timer in the FigView application for creating a slide show for plots created. A toggle button is added to the GUI to allow the user to start and stop the timer to enable and disable the slide show. The periodic rate is set to 2 seconds and the timer loops through all the plots by starting from the first plot after reaching the last plot currently created. Also, an additional timer object is created to update the color of the toggle button while the slide show is activated. The additional code added to FigView is shown below:

figview_OpeningFcn

```
function figview_OpeningFcn(hObject, eventdata, handles, varargin)
```

```
% Choose default command line output for figview
handles.output = hObject;

% initialize handles data structure
handles.user.plot_index = 1;  % plot number index
handles.user.plot_max = 1;    % total number of plots created

handles.enable_zoom = 1;      % enable zoom upon start
handles.zoom_in = 0.5;        % zoom scale, 2x
handles.in_axes = 1;          % assume mouse is not in axes at start
handles.count = 0;            % count for updating toggle button color

% initialize GUI controls, disable until the first plot is created
set(handles.pushbutton_previous, 'Enable', 'off');
set(handles.pushbutton_next, 'Enable', 'off');
set(handles.listbox_plots, 'Enable', 'off');
set(handles.menu_launch_plot, 'Enable', 'off');
set(handles.menu_enable_zoom, 'Checked', 'on');

% create timer objects
handles.plot_timer = timer( 'TimerFcn', ...
                            {@plot_timer_Callback, hObject}, ...
                            'ExecutionMode', 'fixedRate', ...
                            'Period', 1);
handles.button_timer = timer( 'TimerFcn', ...
                            {@button_timer_Callback, hObject}, ...
                            'ExecutionMode', 'fixedRate', ...
                            'Period', 0.05);

% Update handles structure
guidata(hObject, handles);
```

plot_timer_Callback

```
function plot_timer_Callback(timer_object, eventdata, hObject)
    handles = guidata(hObject);
    pushbutton_next_Callback(hObject, [], handles);
```

button_timer_Callback

```
function button_timer_Callback(timer_object, eventdata, hObject)
    handles = guidata(hObject);

    handles.count = handles.count + 0.3;
    c = 0.25*sin(handles.count)+0.75;
```

```
    set(handles.togglebutton_slideshow, 'BackgroundColor', [c 0 0]);
    guidata(hObject, handles);
```

togglebutton_slideshow_Callback

```
function togglebutton_slideshow_Callback(hObject, eventdata, handles)
    if get(hObject, 'Value')
        set(handles.togglebutton_slideshow, 'String', 'Slide Show On');
        start(handles.plot_timer);
        start(handles.button_timer);
    else
        set(handles.togglebutton_slideshow, 'String', 'Slide Show Off');
        stop(handles.plot_timer);
        set(handles.togglebutton_slideshow, 'BackgroundColor', [0.7 0.7
0.7] );
        stop(handles.button_timer);
    end
    guidata(hObject, handles);
```

figure_main_CloseRequestFcn

```
function figure_main_CloseRequestFcn(hObject, eventdata, handles)
    delete(handles.plot_timer);
    delete(handles.button_timer);
    delete(hObject);
```

4.4   Dialog Boxes

GUI applications often use dialog boxes to control program flow, inform the user of the consequences of their next action, report errors, and pop up utility GUIs such as those used for opening and saving files. MATLAB provides the capability to use pre-defined dialog GUIs or design your own custom dialog boxes. Since dialog boxes are an important component of developing comprehensive GUI applications, both built-in and custom dialog boxes are discussed in detail in this section.

4.4.1   MATLAB Built-in Dialog Boxes

MATLAB provides a number of pre-defined dialog box functions for file I/O, selecting the current directory, selecting print settings, etc ... Many of these standard dialog boxes will likely be familiar to you since they are used by many applications that run on GUI operating systems. Built-in dialog boxes are convenient for prompting the user to input data or display information in a popup GUI without the need for you to create a separate GUI figure. For example, MATLAB has a dialog box function named *uigetfile()* that pops up a standard file-browsing window that allows you to select a file, which then is returned to the application:

```
[filename, pathname] = uigetfile({'*.m';'*.fig';'*.*'},'Open File');
```

This example opens a file selector dialog box with file type selection choices of *.m, *.fig, or *.* to list all files. The name of the dialog box is 'Open File'. Once the file is selected, the filename and directory path are returned in separate variables that may be used to open a file or as information for the GUI application. This example produces the following GUI output:

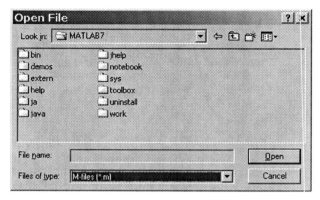

Figure 4.7: Open File default dialog box

The following table lists the pre-defined dialog boxes available in MATLAB:

Table 4.8: MATLAB Pre-defined Dialog Boxes and Parameters

Dialog Box Function	Description	Input Parameters	Output Parameters
errordlg	Error dialog with OK button	('error string', 'dialog name')	handle to dialog box
warndlg	Warning dialog with OK button	('warning string', 'dialog name')	handle to dialog box
helpdlg	Help dialog with OK button	('help string', 'dialog name')	handle to dialog box
msgbox	Creates message box with a specified icon and an OK button	('message', 'title', 'icon', icon_data, icon_cmap) icon = 'none' | 'error' | 'help' | 'warn' | 'custom'	handle to dialog box
questdlg	Prompts user to answer a question, dialog may include up to three buttons, the default is 'Yes', 'No', and 'Cancel' buttons	('question string', 'title string', 'button 1', 'button 2', 'button 3', 'default button')	string, button pressed
inputdlg	Dialog that prompts user to enter responses in edit text boxes	({'input str 1', 'input str 2', ...}, 'dialog_title', num_lines, default answer, resize)	cell of strings corresponding to user input values

		resize = 'on' | 'off'	
listdlg	Dialog that allows the user to select from a list of items and contains OK, Cancel, and Select All buttons	Properties include: 'ListString' 'SelectionMode' 'ListSize' 'InitialValue' 'Name' 'PromptString' 'OKString' 'CancelString' 'uh' (button height) 'fus' (uicontrol spacing) 'ffs' (figure spacing)	[selection number, value of OK]
printdlg	Displays a print dialog box that allows user to print the current figure	(figure, '-crossplatform', '-setup')	[]
pagesetupdlg	Dialog box that displays the page setup properties used for printing a figure	(figure)	[]
uisetcolor	Opens a color selector dialog box	(graphics_handle | RGB color value, 'DialogTitle')	[R G B] color selected
uisetfont	Opens a font selector dialog box	(handle object | font structure, 'DialogTitle')	structure: FontName FontUnits FontSize FontWeight FontAngle
uigetdir	Dialog box that allows user browse and select a directory	('start_path', 'dialog_title')	string, directory name
uigetfile	Opens a dialog that allows user to browse and select a file to open	('Filter', 'dialog_title', 'default_name', 'multiSelect') multiSelect = 'on' | 'off'	[Filename, PathName, FilterIndex]
uiputfile	Opens a dialog that allows user to browse and select a	('Filter', 'dialog_title', 'default_name')	[Filename, PathName,

	file for saving		FilterIndex]
waitbar	Creates a waitbar	(progress, 'title', 'CreateCancelBtn', 'button_callback') progress = 0.0 to 1.0	handle to dialog box

Question and Message Dialogs

Errordlg, *warndlg*, *helpdlg*, *msgbox*, and *questdlg* may be classified together as dialogs that prompt the user with a question or provide information. Error, warning, and help messages simply present information for the user. For example, if an error is detected you may launch an error dialog to inform the user:

```
% detect if value is outside range and display error message if true
if (value < 0) | (value > 1)
errordlg('The value entered is not within the valid range of 0 to 1', ...
        'Input Value Error');
end
```

Figure 4.8: Error dialog box

Warndlg and *helpdlg* dialogs operate in a similar manner as *errordlg*. *questdlg* is a general question dialog box that offers a 'yes', 'no', or 'cancel' response by default. The return value from *questdlg* is the string name of the button that was pressed. For example, the following code asks the user a yes/no question and controls program execution based on the response:

```
% ask user if plots should be deleted
result = questdlg('Do you really want to delete all plots?', ...
                'Delete Plots');

switch result
        case 'Yes'
                %delete(handles.plot);
                'Plots deleted'
        case 'No'
                'Plots not deleted'
        case 'Cancel'
                'Operation cancelled'
end
```

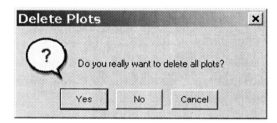

Figure 4.9: Question dialog box, 3 buttons

questdlg is not limited to yes/no questions since you may label the buttons however you wish. For example, you could set two buttons to 'Save' and 'Cancel' to ask the user to save a file as follows:

```
result = questdlg('Do you want to save the file?', ...
                'Save File', 'Save', 'Cancel', 'Save');
```

Figure 4.10: Question dialog box, 2 buttons

The last input argument, 'Save', is the default highlighted button that has focus and executes when the user presses the return key.

Input Dialogs

Inputdlg dialogs allow the user to enter text or numerical information and contain edit boxes that are defined using a cell array of strings. You have as many inputs as you wish and also define default text that appears in each edit box. Also, you can allow each edit box to use multiple line text input by choosing the number of lines. The following code demonstrates how to setup a dialog box that has three inputs and the first input should allow up to three text lines:

```
output = inputdlg(    {'input 1', 'input 2', 'input3'}, ...
                      'Input Dialog Box', ...
                      [3 1 1], ...
                      {'line1', 'line2', 'line3'});
```

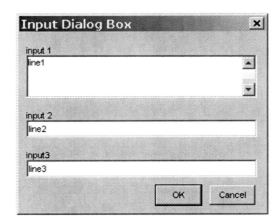

Figure 4.11: Input text dialog box

The vector of numerical values, [3 1 1], corresponds to the number of input lines that are defined for the first, second, and third edit boxes respectively. The return argument, *output* in this case, contains a cell array of strings that contain the strings that are entered by the user. The output argument only contains the input strings when the user presses return, a cancel action returns an empty cell.

Listdlg dialogs create a listbox figure that displays the contents of a cell array of strings defined by the **ListString** property. The return values from the function when the user clicks the OK button are

the list item number and the detection of the OK button click. The
example below demonstrates *listdlg*:

```
list = {'Plot 1', 'Plot 2', 'Plot 3'};
[listnum, ok_click] = listdlg(  'PromptString','Select a plot:',...
                                'SelectionMode','single',...
                                'ListString', list, ...
                                'Name', 'Select Plot')
```

Figure 4.12: List box dialog

Setup Dialogs

Setup dialog functions *pagesetupdlg*, *printdlg*, *uisetcolor*, and *uisetfont*
allow you to access common operating system setup parameters such
as the default printer or selecting a system font for your text. Both
pagesetupdlg and *printdlg* accept a figure handle as an input
parameter to set the page and print properties of a figure window. The
uisetcolor function pops up a color selector figure that allows you to
choose an RGB color value that is then returned by the function.
uisetfont is similar to *uisetcolor* and opens a font selector that returns
FontName,   FontUnits,   FontSize,   FontWeight,   and   FontAngle

parameters in a single structure variable. The following code demonstrates the *uisetfont* dialog function:

```
font_info = uisetfont('Choose Font')
```

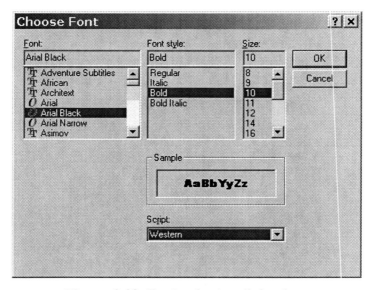

Figure 4.13: Font selector dialog box

```
>> font_info =

    FontName: 'Arial Black'
   FontUnits: 'points'
    FontSize: 10
  FontWeight: 'bold'
   FontAngle: 'normal'
```

File Dialogs

Some of the most important types of dialog boxes are those that allow you to interactively browse and select files from the local computer or network. All GUI operating systems contain standard types of file and directory browsing dialog GUIs. MATLAB provides three dialog box functions, *uigetdir*, *uigetfile*, and *uiputfile*, for performing file system browsing and file information retrieval.

uigetdir, as indicated by the function name, provides a GUI interface figure that shows the current directory or directory of the start path property that you specify and then allows you to browse through the directory trees of the computer system or network. Once a selection is made and the OK button is clicked, the function returns a string with the directory path that was chosen. For example, the following code instantiates a directory selection dialog with the start path as *C:\Matlab7* and then changes the current directory of MATLAB based on the selection:

```
pathname = uigetdir('c:\matlab7', 'Choose Directory');
cd(pathname);
```

Figure 4.14: Directory selector dialog box

Both *uigetfile* and *uiputfile* operate in a similar manner as *uigetdir* except they both return the name of the selected file and directory path name. You can also choose file filters to control which file names are visible in the file list. You can create an open file dialog that initially displays *.m files and then opens the MATLAB editor with the M-file that is selected by using the following code:

```
[filename, pathname] = uigetfile({'*.m', 'M-files (*.m)'}, 'Open M-file');
edit([pathname filename]);
```

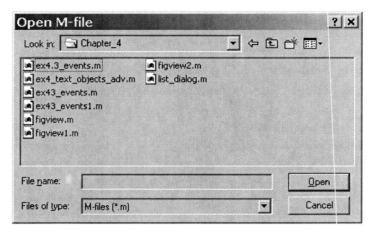

Figure 4.15: Open file selector dialog box

Exercise 4.3: Dialog Boxes

Currently, FigView does not contain dialog boxes to control program flow or allow the user to load and save files. The following three dialog box additions to FigView will provide a more versatile application:

- Add the ability to save a special M-file containing the plot commands that the user has created in the current FigView session

- Add the ability to open the same M-file and load the plot commands into FigView

- Add a dialog box to warn the user that all plots are about to be deleted when the 'Delete Plots' item is clicked on the menu

To accomplish the above requirements, you will need to add 'Open ...' and 'Save ...' items to the File menu as well as callback functions.

Exercise 4.3 Solution: Dialog Boxes Added to FigView

menu_open_Callback

```
function menu_open_Callback(hObject, eventdata, handles)


    % open uigetfile dialog GUI

    [filename, pathname] = uigetfile({'*.plt'}, 'Open Plot Command File
*.plt');


    % read plot command text file

    [handles.user.plot_names, ...

     handles.user.plot_commands] = textread([pathname filename], '%s %s',
'delimiter', '=');


    % reset plot_index to 1 and

    % plot_max = number of plot command read from file

    handles.user.plot_index = 1;

    [mx, dummy] = size(handles.user.plot_names);

    handles.user.plot_max = mx + 1;


    % update listbox text with the list of plot names read in from file

    set(handles.listbox_plots,    'String', handles.user.plot_names, ...

                                  'Value', handles.user.plot_index );


    % make sure controls are enabled

    set(handles.pushbutton_previous, 'Enable', 'on');

    set(handles.pushbutton_next, 'Enable', 'on');

    set(handles.listbox_plots, 'Enable', 'on');

    set(handles.menu_launch_plot, 'Enable', 'on');


    % draw first plot in the list

    update_plot(handles);


    guidata(hObject, handles);
```

menu_save_Callback

```
function menu_save_Callback(hObject, eventdata, handles)


    % open uiputfile dialog GUI

    filename = uiputfile({'*.plt'}, 'Save Plot Command File *.plt');


    % write plot names and plot command strings to a text file
```

```
    % using an = sign as a delimiter
    fid = fopen(filename, 'wt');
        for i = 1:handles.user.plot_max-1
            fprintf(fid, '%s = %s\n', ...
                char(handles.user.plot_names{i}), ...
                char(handles.user.plot_commands{i}));
        end
    fclose(fid);
```

menu_delete_all_Callback

```
function menu_delete_all_Callback(hObject, eventdata, handles)

    result = questdlg('Are you sure you want to delete all plots?', ...
                    'Deleting Plots!', 'Yes', 'Cancel', 'Cancel');
    if strcmp(result, 'Yes')

        handles.user.plot_index = 1;
        handles.user.plot_max = 1;
        handles.user.plot_commands = {};
        handles.user.plot_names = {};

        % update listbox text with the list of plot names created
        set(handles.listbox_plots, 'String', '', 'Value', 1);

        % disable current plot controls
        set(handles.pushbutton_previous, 'Enable', 'off');
        set(handles.pushbutton_next, 'Enable', 'off');
        set(handles.listbox_plots, 'Enable', 'off');

        % reset axes
        plot(handles.axes_main, 1);
        set(handles.axes_main, 'XGrid', 'on', 'YGrid', 'on');

    end

    % Update handles structure
    guidata(hObject, handles);
```

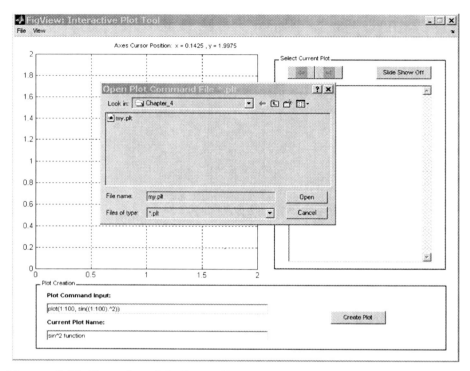

Figure 4.16: Exercise 4.3, Open File selector dialog added to FigView

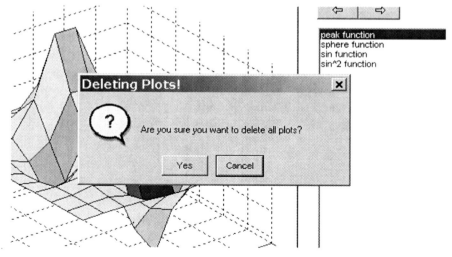

Figure 4.17: Exercise 4.3, Question dialog added to FigView

4.4.2   Custom Dialog Boxes

Predefined dialog box functions don't always meet the requirements for GUI applications and custom development of dialogs or popup GUIs is required. MATLAB allows you to easily create custom dialogs by simply creating a separate project in GUIDE for a dialog. There are two basic approaches for generating custom dialogs using GUIDE:

- Create a Modal Dialog Box project
- Create a custom GUI project

Choosing the Modal Dialog Box option when creating a new project generates a custom question dialog that appears as follows:

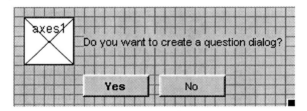

Figure 4.18: Default Modal Dialog Box in GUIDE

This GUI may be altered to meet any requirements necessary for your application. The only main differences between using the Modal Dialog Box project as compared to a blank GUI project are that the Modal Dialog project provides basic controls that may be useful for a question dialog and the automatically generated M-file code contains additional sections that perform the following functions:

- Set title based on input arguments
- Center the dialog box over the parent figure if possible
- Load a question dialog icon and display in an axes object
- Set the figure to a modal window style and use the uiwait function to halt program execution until the user responds to the dialog
- Processes pushbutton controls

For example, input arguments are processed using the automatically generated code shown below:

Set title based on input arguments

```
% Insert custom Title and Text if specified by the user
% Hint: when choosing keywords, be sure they are not easily confused
% with existing figure properties.  See the output of set(figure) for
% a list of figure properties.
if(nargin > 3)
    for index = 1:2:(nargin-3),
        if nargin-3==index, break, end
        switch lower(varargin{index})
         case 'title'
          set(hObject, 'Name', varargin{index+1});
         case 'string'
          set(handles.text1, 'String', varargin{index+1});
        end
    end
end
```

If you desire to have a dialog that has a completely different structure than a question dialog, then it may be more advantageous to create your dialog using a blank GUI project from GUIDE. Otherwise, you will need to change much of the additional auto-generated code that is specific to the question Modal Dialog structure.

Passing Arguments Between Dialogs and Parent GUIs

Each GUI application created using GUIDE may be launched from another GUI application generating a parent-child relationship. The main differentiating factor between a main parent GUI and a child dialog GUI is that information must be exchanged in order for properties and data values to be accessible between one another. The *varargin* and *varargout* variable input and output arguments allow you to transfer information to and from the main GUI and the dialog GUI. For example, if you wish to instantiate a dialog with a custom title and also want to pass data to and from the main GUI you may code something similar to the following:

Dialog GUI M-file

Retrieve Input Arguments In The OpeningFcn

```
function my_dialog_OpeningFcn(hObject, eventdata, handles, varargin)
        handles.title = varargin{1};
        handles.data = varargin{2};
        set(handles.text_dialog_title, 'String', handles.title);
        guidata(hObject, handles);
```

Send Output Arguments In The OutputFcn

```
function varargout = my_dialog_OutputFcn(hObject, eventdata, handles)
        varargout{1} = handles.data;
        guidata(hObject, handles);
```

Main GUI M-file

Call Dialog GUI and Pass Arguments

```
handles.data = my_dialog(handles.title, handles.data);
```

It is important to note that the output arguments are only returned when the GUI is closed after the user has responded. Passing data between two GUI applications while both GUIs remain active is not the general intent for dialogs. Passing data between multiple GUIs that are not dialogs is discussed in chapter 5. The following example will demonstrate how to create a custom dialog GUI that is quite different than the built-in dialogs provided by MATLAB.

Example 4.5: Custom Dialog GUI

This example shows how to create a dialog GUI that allows the user to select a plot style by clicking on axes objects within the dialog GUI. The plot style is then returned using the *varargout* parameter. This dialog is then incorporated into FigView to allow the user to change the plot style of the FigView axes. A menu item entitled 'Plot Style' is added to FigView to open the plot style dialog box. The code and figures below show how to implement the plot style dialog.

Plot Style Selector Dialog GUI

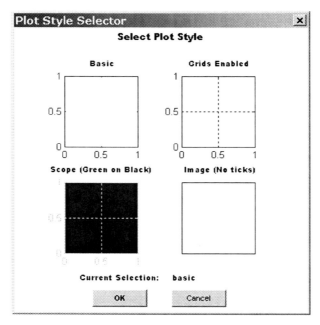

Figure 4.19: Example 4.5 output, custom plot selector dialog box

my_dialog.m Dialog GUI M-file

my_dialog_OpeningFcn

```
function my_dialog_OpeningFcn(hObject, eventdata, handles, varargin)

% Insert custom Title and Text if specified by the user
% Hint: when choosing keywords, be sure they are not easily confused
% with existing figure properties.  See the output of set(figure) for
% a list of figure properties.
if(nargin > 3)
    for index = 1:2:(nargin-3),
        if nargin-3==index, break, end
        switch lower(varargin{index})
         case 'title'
          set(hObject, 'Name', varargin{index+1});
         case 'string'
          set(handles.text1, 'String', varargin{index+1});
        end
    end
```

```
end

% Determine the position of the dialog - centered on the callback figure
% if available, else, centered on the screen
FigPos=get(0,'DefaultFigurePosition');
OldUnits = get(hObject, 'Units');
set(hObject, 'Units', 'pixels');
OldPos = get(hObject,'Position');
FigWidth = OldPos(3);
FigHeight = OldPos(4);
if isempty(gcbf)
    ScreenUnits=get(0,'Units');
    set(0,'Units','pixels');
    ScreenSize=get(0,'ScreenSize');
    set(0,'Units',ScreenUnits);

    FigPos(1)=1/2*(ScreenSize(3)-FigWidth);
    FigPos(2)=2/3*(ScreenSize(4)-FigHeight);
else
    GCBFOldUnits = get(gcbf,'Units');
    set(gcbf,'Units','pixels');
    GCBFPos = get(gcbf,'Position');
    set(gcbf,'Units',GCBFOldUnits);
    FigPos(1:2) = [(GCBFPos(1) + GCBFPos(3) / 2) - FigWidth / 2, ...
                   (GCBFPos(2) + GCBFPos(4) / 2) - FigHeight / 2];
end
FigPos(3:4)=[FigWidth FigHeight];
set(hObject, 'Position', FigPos);
set(hObject, 'Units', OldUnits);


% draw plot styles into axes objects
for i =1:4
    str = ['handles.axes' num2str(i)];
    image([], 'Parent', eval(str));
end

set(handles.axes1, 'Box', 'on', ...
                    'ButtonDownFcn', {@axes1_ButtonDownFcn, handles});

set(handles.axes2, 'XGrid', 'on', ...
                    'YGrid', 'on', ...
                    'ButtonDownFcn', {@axes2_ButtonDownFcn, handles});
```

```
set(handles.axes3, 'Color', [0 0 0], ...
                   'XColor', [0 1 0], ...
                   'YColor', [0 1 0], ...
                   'XGrid', 'on', 'YGrid', 'on', ...
                   'ButtonDownFcn', {@axes3_ButtonDownFcn, handles});

set(handles.axes4, 'XTick', [], 'YTick', [], ...
                   'ButtonDownFcn', {@axes4_ButtonDownFcn, handles});

handles.plot_style = 'basic';

% Make the GUI modal
set(handles.figure1,'WindowStyle','modal')

% Update handles structure
guidata(hObject, handles);

% UIWAIT makes my_dialog wait for user response (see UIRESUME)
uiwait(handles.figure1);
```

my_dialog_OutputFcn

```
function varargout = my_dialog_OutputFcn(hObject, eventdata, handles)

        % Get default command line output from handles structure
        varargout{1} = handles.plot_style;

        % The figure can be deleted now
        delete(handles.figure1);
```

pushbutton_ok_Callback

```
function pushbutton_ok_Callback(hObject, eventdata, handles)

        % Use UIRESUME instead of delete because the OutputFcn needs
        % to get the updated handles structure.
        uiresume(handles.figure1);
```

pushbutton_cancel_Callback

```
function pushbutton_cancel_Callback(hObject, eventdata, handles)
        handles.plot_style = 'cancel';
```

```
        % Update handles structure
        guidata(hObject, handles);


        % Use UIRESUME instead of delete because the OutputFcn needs
        % to get the updated handles structure.
        uiresume(handles.figure1);
```

figure1_CloseReqestFcn

```
function figure1_CloseRequestFcn(hObject, eventdata, handles)

        if isequal(get(handles.figure1, 'waitstatus'), 'waiting')
                % The GUI is still in UIWAIT, us UIRESUME
                uiresume(handles.figure1);
        else
        % The GUI is no longer waiting, just close it
                delete(handles.figure1);
        end
```

figure1_KeypressFcn

```
function figure1_KeyPressFcn(hObject, eventdata, handles)

% Check for "enter" or "escape"
if isequal(get(hObject,'CurrentKey'),'escape')
    % User said no by hitting escape
    handles.plot_style = 'cancel';

    % Update handles structure
    guidata(hObject, handles);

    uiresume(handles.figure1);
end

if isequal(get(hObject,'CurrentKey'),'return')
    uiresume(handles.figure1);
end
```

axes1_ButtonDownFcn

```
function axes1_ButtonDownFcn(hObject, eventdata, handles)
    set(handles.axes1, 'XColor', [1 0 0], 'YColor', [1 0 0], ...
                       'LineWidth', 2);
```

```
    handles.plot_style = 'basic';
    guidata(hObject, handles);
```

axes2_ButtonDownFcn

```
function axes2_ButtonDownFcn(hObject, eventdata, handles)
    set(handles.axes2, 'XColor', [1 0 0], 'YColor', [1 0 0], ...
                       'LineWidth', 2);
    handles.plot_style = 'grid_on';
    guidata(hObject, handles);
```

axes3_ButtonDownFcn

```
function axes3_ButtonDownFcn(hObject, eventdata, handles)
    set(handles.axes3, 'XColor', [1 0 0], 'YColor', [1 0 0], ...
                       'LineWidth', 2);
    handles.plot_style = 'scope';
    guidata(hObject, handles);
```

axes4_ButtonDownFcn

```
function axes4_ButtonDownFcn(hObject, eventdata, handles)
    set(handles.axes4, 'XColor', [1 0 0], 'YColor', [1 0 0], ...
                       'LineWidth', 2);
    handles.plot_style = 'image';
    guidata(hObject, handles);
```

figure1_WindowButtonUpFcn

```
function figure1_WindowButtonUpFcn(hObject, eventdata, handles)


    switch handles.plot_style

        case 'basic'
            set(handles.axes1, 'XColor', [0 0 0], 'YColor', [0 0 0], ...
                               'LineWidth', 0.5);
        case 'grid_on'
            set(handles.axes2, 'XColor', [0 0 0], 'YColor', [0 0 0], ...
                               'LineWidth', 0.5);
        case 'scope'
            set(handles.axes3, 'XColor', [0 1 0], 'YColor', [0 1 0], ...
                               'LineWidth', 0.5);
        case 'image'
            set(handles.axes4, 'XColor', [0 0 0], 'YColor', [0 0 0], ...
```

```
                                    'LineWidth', 0.5);
    end


    % update Current Selection text
    set(handles.text_plot_style, 'String', handles.plot_style);


    guidata(hObject, handles);
```

Additions to figview.m GUI M-file

figview_OpeningFcn

```
% default value for handles.plot_style added
handles.plot_style = 'basic';
```

menu_plot_style_Callback

```
function menu_plot_style_Callback(hObject, eventdata, handles)
    handles.plot_style = my_dialog();
    update_plot(handles);
    guidata(hObject, handles);
```

update_plot

```
function update_plot(handles)


    % make sure GUI figure is current figure
    figure(handles.figure_main);


    % set plot command and name fields for current plot selected
    set(handles.edit_plot_command, 'String',
handles.user.plot_commands{handles.user.plot_index});
    set(handles.edit_plot_name, 'String',
handles.user.plot_names{handles.user.plot_index});


    % evaluate plot string
    eval(handles.user.plot_commands{handles.user.plot_index});


    switch handles.plot_style
        case 'basic'
            set(handles.axes_main, 'Box', 'on', ...
                                   'Color', [1 1 1], ...
                                   'XColor', [0 0 0], ...
                                   'YColor', [0 0 0], ...
                                   'ZColor', [0 0 0], ...
                                   'XGrid', 'off', ...
```

```
                                    'YGrid', 'off', ...
                                    'ZGrid', 'off');
        case 'grid_on'
            set(handles.axes_main, 'Box', 'on', ...
                                    'Color', [1 1 1], ...
                                    'XColor', [0 0 0], ...
                                    'YColor', [0 0 0], ...
                                    'ZColor', [0 0 0], ...
                                    'XGrid', 'on', ...
                                    'YGrid', 'on', ...
                                    'ZGrid', 'on');
        case 'scope'
            set(handles.axes_main, 'Box', 'on', ...
                                    'Color', [0 0 0], ...
                                    'XColor', [0 0.3 0], ...
                                    'YColor', [0 0.3 0], ...
                                    'ZColor', [0 0.3 0], ...
                                    'XGrid', 'on', ...
                                    'YGrid', 'on', ...
                                    'ZGrid', 'on');
        case 'image'
            set(handles.axes_main, 'Box', 'on', ...
                                    'Color', [1 1 1], ...
                                    'XColor', [0 0 0], ...
                                    'YColor', [0 0 0], ...
                                    'ZColor', [0 0 0], ...
                                    'XGrid', 'off', ...
                                    'YGrid', 'off', ...
                                    'ZGrid', 'off', ...
                                    'XTick', [], ...
                                    'YTick', [], ...
                                    'ZTick', []);
    end
```

Chapter 5
Advanced GUI Designs

With the completion of chapter 4, you have now learned how to construct a complete interactive GUI application that uses a single main interface figure. This chapter expands on the system level architecture of MATLAB GUI development by introducing techniques for creating multiple interactive figure GUI applications. Additional topics discussed here include the development of real-time GUIs and animation, custom GUI control design and programming, and compiling GUIs into stand-alone executable applications.

5.1   Multiple Figure GUIs

The specification of a GUI design often requires multiple GUI windows for controls and/or data. You are likely familiar with many applications that utilize popup GUI windows that contain controls for the main application or separate windows to show data such as images or plots. Until this chapter we have concentrated on GUI designs that incorporate all interactive UI controls within a single figure instantiation, aside from dialog boxes. We have seen how to launch additional data figures to simply display information, although these figures were not interactive in the sense that they didn't pass information back to the main application. This section discusses the use of global variables for constructing GUI applications that can have multiple interactive control and/or data figures.

5.1.1   Global Variables

Most of the examples throughout this book use the local *handles* variable structure within functions to store information about the application. Often, local variables are then used to pass information between functions. One major limitation of this GUI architecture is that all the information regarding uicontrol states and callback functions remains local while the application is running. You can easily pass information to and from a GUI during startup or upon closing by using the *varargin* and *varargout* input and output parameters. The problem here is that you wish to have multiple figures remaining open and still allowing each to share control state information and other data between figures. The following block diagram demonstrates a typical multiple GUI application:

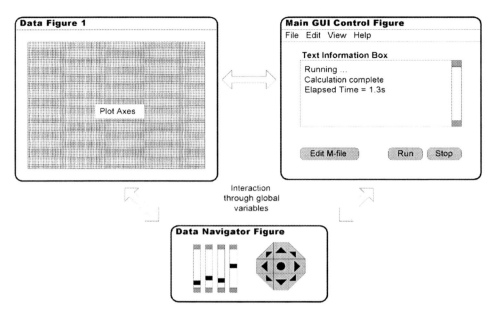

Figure 5.1: Conceptual drawing of a multiple figure GUI

To accomplish this, you can declare global variables and structures that are common in all separate target GUI M-files. If you create a global variable structure in each M-file similar to the *handles* structure and save control state information and data, then this information will be available for each GUI figure while each remains open. For example, you can declare a global variable structure as follows:

```
global my_handles
```

Global variables must be defined in each function that you intend to use the variable within:

```
function figure_OpeningFcn(hObject, eventdata, handles)
        global my_handles
        my_handles.figure = handles.figure;
        my_handles.color = [0 0 0];

function figure_Callback1(hObject, eventdata, handles)
        global my_handles
        set(my_handles.figure, 'Color', my_handles.color);
```

This methodology extends to multiple GUI designs by simply declaring global variables for each function that requires sharing of common information:

GUI Figure 1 M-file

```
function figure1_OpeningFcn(hObject, eventdata, handles)

    global my_handles

    my_handles.figure1 = handles.figure1;

    my_handles.color = [0 0 0];
```

GUI Figure 2 M-file

```
function figure2_Callback1(hObject, eventdata, handles)

    global my_handles

    set(my_handles.figure, 'Color', my_handles.color);
```

In the above example, the *my_handles* variable will be visible in both GUIs for the functions where you declare *my_handles* as global. Although this is not an ideal architecture for developing multiple interactive figure GUIs, it is a simple method and also circumnavigates some of the GUI development limitations within MATLAB.

Defining Global Structures and Potential Pitfalls

In order to avoid confusion and possibly overwriting GUI control handle data, it is very important to construct a global structure that incorporates figure name designators that act as tags. This methodology allows you to utilize uicontrol handles from GUIs with assurance that variable name duplication will not accidentally occur. This is especially useful for complex applications where a large number of handle objects exist for each GUI. The following global structure provides an example of how you might tag global handles structures:

GUI Figure 1 M-file OpeningFcn

```
function figure_OpeningFcn(hObject, eventdata, handles, varargin)
        % declare global structure variables for both figures
        global hFig1
        global hFig2


        % save figure 1 handles to global structure hFig1
        hFig1.figure = handles.figure;
        hFig1.axes = handles.axes;
        hFig1.pushbutton = handles.pushbutton;
```

GUI Figure 2 M-file OpeningFcn

```
function figure_OpeningFcn(hObject, eventdata, handles, varargin)
        % declare global structure variables for both figures
        global hFig1
        global hFig2


        % save figure 2 handles to global structure hFig2
        hFig2.figure = handles.figure;
        hFig2.axes = handles.axes;
        hFig2.pushbutton = handles.pushbutton;
```

Once you save all GUI handles to the global structures in both M-files, then you are free to get or set properties of both figures within both figures thus establishing mutual interactive capability. For example, the global *hFig1.figure* handle object properties may be set within the Figure 2 GUI M-file. This program structure enables an action from one figure to cause a reaction in another.

Another potential pitfall encountered when using global variables, aside from data confusion for handles naming, is that global variables may be deleted from the MATLAB run-time environment when the following commands are entered at the command prompt:

>> clear globals

>> clear all

Even when a GUI application does not show any variables in the workspace during run-time, the global variables are still affected by the above listed clear commands. Avoid using these commands in scripts that you intend to run along with your GUI application. One way to avoid this situation is to compile your GUI into a stand-alone executable application that does not rely on a MATLAB session. This is discussed further in the last section of this chapter.

5.1.2   Interactive Multiple Control GUIs

This section discusses the structure of multi-figure GUIs in more detail. As mentioned in section 5.1.1, clearly defining a global variable structure for a multi-figure GUI is essential for avoiding confusion during development. Before the global variable structure is defined it is important to create a basic GUI interaction diagram that shows what parameters need to be shared between GUI figures. Once this is established, the global variable structure may be defined.

GUI Interaction Diagrams and Lists

Interaction diagrams and lists can clarify the interface needs between each GUI figure in an application. A simple diagram and list of interactions can show what parameters need to be passed to and from each GUI module. All properties and handles from one GUI figure may not need to be accessed by another GUI figure and therefore the global variable structure can be simplified if a clear interaction diagram is established.

For example, if you wish to have a slider in your main GUI figure that controls an axis parameter in a separate plot figure and also have the mouse position within the axis from the plot figure displayed in a separate control figure, then you might create a diagram similar to the one show below:

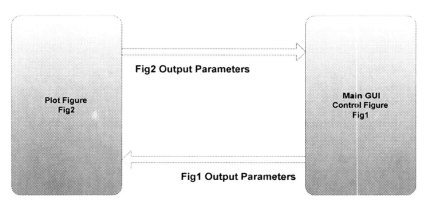

Plot Figure
Fig2

Fig2 Output Parameters

Fig1 Output Parameters

Main GUI
Control Figure
Fig1

Figure 5.2: Parameter passing between GUI figures

Fig1 Output Parameters

1. Text handle for figure 2 to display mouse cursor values

Fig2 Output Parameters

1. Axes handle to give figure 1 access

The output parameters must be clearly defined since they must be saved to the global variable structure during the *OpeningFcn()* function to ensure the parameters will be available to the other GUI figures. Once the output parameters are specified, we can define the global variable structure:

GUI Figure 1 M-file

OpeningFcn

```
function figure_OpeningFcn(hObject, eventdata, handles, varargin)
% declare global structure variables for both figures
global hFig1
global hFig2

% Fig1 output objects
hFig1.text_cursor_pos = handles.text_cursor_pos;

% plot data in Figure 2 axes
plot(hFig2.axes, function);
```

slider1_Callback

```
function slider1_Callback(hObject, eventdata, handles, varargin)
% declare global structure variables for both figures
global hFig1
global hFig2

slider_value = get(hFig1.slider1, 'Value');
% call zoom_axes function to modify the axes of Figure 2
zoom_axes(hFig2.axes, slider_value);
```

GUI Figure 2 M-file

OpeningFcn

```
function figure_OpeningFcn(hObject, eventdata, handles, varargin)
% declare global structure variables for both figures
global hFig1
global hFig2


% Fig2 output objects
hFig2.axes = handles.axes;
```

WindowButtonMotionFcn

```
function figure_WindowButtonMotionFcn(hObject, eventdata, handles)
global hFig1
global hFig2


mouse_pos = get(handles.axes, 'CurrentPoint');
set(hFig1.text_cursor_pos, ...
    'String', [num2str(mouse_pos(1,1)) ', ' num2str(mouse_pos(2,1))]);
```

Although the above example is quite simple, this method becomes very useful as the number of interactive parameters increases.

Global Handle Sharing, GHS

You may be wondering why not just set *hFig1* and *hFig2* to the handles structure of the figures to avoid needing to track each output parameter. For example:

```
global hFig1
hFig1.handles = handles;
```

A technique referred to as Global Handle Sharing, or GHS, allows you to simplify your code significantly while providing access to each figure's handles by using passing the entire handles structure for each figure into a global variable that is accessible by all other figures in your application. You must be careful since handle parameters that change during program execution are not updated unless you repeatedly save the handles to the global structure. In general, you need to add the two lines of code above to each function to ensure the handles data remains updated. For example:

GUI Figure 1 M-file

OpeningFcn

```
function figure1_OpeningFcn(hObject, eventdata, handles, varargin)
% declare global structure variables for all figures
global hFig1 hFig2 hFig3

% initialize user fields
handles.slider_value = 0;

% Save local figure handles to global variable
hFig1.handles = handles;
```

slider_Callback

```
function slider_Callback(hObject, eventdata, handles, varargin)
% declare global structure variables for all figures
global hFig1 hFig2 hFig3

handles.slider_value = get(hObject, 'Value');

% Save local figure handles to global variable
hFig1.handles = handles;
```

The diagram shown below demonstrates the GHS methodology:

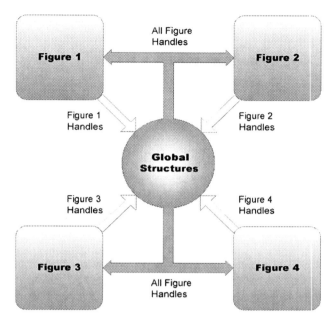

Figure 5.3: Global Handle Sharing architecture for multi-figure GUIs

The GHS architecture allows you to access any **UIControl**, **Axes**, or **HG Object** that is contained in a figure's handles. One important general rule to follow when using this architecture is to make sure that user fields that are added to the *handles* structure are initialized in the *OpeningFcn()* function to avoid other GUIs from trying to access non-existent fields. The examples throughout this chapter will focus on this architecture since it provides a simple yet powerful design model.

5.1.3   EquationAnimator: Multiple Figure GUI Design Example

Example 5.1: EquationAnimator: Multiple Figure GUI Design

This section introduces a fun new example project named **EquationAnimator** that allows you to view and modify the progression, over time, of a set of recursive equations that exhibit chaotic behavior. Often there are GUI applications that require real-time graphical animation of equations, parameters, images, etc ... This example uses a multiple figure GUI design along with real-time animation techniques to demonstrate how these types of applications are developed in MATLAB.

Project File Names:

1. ea_main.m, ea_main.fig

2. ea_graphics.m, ea_graphics.fig

3. ea_control.m, ea_control.fig

Basic Description:

Multiple figure GUI application for processing and viewing the evolution of a recursive set of equations in real-time.

Application Goals:

This application should generate and display the following set of quadratic recursive equations (Julien Sprott, *Strange Attractors: Creating Patterns in Chaos*, 1993) and allow the user to vary parameters to control the behavior of the output:

$$x(n+1) \leftrightarrow a_1 + a_2 x(n) + a_3 x(n)^2 + a_4 x(n)y(n) + a_5 y(n) + a_6 y(n)^2$$
$$y(n+1) \leftrightarrow a_7 + a_8 x(n) + a_9 x(n)^2 + a_{10} x(n)y(n) + a_{11} y(n) + a_{12} y(n)^2$$
$$n = 1,2,3...$$

The evolution of this recursive set of equations may be viewed over time by holding a sequence of *N* values that contain the values for each iteration of the equation. For example, if *N* = 1000, then a snapshot of the last 1000 iterations may be viewed in the xy plane to observe the behavior of the equations.

     Coefficients *a(1:12)* may be altered in real-time to observe chaotic states and strange attractors. Some solutions are stable and some diverge to infinity.

A total of three figures should be designed for the application:

- **ea_main**: Main parent GUI that should appear upon startup and control file I/O and launching the *ea_graphics* figure and *ea_control* figure GUIs. This GUI should possess the following functionality:

o Menu items for loading and saving an equation parameter file

o Menu items for displaying/hiding the graphics and control figures

o Display the set of iterative equations using LaTex format

o A parameters panel should allow the user to input *N*, the value of *n* at which a plot of either *x(n)* or *y(n)* should be displayed, two radiobuttons that control if the plot should show *x(n)* or *y(n)* data, and a pushbutton for launching the parameter control figure.

o Pushbuttons for Run, Stop, and Reset

- **ea_graphics**: Graphical data figure for rendering the iterative equations in x/y coordinates at each step, *n*, using line objects with only the markers enabled. An additional plot axes should be used to display the cumulative plot of *x* or *y*. The rendering axes should display the updated *x* and *y* values at a frame rate defined using a **Timer Object.** Also, the GUI should allow zooming in and out using the keyboard.

- **ea_control**: A popup GUI with slider and edit controls for manipulating equation parameters and the rendering frame rate

Design Styles:

ea_main figure: A combination of a menu bar and UIControl objects

ea_graphics figure: A figure with axes objects for displaying data

ea_control figure: UIControls only

Graphical Layout:

The GUI layouts for each figure in the application are shown below:

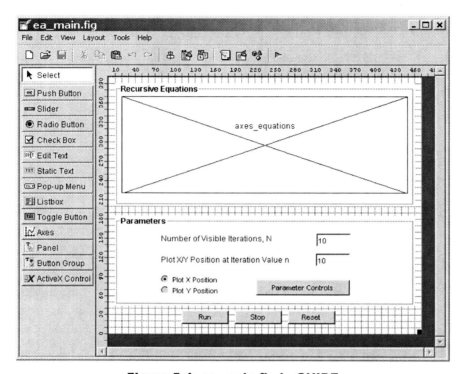

Figure 5.4: ea_main.fig in GUIDE

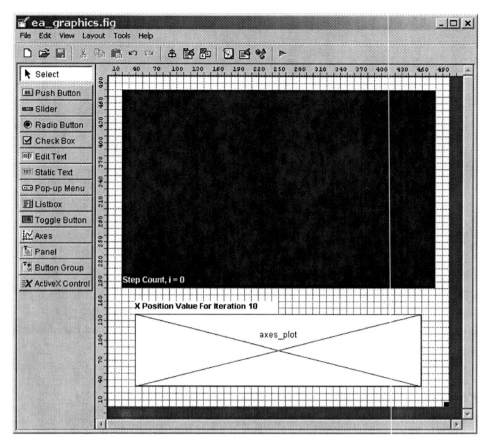

Figure 5.5: ea_graphics.fig in GUIDE

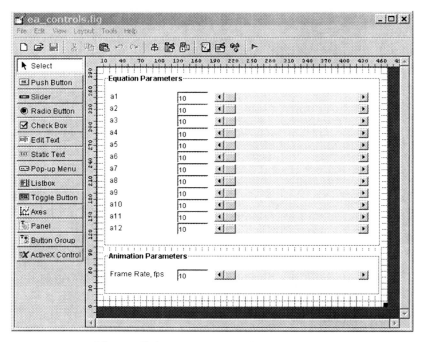

Figure 5.6: ea_controls.fig in GUIDE

Menus:

The menu bar hierarchy is shown below:

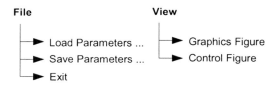

Exercise 5.1: GHS Architecture For EquationAnimator

Design a GHS architecture for the above **EquationAnimator** example application. Create a basic block diagram to demonstrate how each figure will interact and the global variable structure tree that will be used.

Example 5.1 Solution:

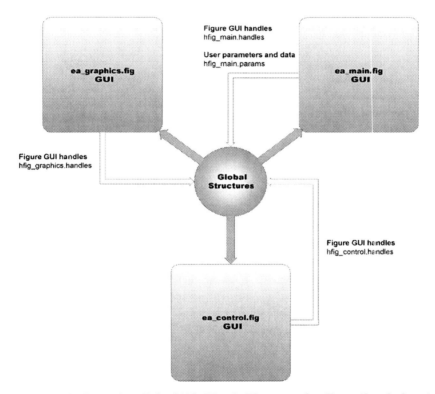

Figure 5.7: Exercise 5.1, GHS Block Diagram for EquationAnimator

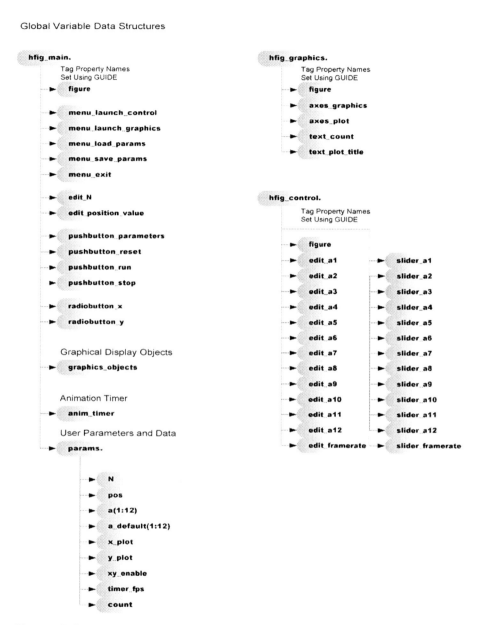

Global Variable Data Structures

Figure 5.8: Exercise 5.1, Global Variable Structure for EquationAnimator

5.2   Real-time GUIs and Animation

Graphical representation of data or GUI controls as static entities is often not sufficient for complex applications that contain streaming information or dynamic control elements. Real-time GUIs and animation offer solutions for managing the display of dynamic information and creating interactive controls. Some common examples of GUI applications that often require a real-time or animation GUI design are:

- Video Applications

- Audio Signal Processing

- Communications Signal Processing

- Simulation of Complex Systems

- Instrumentation and Data Acquisition Interfaces

- Control Systems

- Real-time Financial Market Analysis

- Animation of 2D or 3D Graphical Data

This section expands upon the knowledge you have learned throughout the previous chapters regarding the use of **Timer** functions for generating real-time events and describes a general framework for real-time GUIs.

5.2.1   Using Timers For Loops

In section 4.3.4 you were introduced to the MATLAB *timer()* function as a tool for controlling dynamic events. **Timer Objects** are essentially the heart of a real-time or animation application in that they provide a precise periodic or single shot event that executes a core segment of code for updating plots, data, GUI objects, etc ... Attempting to create such an application using *for* loops is generally plagued with problems. Examples include unpredictable loop processing speed and forcing MATLAB to consume processing resources within *for* loops. This often leaves input events, such as mouse or keyboard events, unprocessed and can cause the application to not respond to input commands and/or have jerky operation. The following diagram demonstrates the use of **Timer Objects** for controlling periodic event calls:

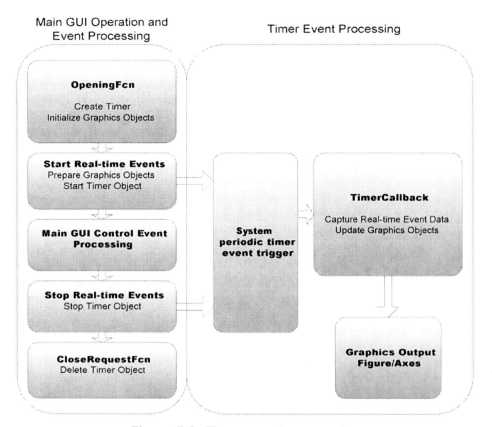

Figure 5.9: Timer event processing

Timer Objects are part of the event queue and this feature allows the timer processing callback to be called when resources are available. Conventional *for* loops or *while* loops simply consume the processing thread until the loop is complete. Although it is possible to poll variables within conventional loops it is not recommended for real-time or animation applications.

5.2.2   Animating HG Objects

Real-time or animation applications generally require updating a figure or axes with **HG Objects**. Often the rendering speed of the figure or axes depends upon the number or complexity of **HG Objects** that must be updated and how often these objects are updated. The best way to ensure **HG Objects** are updated efficiently is to instantiate the **HG Objects** prior to the first **Timer** callback function such as within a start command pushbutton event.

Once the graphics object handles are created, the properties of the objects may be manipulated. Creating **HG Objects** within the **Timer** callback function is not recommended and will slow down the application significantly. For example, if you have an application that requires you to acquire a frame of video from a camera and display the image in a figure, you should create an image object handle prior to starting the video capture timer and use the **CData** property to update the image data for each frame.

Animation of plot data may also be efficiently rendered by first generating a handle to a **Line Object** using a plot command and then updating the **XData** and **YData** properties as new data is acquired or generated within the **Timer** callback. The following example demonstrates this approach by generating a sinusoidal plot upon opening the GUI and then increasing the frequency and displaying the updated waveform using a counter within the **Timer** callback:

Example 5.2: Animation of Plot Data

Animation of Plot Data

```
function figure_OpeningFcn(hObject, [], handles)
global hfig_main
    x = 1:100;
    y = sin(x).^2;
    hfig_main.count = 0;
    hfig_main.my_plot = plot(x, y);
    hfig_main.timer = timer( 'TimerFcn', ...
                        {@timer_Callback, hObject}, ...
                        'ExecutionMode', 'fixedRate', ...
                        'Period', 0.1);

function pushbutton_start_Callback(hObject, [], handles)
global hfig_main
    start(hfig_main.timer);

function timer_Callback(hObject, handles)
global hfig_main
    hfig_main.count = hfig_main.count + 1;
    x = 1:100;
    y = sin(x.*i./10).^2;
    set(hfig_main.my_plot, 'XData', x, 'YData', y);

function pushbutton_start_Callback(hObject, [], handles)
global hfig_main
```

```
        stop(hfig_main.timer);


function figure_CloseRequest(hObject, [], handles)
global hfig_main
        delete(hfig_main.timer);
```

The above example illustrates the use of the *set()* function within the **Timer** callback to perform the updating of an **HG object**. Calling the plot function itself within the **Timer** callback will cause a slower update time and may have flicker from rendering the entire axes.

As you can imagine, there are numerous ways to animate or update **HG Objects** based on properties. Some examples of properties that are often used in real-time or animation applications are listed in the table below:

Table 5.1: HG Objects and Properties Useful For Animation Applications

HG Object	Property	Application
Line (plots)	XData, YData, ZData	Updating plot data or generating graphics
Line	Color	Changing color of plot data
Image	CData	Update pixel data in an image
Image	AlphaData	Update alpha transparency of an image's pixel data
Light	Color	Update light color
Light	Position	Animate the position of a light
Patch	Faces, XData, YData, ZData	Animate vertices for graphics generation
Patch	FaceColor, CData	Manipulate color of patches
Text	String, Color	Periodically update text data
Surface	XData, YData, ZData, CData	Animation of 2D functions
Axes	XLim, YLim, ZLim	Zooming in and out of an axes

UIControls (Text, Edit Boxes)	String	Update text information timer events
UIControls (Pushbutton, Togglebutton)	CData	Animate a button's image icon

The above list is certainly not exhaustive but gives you an idea of common properties that may be used dynamically within a GUI application.

5.2.3   Real-time Controls

Local handle object architectures are built around the concept of passing the *handles* structure to a callback function, updating the *handles* structure within the callback, and then passing control back to the main application. One drawback of this program structure is that callback functions must complete execution before the handles data modified in the callback is available to other callback functions. Any time you have a *for* loop or a lengthy calculation within a callback, other GUI control properties will not have any affect on the current executing callback function. The *handles* data is basically static within a callback except for the *handles* data that you modify within a callback.

In contrast to local handles passing to each callback, the GHS architecture allows an executing callback to access the current state of any field of the global handles structure. This allows GUI controls to update information smoothly within a real-time application where events are constantly being triggered. Smooth operation is very important for real-time applications since it affects the user's ability to effectively interact with the GUI.

Real-time Sliders

One UIControl that requires a bit more effort to achieve truly smooth operation is the slider control. In MATLAB, slider values are updated through callback or keypress functions when the following actions occur:

* Either arrow button is clicked using the mouse

- Either arrow button is clicked and held down using the mouse causing the slider to increase or decrease in value

- The trough of the slider is clicked and/or held down using the mouse

- The slider bar is clicked and held and then moved to a new position

- The mouse is clicked within the slider control and the arrow keys on the keyboard are pressed or held down

The callback and keypress functions are called repetitively when the arrow keys are held down, the arrow buttons are held down, or when the mouse button is held down when the cursor is in the trough. However, when the slider bar is grabbed and moved to a different value, the callback function does not execute during the dragging of the mouse. The callback is only executed twice, once when the slider bar starts to move and once when the user depresses the mouse button with the slider bar in the final position.

To achieve truly smooth operation, such that the slider value is acquired while the slider bar is in motion, you can use the figure's *WindowButtonMotionFcn()* callback. You can create a conditional case to check if the mouse cursor is within the slider's area and get the slider value if the case is true. This allows you to read the slider value as the slider bar is being repositioned. The following example code demonstrates this trick:

Example 5.3: Real-time Slider Control

Real-time Slider

```
function figure_WindowButtonMotionFcn(hObject, eventdata, handles)
global hfig


    % check if mouse is over a slider object and get the current
    % slider value and update the edit box and global variable
    obj = get(hfig.figure, 'CurrentObject');

    if ~isempty(obj)
        if obj == hfig.slider

                % get the slider value
                hfig.params.slider_val = get(hfig.slider, 'Value');
        end
    end
```

Exercise 5.2: Implementing EquationAnimator

In this example you will develop the detailed code for each of the following GUI figures for EquationAnimator:

- ea_main.fig
- ea_graphics.fig
- ea_control.fig

The following list defines specific requirements and guidelines for developing the application:

ea_main

- The 'Load Parameters' menu item should generate a simple M-file containing the equation coefficients while the 'Save Parameters' item should read the M-file and update the global variables and controls

- Upon startup of *ea_main*, the graphics figure window should also be launched by default and its menu item under the 'View' menu should be checked

- The 'View' menu items should simply hide the graphics and control figures by using the **Visible** property although they should always exist as figure objects as long as *ea_main* remains open

- The Parameter Controls pushbutton should make the *ea_control* figure visible and check mark the 'Control Figure' menu item

- The Run button should initialize the graphics objects by using the plot command to create a line object and then start the animation timer

- While the timer is running the frame rate slider control should be disabled since the timer object period property cannot be changed while the timer is active

- The Stop button should stop the timer function

- The Reset button should set the *count*, *x_plot*, *y_plot*, *x*, and *y* parameters to zero and reload the current default coefficient values *a(1:12)*

- The *anim_timer()* callback function should calculate the next *N* iterations of the *x* and *y* recursive functions, save them to vectors *x(n)* and *y(n)*, and update the line object in the graphics figure using these vectors

ea_graphics

- The graphics figure should include a *KeyPressFcn()* and *WindowButtonMotionFcn()* callback functions to allow the user to zoom in and out of the graphics axes similar to the code developed in chapter 4

- The plot axes should be used to display the a cumulative plot of *x(n)* or *y(n)* based on the state of the x-plot and y-plot radiobuttons

ea_controls

- Real-time slider controls should be used for each slider such that the edit box and global variable associated with each slider value is updated while the slider is moving by using the *WindowButtonMotionFcn()* callback function

- The range of values for the slider and edit box for *a(1:12)* coefficients should be limited to -2 to +2 with slider increments of 0.001 for fine control

- The frame rate slider and edit box should have a range from 1 to 30 frames per second with fractional values rounded to the nearest integer value

Screen Shots of EquationAnimator Running

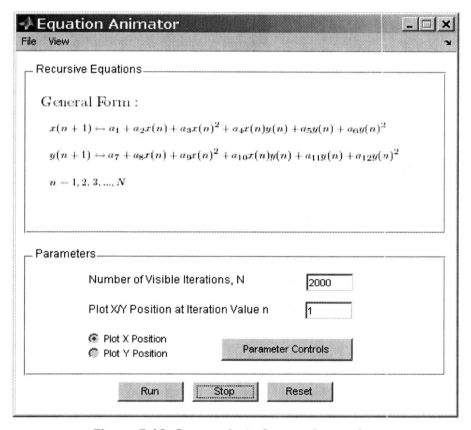

Figure 5.10: Screenshot of ea_main running

ea_graphics - Note the multiple strange attractor points that may be visualized in real-time. As you increase *N*, more points are plotted on the screen and the geometry of the recursive mapping of *x(n)* and *y(n)* becomes more evident. Small changes in coefficients *a(1:12)* can change the behavior to form many intriguing mappings. Many combinations of *a(1:12)* will cause divergence as well. If this occurs you can simply stop the animation and press reset.

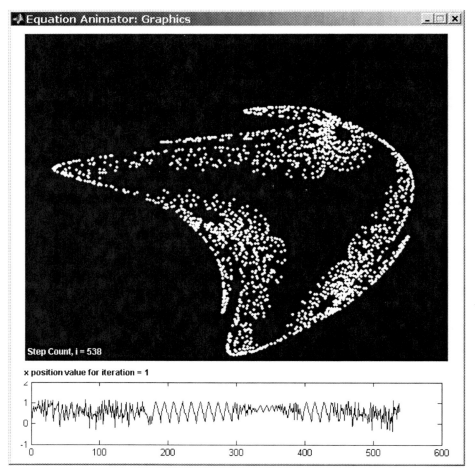

Figure 5.11: Screenshot ea_graphics running

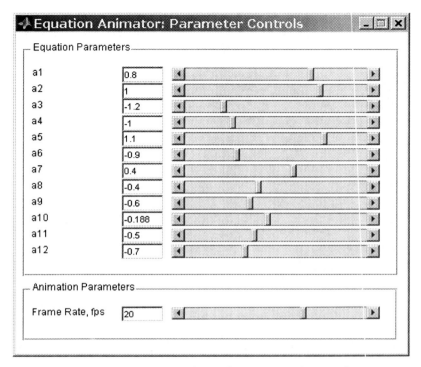

Figure 5.12: Screenshot of ea_controls running

Exercise 5.2 Example Code For EquationAnimator

ea_main.m

```
% ----------------------------------------------------------------------
function varargout = ea_main(varargin)
    gui_Singleton = 1;
    gui_State = struct('gui_Name',       mfilename, ...
                       'gui_Singleton',  gui_Singleton, ...
                       'gui_OpeningFcn', @figure_OpeningFcn, ...
                       'gui_OutputFcn',  @figure_OutputFcn, ...
                       'gui_LayoutFcn',  [] , ...
                       'gui_Callback',   []);
    if nargin && ischar(varargin{1})
        gui_State.gui_Callback = str2func(varargin{1});
    end

    if nargout
        [varargout{1:nargout}] = gui_mainfcn(gui_State, varargin{:});
    else
        gui_mainfcn(gui_State, varargin{:});
    end
```

figure_OpeningFcn

```
% ----------------------------------------------------------------------
function figure_OpeningFcn(hObject, eventdata, handles, varargin)
global hfig_main
global hfig_control
global hfig_graphics

    hfig_main = handles;

    % initialize equation parameters
    hfig_main.params.N = 500;    % max iterations
    hfig_main.params.pos = 1;    % iteration plot position value
    hfig_main.params.xy_enable = 'x'; % enable x position plotting
    hfig_main.params.count = 0;  % time step counter

    hfig_main.params.a_default = [0.8 1.0 -1.2 -1.0 1.1 -0.9 0.4 -0.4 -0.6
-0.2 -0.5 -0.7];
    hfig_main.params.a = hfig_main.params.a_default;

    hfig_main.params.x = zeros(hfig_main.params.N, 1);
    hfig_main.params.y = zeros(hfig_main.params.N, 1);
```

```
hfig_main.params.timer_fps = 20;  % frequency of animation timer


% update edit box text with parameters
set(hfig_main.edit_N, ...
    'String', num2str(hfig_main.params.N));
set(hfig_main.edit_position_value, ...
    'String', num2str(hfig_main.params.pos));


% set the axes_equation axes to current to display Latex equations
set(hfig_main.figure, 'CurrentAxes', hfig_main.axes_equations);


% Equations With Specified Parameters
text(   'Position', [10 130], ...
        'BackgroundColor', [1 1 0.9], ...
        'Color', [0 0 0], ...
        'FontName', 'Arial', ...
        'FontSize', 9, ...
        'FontUnits', 'pixels', ...
        'Interpreter', 'Latex', ...
        'String', 'General Form :', ...
        'Units', 'Pixels');


% x(n) equation
text(   'Position', [20 100], ...
        'BackgroundColor', [1 1 0.9], ...
        'Color', [0 0 0], ...
        'FontName', 'Arial', ...
        'FontSize', 7, ...
        'FontUnits', 'pixels', ...
        'Interpreter', 'Latex', ...
        'String', '$${x(n+1) \leftrightarrow a_1 + a_2x(n) + a_3x(n)^2
+ a_4x(n)y(n) + a_5y(n) + a_6y(n)^2}$$', ...
        'Units', 'Pixels');


% y(n) equation
text(   'Position', [20 70], ...
        'BackgroundColor', [1 1 0.9], ...
        'Color', [0 0 0], ...
        'FontName', 'Arial', ...
        'FontSize', 7, ...
        'FontUnits', 'pixels', ...
        'Interpreter', 'Latex', ...
```

```
            'String', '$${y(n+1) \leftrightarrow a_7 + a_8x(n) + a_9x(n)^2
+ a_{10}x(n)y(n) + a_{11}y(n) + a_{12}y(n)^2}$$', ...
            'Units', 'Pixels');


    % n = 1:N equation
    text(   'Position', [20 40], ...
            'BackgroundColor', [1 1 0.9], ...
            'Color', [0 0 0], ...
            'FontName', 'Arial', ...
            'FontSize', 7, ...
            'FontUnits', 'pixels', ...
            'Interpreter', 'Latex', ...
            'String', '$${n = 1,2,3, ... ,N}$$', ...
            'Units', 'Pixels');


% initialize animation timer
    hfig_main.anim_timer = timer( 'TimerFcn', ...
                                {@anim_timer_Callback, hObject}, ...
                                'ExecutionMode', 'fixedRate', ...
                                'Period',
round(1/hfig_main.params.timer_fps*1000)/1000);


% open graphics figure
eval('ea_graphics')
set(hfig_main.menu_launch_graphics, 'Checked', 'on');
set(hfig_graphics.text_plot_title, ...
    'String', [hfig_main.params.xy_enable ...
            ' position value for iteration = ' ...
            num2str(hfig_main.params.pos)]);


% open parameter controls figure with the Visible property set to 'off'
eval('ea_controls')
set(hfig_control.figure, 'Visible', 'off');


% Choose default command line output for figure
handles.output = hObject;


% Update handles structure
guidata(hObject, handles);
```

figure_OutputFcn

```
% --- Outputs from this function are returned to the command line.
```

```
function varargout = figure_OutputFcn(hObject, eventdata, handles)
varargout{1} = handles.output;
```

anim_timer_Callback

```
% -------------------------------------------------------------------
function anim_timer_Callback(timer_object, eventdata, hObject)
global hfig_main
global hfig_control
global hfig_graphics

    handles = guidata(hObject);

    % use local variables simplify equations
    x = hfig_main.params.x;
    y = hfig_main.params.y;
    a = hfig_main.params.a;

    % set the first element in vector x(n) and y(n) to the last element
value from
    % the previous timer iteration
    x(1) = x(end);
    y(1) = y(end);

    % update graphics objects in graphics figure
    set(hfig_main.graphic_objects, 'XData', x, 'YData', y);

    % calculate N iterations for x(n) and y(n)
    for n = 1:hfig_main.params.N-1

        % quadratic recursive equation
        x(n+1) = a(1) + a(2)*x(n) + a(3)*x(n)^2 + a(4)*x(n)*y(n) +
a(5)*y(n) + a(6)*y(n)^2;
        y(n+1) = a(7) + a(8)*x(n) + a(9)*x(n)^2 + a(10)*x(n)*y(n) +
a(11)*y(n) + a(12)*y(n)^2;

        if n == hfig_main.params.pos
            hfig_main.params.x_plot(hfig_main.params.count+1) = x(n);
            hfig_main.params.y_plot(hfig_main.params.count+1) = y(n);
        end

    end

    % check if x or y plot radiobutton is enabled and draw plots
```

```
if hfig_main.params.xy_enable == 'x'
    plot(hfig_graphics.axes_plot, hfig_main.params.x_plot, '-k');
elseif hfig_main.params.xy_enable == 'y'
    plot(hfig_graphics.axes_plot, hfig_main.params.y_plot, '-k');
end

% flush event queue and update graphics
drawnow

% save x and y params
hfig_main.params.x = x;
hfig_main.params.y = y;

% update frame counter text
set(hfig_graphics.text_count, ...
    'String', ['Step Count, i = ' num2str(hfig_main.params.count)]);

% update frame counter
hfig_main.params.count = hfig_main.params.count + 1;
```

edit_N_Callback

```
% -------------------------------------------------------------------
function edit_N_Callback(hObject, eventdata, handles)
global hfig_main

    % initialize equation parameters
    hfig_main.params.N = str2num(get(hObject, 'String')); % max iterations
    hfig_main.params.count = 0;  % time step counter
    hfig_main.params.x = zeros(hfig_main.params.N, 1);
    hfig_main.params.y = zeros(hfig_main.params.N, 1);
```

pushbutton_parameters_Callback

```
% -------------------------------------------------------------------
function pushbutton_parameters_Callback(hObject, eventdata, handles)
global hfig_main

    eval('ea_controls');
    hfig_main.controls_open = 1;     % controls figure is open
    set(hfig_main.menu_launch_control, 'Checked', 'on');
```

menu_exit_Callback

```
% ----------------------------------------------------------------
function menu_exit_Callback(hObject, eventdata, handles)
global hfig_main
global hfig_control
global hfig_graphics

    % make sure timer object is deleted before closing
    delete(hfig_main.anim_timer);

    % close ea_control figure
    if ishandle(hfig_control.figure)
        delete(hfig_control.figure);
    end

    % close ea_graphics figure
    if ishandle(hfig_graphics.figure)
        delete(hfig_graphics.figure);
    end

    % close ea_main figure last
    delete(hfig_main.figure);
```

menu_launch_graphics_Callback

```
% ----------------------------------------------------------------
function menu_launch_graphics_Callback(hObject, eventdata, handles)
global hfig_main
global hfig_graphics

    switch get(hfig_main.menu_launch_graphics, 'Checked')
        case 'on'
            set(hfig_main.menu_launch_graphics, 'Checked', 'off');
            set(hfig_graphics.figure, 'Visible', 'off');
        case 'off'
            set(hfig_main.menu_launch_graphics, 'Checked', 'on');
            if ishandle(hfig_graphics.figure)
                set(hfig_graphics.figure, 'Visible', 'on');
            else
                eval('ea_graphics')
            end
```

```
    end
```

menu_launch_control_Callback

```
% -------------------------------------------------------------------
function menu_launch_control_Callback(hObject, eventdata, handles)
global hfig_main
global hfig_control

    switch get(hfig_main.menu_launch_control, 'Checked')
        case 'on'
            set(hfig_main.menu_launch_control, 'Checked', 'off');
            set(hfig_control.figure, 'Visible', 'off');
        case 'off'
            set(hfig_main.menu_launch_control, 'Checked', 'on');
            if ishandle(hfig_control.figure)
                set(hfig_control.figure, 'Visible', 'on');
            else
                eval('ea_controls')
            end
    end
```

pushbutton_run_Callback

```
% -------------------------------------------------------------------
function pushbutton_run_Callback(hObject, eventdata, handles)
global hfig_main
global hfig_control
global hfig_graphics

    % reset parameters
    hfig_main.params.x = zeros(hfig_main.params.N, 1);
    hfig_main.params.y = zeros(hfig_main.params.N, 1);
    hfig_main.params.x_plot = 0;

    % disable frame rate parameter controls, these can only be
    % modified when the timer is stopped
    set(hfig_control.edit_framerate, 'Enable', 'off');
    set(hfig_control.slider_framerate, 'Enable', 'off');

    % initialize graphics objects
    plot(hfig_graphics.axes_graphics, 0, 'k'); % reset plot
```

```
    set(hfig_graphics.axes_graphics, 'NextPlot', 'Add');

    hfig_main.graphic_objects = plot(hfig_graphics.axes_graphics, ...
            hfig_main.params.x, ...
            hfig_main.params.y, ...
            'Color', [1 1 1], ...
            'LineStyle', 'none', ...
            'Marker', '.');

    % set nextplot property to ensure graphics screen is erased for
    % each frame
    set(hfig_graphics.axes_graphics, 'NextPlot', 'ReplaceChildren');

    % start timer
    start(hfig_main.anim_timer);
```

pushbutton_stop_Callback

```
% ------------------------------------------------------------------
function pushbutton_stop_Callback(hObject, eventdata, handles)
global hfig_main
global hfig_control
    stop(hfig_main.anim_timer);

    % enable frame rate parameter controls
    set(hfig_control.edit_framerate, 'Enable', 'on');
    set(hfig_control.slider_framerate, 'Enable', 'on');
    set(hfig_control.slider_framerate, 'Value', ...
hfig_main.params.timer_fps);
```

radiobutton_x_Callback

```
% ------------------------------------------------------------------
function radiobutton_x_Callback(hObject, eventdata, handles)
global hfig_main
global hfig_graphics
    val = get(hObject,'Value');
    if val
        hfig_main.params.xy_enable = 'x';
        set(hfig_main.radiobutton_y, 'Value', 0);
    end
    set(hfig_graphics.text_plot_title, ...
```

```
                  'String', [hfig_main.params.xy_enable ...
                        ' position value for iteration = ' ...
                        num2str(hfig_main.params.pos)]);
```

radiobutton_y_Callback

```
% -----------------------------------------------------------------------
function radiobutton_y_Callback(hObject, eventdata, handles)
global hfig_main
global hfig_graphics
    val = get(hObject,'Value');
    if val
        hfig_main.params.xy_enable = 'y';
        set(hfig_main.radiobutton_x, 'Value', 0);
    end
    set(hfig_graphics.text_plot_title, ...
        'String', [hfig_main.params.xy_enable ...
                        ' position value for iteration = ' ...
                        num2str(hfig_main.params.pos)]);
```

edit_position_value_Callback

```
% -----------------------------------------------------------------------
function edit_position_value_Callback(hObject, eventdata, handles)
global hfig_main
global hfig_graphics
    hfig_main.params.pos = str2num(get(hObject, 'String'));
    set(hfig_graphics.text_plot_title, ...
        'String', [hfig_main.params.xy_enable ...
                        ' position value for iteration = ' ...
                        num2str(hfig_main.params.pos)]);
```

menu_load_params_Callback

```
% -----------------------------------------------------------------------
function menu_load_params_Callback(hObject, eventdata, handles)
global hfig_main

    [filename, pathname] = uigetfile( ...
    {'*.m','M-Files (*.m)'; ...
    '*.m',   'M-files (*.m)'}, ...
    'Select Parameter M-file');

    hfig_main.params.file = [pathname filename];
```

```
    eval(['run ' hfig_main.params.file ';']);
    update_controls;
```

menu_save_params_Callback

```
% ------------------------------------------------------------------
function menu_save_params_Callback(hObject, eventdata, handles)
global hfig_main

    [filename, pathname] = uiputfile( ...
    {'*.m','M-Files (*.m)'; ...
    '*.m',   'M-files (*.m)'}, ...
    'Select Parameter M-file');

    str = ['hfig_main.params.a = [' num2str(hfig_main.params.a(1)) ' ' ...
        num2str(hfig_main.params.a(2)) ' ' ...
        num2str(hfig_main.params.a(3)) ' ' ...
        num2str(hfig_main.params.a(4)) ' ' ...
        num2str(hfig_main.params.a(5)) ' ' ...
        num2str(hfig_main.params.a(6)) ' ' ...
        num2str(hfig_main.params.a(7)) ' ' ...
        num2str(hfig_main.params.a(8)) ' ' ...
        num2str(hfig_main.params.a(9)) ' ' ...
        num2str(hfig_main.params.a(10)) ' ' ...
        num2str(hfig_main.params.a(11)) ' ' ...
        num2str(hfig_main.params.a(12)) '];'];

    fid = fopen([pathname filename], 'w');
        fwrite(fid, str, 'char');
    fclose(fid);
```

figure_DeleteFcn

```
% ------------------------------------------------------------------
function figure_DeleteFcn(hObject, eventdata, handles)
global hfig_main
global hfig_control
global hfig_graphics

    % make sure all global variables are removed from the workspace
    % just prior to deleting ea_main
    clear hfig_main hfig_control hfig_graphics
```

figure_CloseRequestFcn

```
% --- Executes when user attempts to close figure.
function figure_CloseRequestFcn(hObject, eventdata, handles)
global hfig_main
global hfig_control
global hfig_graphics

    % make sure timer object is deleted before closing
    delete(hfig_main.anim_timer);

    % close ea_control figure
    if ishandle(hfig_control.figure)
        delete(hfig_control.figure);
    end

    % close ea_graphics figure
    if ishandle(hfig_graphics.figure)
        delete(hfig_graphics.figure);
    end

    % close ea_main figure last
    delete(hfig_main.figure);
```

pushbutton_reset_Callback

```
% ------------------------------------------------------------------
function pushbutton_reset_Callback(hObject, eventdata, handles)
global hfig_main
global hfig_graphics

    % reset counter and x/y data
    hfig_main.params.x_plot = 0;
    hfig_main.params.y_plot = 0;
    hfig_main.params.count = 0;  % time step counter
    hfig_main.params.x = zeros(hfig_main.params.N, 1);
    hfig_main.params.y = zeros(hfig_main.params.N, 1);

    set(hfig_graphics.text_count, ...
        'String', ['Step Count, i = ' num2str(hfig_main.params.count)]);
```

```matlab
% reload current default parameters
if isfield(hfig_main.params, 'file')
    eval(['run ' hfig_main.params.file ';']);
else
    hfig_main.params.a = hfig_main.params.a_default;
end
update_controls;
```

ea_graphics.m

```matlab
function varargout = ea_graphics(varargin)

    gui_Singleton = 1;
    gui_State = struct('gui_Name',        mfilename, ...
                       'gui_Singleton',   gui_Singleton, ...
                       'gui_OpeningFcn',  @figure_OpeningFcn, ...
                       'gui_OutputFcn',   @figure_OutputFcn, ...
                       'gui_LayoutFcn',   [] , ...
                       'gui_Callback',    []);
    if nargin && ischar(varargin{1})
        gui_State.gui_Callback = str2func(varargin{1});
    end

    if nargout
        [varargout{1:nargout}] = gui_mainfcn(gui_State, varargin{:});
    else
        gui_mainfcn(gui_State, varargin{:});
    end
```

figure_OpeningFcn

```matlab
% -------------------------------------------------------------------------
-
function figure_OpeningFcn(hObject, eventdata, handles, varargin)
global hfig_graphics

    hfig_graphics = handles;

    % Choose default command line output for figure
    handles.output = hObject;

    % Update handles structure
```

```
    guidata(hObject, handles);
```

figure_OutputFcn

```
% -------------------------------------------------------------------------
-
function varargout = figure_OutputFcn(hObject, eventdata, handles)
    varargout{1} = handles.output;
```

figure_KeyPressFcn

```
% -------------------------------------------------------------------------
-
function figure_KeyPressFcn(hObject, eventdata, handles)
global hfig_graphics

    % capture the current key press
    keycode = double(get(hfig_graphics.figure, 'CurrentCharacter'));

    % process the current key press, zoom in and out if i or o is pressed
    if ~isempty(keycode)
        switch keycode
            case double('i')
                zoom_axes(hfig_graphics.axes_graphics, 0.95, ...
                    hfig_graphics.axes_mouse_pos);
            case double('o')
                zoom_axes(hfig_graphics.axes_graphics, 1/0.95, ...
                    hfig_graphics.axes_mouse_pos);

        end
    end
```

zoom_axes

```
% -------------------------------------------------------------------------
-
function zoom_axes(hAxes, zoom_scale, mouse_pos)

    xlim = get(hAxes, 'XLim');
    xmax = xlim(2);
    xmin = xlim(1);
    x = mouse_pos(1,1);

    ylim = get(hAxes, 'YLim');
```

```
    ymax = ylim(2);

    ymin = ylim(1);

    y = mouse_pos(1,2);


    sx_zoom = zoom_scale;

    xmax_zoom = (xmax - x )*sx_zoom + x;

    xmin_zoom = (xmin - x)*sx_zoom + x;

    set(hAxes, 'XLim', [xmin_zoom xmax_zoom]);


    sy_zoom = zoom_scale;

    ymax_zoom = (ymax - y)*sy_zoom + y;

    ymin_zoom = (ymin - y)*sy_zoom + y;

    set(hAxes, 'YLim', [ymin_zoom ymax_zoom]);
```

figure_WindowButtonMotionFcn

```
% -------------------------------------------------------------------------
-
function figure_WindowButtonMotionFcn(hObject, eventdata, handles)
global hfig_graphics

    % first determine if mouse is within the graphics axes
    mouse_pos = get(hfig_graphics.figure, 'CurrentPoint');
    axes_area = get(hfig_graphics.axes_graphics, 'Position');

    if (mouse_pos(1) < ...
        (axes_area(1) + axes_area(3))) & ...
        (mouse_pos(1) > ...
        (axes_area(1))) & ...
        (mouse_pos(2) < ...
        (axes_area(2) + axes_area(4))) & ...
        (mouse_pos(2) > ...
        (axes_area(2)))

        hfig_graphics.in_axes = 1;


        % update axes mouse position
        hfig_graphics.axes_mouse_pos = get(hfig_graphics.axes_graphics,
'CurrentPoint');
    else
        hfig_graphics.in_axes = 0;
    end
```

figure_CloseRequestFcn

```
% --- Executes when user attempts to close figure.
function figure_CloseRequestFcn(hObject, eventdata, handles)
global hfig_main


    % make sure the the main figure menu item is not checked when
    % the graphics figure is closed
    set(hfig_main.menu_launch_graphics, 'Checked', 'off');
    delete(hObject);
```

ea_controls.m

```
function varargout = ea_controls(varargin)
    gui_Singleton = 1;
    gui_State = struct('gui_Name',        mfilename, ...
                        'gui_Singleton',  gui_Singleton, ...
                        'gui_OpeningFcn', @figure_OpeningFcn, ...
                        'gui_OutputFcn',  @figure_OutputFcn, ...
                        'gui_LayoutFcn',  [] , ...
                        'gui_Callback',   []);
    if nargin && ischar(varargin{1})
        gui_State.gui_Callback = str2func(varargin{1});
    end

    if nargout
        [varargout{1:nargout}] = gui_mainfcn(gui_State, varargin{:});
    else
        gui_mainfcn(gui_State, varargin{:});
    end
```

figure_OpeningFcn

```
%--------------------------------------------------------------------
function figure_OpeningFcn(hObject, eventdata, handles, varargin)
global hfig_main
global hfig_control
global hfig_graphics


    hfig_control = handles;
```

```
% update edit boxes and sliders with current param values
update_controls;

% Choose default command line output for figure
handles.output = hObject;

% Update handles structure
guidata(hObject, handles);
```

figure_OutputFcn

```
%------------------------------------------------------------------------
function varargout = figure_OutputFcn(hObject, eventdata, handles)
    % Get default command line output from handles structure
    varargout{1} = handles.output;
```

figure_CloseRequestFcn

```
%------------------------------------------------------------------------
function figure_CloseRequestFcn(hObject, eventdata, handles)
global hfig_main

    % make sure the the main figure menu item is not checked when
    % the control figure is closed
    set(hfig_main.menu_launch_control, 'Checked', 'off');

    delete(hObject);
```

figure_WindowButtonMotionFcn

```
%------------------------------------------------------------------------
function figure_WindowButtonMotionFcn(hObject, eventdata, handles)
global hfig_main
global hfig_control

    obj = get(hfig_control.figure, 'CurrentObject');

    % check if mouse is over a slider object and get the current
    % slider value and update the edit box and global variable
    if ~isempty(obj)
```

```
switch obj

    case hfig_control.slider_a1
        % update slider params from slider object values
        hfig_main.params.a(1) = get(hfig_control.slider_a1,
'Value');
        set(hfig_control.edit_a1, ...
            'String', num2str(hfig_main.params.a(1)));

    case hfig_control.slider_a2
        hfig_main.params.a(2) = get(hfig_control.slider_a2,
'Value');
        set(hfig_control.edit_a2, ...
            'String', num2str(hfig_main.params.a(2)));

    case hfig_control.slider_a3
        hfig_main.params.a(3) = get(hfig_control.slider_a3,
'Value');
        set(hfig_control.edit_a3, ...
            'String', num2str(hfig_main.params.a(3)));

    case hfig_control.slider_a4
        hfig_main.params.a(4) = get(hfig_control.slider_a4,
'Value');
        set(hfig_control.edit_a4, ...
            'String', num2str(hfig_main.params.a(4)));

    case hfig_control.slider_a5
        hfig_main.params.a(5) = get(hfig_control.slider_a5,
'Value');
        set(hfig_control.edit_a5, ...
            'String', num2str(hfig_main.params.a(5)));

    case hfig_control.slider_a6
        hfig_main.params.a(6) = get(hfig_control.slider_a6,
'Value');
        set(hfig_control.edit_a6, ...
            'String', num2str(hfig_main.params.a(6)));

    case hfig_control.slider_a7
        hfig_main.params.a(7) = get(hfig_control.slider_a7,
'Value');
        set(hfig_control.edit_a7, ...
            'String', num2str(hfig_main.params.a(7)));

    case hfig_control.slider_a8
```

```
                    hfig_main.params.a(8) = get(hfig_control.slider_a8,
    'Value');

                    set(hfig_control.edit_a8, ...
                        'String', num2str(hfig_main.params.a(8)));

            case hfig_control.slider_a9
                    hfig_main.params.a(9) = get(hfig_control.slider_a9,
    'Value');

                    set(hfig_control.edit_a9, ...
                        'String', num2str(hfig_main.params.a(9)));

            case hfig_control.slider_a10
                    hfig_main.params.a(10) = get(hfig_control.slider_a10,
    'Value');

                    set(hfig_control.edit_a10, ...
                        'String', num2str(hfig_main.params.a(10)));

            case hfig_control.slider_a11
                    hfig_main.params.a(11) = get(hfig_control.slider_a11,
    'Value');

                    set(hfig_control.edit_a11, ...
                        'String', num2str(hfig_main.params.a(11)));

            case hfig_control.slider_a12
                    hfig_main.params.a(12) = get(hfig_control.slider_a12,
    'Value');

                    set(hfig_control.edit_a12, ...
                        'String', num2str(hfig_main.params.a(12)));

            case hfig_control.slider_framerate
                    hfig_main.params.timer_fps =
    round(get(hfig_control.slider_framerate, 'Value'));
                    set(hfig_control.edit_framerate, ...
                        'String', num2str(hfig_main.params.timer_fps));
                    set(hfig_main.anim_timer, ...
                        'Period',
    round(1/hfig_main.params.timer_fps*1000)/1000);
        end
    end
```

edit_framerate_Callback

```
%-------------------------------------------------------------------
function edit_framerate_Callback(hObject, eventdata, handles)
global hfig_main
```

```
global hfig_control

    % retrieve value and round to integer
    hfig_main.params.timer_fps = round(str2num(get(hObject,'String')));

    % check if the user enters a value greater than the max or
    % less than the min range of the slider
    smax = get(hfig_control.slider_framerate, 'Max');
    smin = get(hfig_control.slider_framerate, 'Min');

    if hfig_main.params.timer_fps > smax
        hfig_main.params.timer_fps = smax;
        set(hfig_control.edit_framerate, ...
            'String', num2str(hfig_main.params.timer_fps));

    elseif hfig_main.params.timer_fps < smin
        hfig_main.params.timer_fps = smin;
        set(hfig_control.edit_framerate, ...
            'String', num2str(hfig_main.params.timer_fps));
    end

    % set the slider value
    set(hfig_control.slider_framerate, ...
        'Value', hfig_main.params.timer_fps);

    % set the timer period
    set(hfig_main.anim_timer, 'Period',
round(1/hfig_main.params.timer_fps*1000)/1000);
```

slider_framerate_Callback

```
%-----------------------------------------------------------------------
function slider_framerate_Callback(hObject, eventdata, handles)
global hfig_main
global hfig_control
global hfig_graphics

    % retrieve value and round to integer
    hfig_main.params.timer_fps = round(get(hObject,'Value'));
    set(hfig_control.edit_framerate, ...
        'String', num2str(hfig_main.params.timer_fps));
```

```
    set(hfig_main.anim_timer, 'Period',
round(1/hfig_main.params.timer_fps*1000)/1000);
```

edit_a6_Callback

```
%-----------------------------------------------------------------
function edit_a6_Callback(hObject, eventdata, handles)
global hfig_main
global hfig_control
global hfig_graphics

    hfig_main.params.a(6) = str2num(get(hObject,'String'));
    hfig_main.params.a(6) = edit_control(hfig_main.params.a(6), ...
                        hfig_control.slider_a6, ...
                        hfig_control.edit_a6);
```

slider_a6_Callback

```
%-----------------------------------------------------------------
function slider_a6_Callback(hObject, eventdata, handles)
global hfig_main
global hfig_control

    hfig_main.params.a(6) = get(hObject,'Value');
    set(hfig_control.edit_a6, ...
        'String', num2str(hfig_main.params.a(6)));
```

edit_a7_Callback

```
%-----------------------------------------------------------------
function edit_a7_Callback(hObject, eventdata, handles)
global hfig_main
global hfig_control

    hfig_main.params.a(7) = str2num(get(hObject,'String'));
    hfig_main.params.a(7) = edit_control(hfig_main.params.a(7), ...
                        hfig_control.slider_a7, ...
                        hfig_control.edit_a7);
```

slider_a7_Callback

```
%-----------------------------------------------------------------
function slider_a7_Callback(hObject, eventdata, handles)
global hfig_main
```

```
global hfig_control

    hfig_main.params.a(7) = get(hObject,'Value');
    set(hfig_control.edit_a7, ...
        'String', num2str(hfig_main.params.a(7)));
```

edit_a8_Callback

```
%-------------------------------------------------------------------
function edit_a8_Callback(hObject, eventdata, handles)
global hfig_main
global hfig_control

    hfig_main.params.a(8) = str2num(get(hObject,'String'));
    hfig_main.params.a(8) = edit_control(hfig_main.params.a(8), ...
                        hfig_control.slider_a8, ...
                        hfig_control.edit_a8);
```

slider_a8_Callback

```
%-------------------------------------------------------------------
function slider_a8_Callback(hObject, eventdata, handles)
global hfig_main
global hfig_control

    hfig_main.params.a(8) = get(hObject,'Value');
    set(hfig_control.edit_a8, ...
        'String', num2str(hfig_main.params.a(8)));
```

edit_a9_Callback

```
%-------------------------------------------------------------------
function edit_a9_Callback(hObject, eventdata, handles)
global hfig_main
global hfig_control

    hfig_main.params.a(9) = str2num(get(hObject,'String'));
    hfig_main.params.a(9) = edit_control(hfig_main.params.a(9), ...
                        hfig_control.slider_a9, ...
                        hfig_control.edit_a9);
```

slider_a9_Callback

```
%------------------------------------------------------------------
function slider_a9_Callback(hObject, eventdata, handles)
global hfig_main
global hfig_control

   hfig_main.params.a(9) = get(hObject,'Value');
   set(hfig_control.edit_a9, ...
       'String', num2str(hfig_main.params.a(9)));
```

edit_a10_Callback

```
%------------------------------------------------------------------
function edit_a10_Callback(hObject, eventdata, handles)
global hfig_main
global hfig_control
global hfig_graphics

   hfig_main.params.a(10) = str2num(get(hObject,'String'));
   hfig_main.params.a(10) = edit_control(hfig_main.params.a(10), ...
                       hfig_control.slider_a10, ...
                       hfig_control.edit_a10);
```

slider_a10_Callback

```
%------------------------------------------------------------------
function slider_a10_Callback(hObject, eventdata, handles)
global hfig_main
global hfig_control

   hfig_main.params.a(10) = get(hObject,'Value');
   set(hfig_control.edit_a10, ...
       'String', num2str(hfig_main.params.a(10)));
```

edit_a11_Callback

```
%------------------------------------------------------------------
function edit_a11_Callback(hObject, eventdata, handles)
global hfig_main
global hfig_control
global hfig_graphics
```

```
    hfig_main.params.a(11) = str2num(get(hObject,'String'));
    hfig_main.params.a(11) = edit_control(hfig_main.params.a(11), ...
                        hfig_control.slider_a11, ...
                        hfig_control.edit_a11);
```

edit_a11_Callback

```
%-------------------------------------------------------------------
function slider_a11_Callback(hObject, eventdata, handles)
global hfig_main
global hfig_control


    hfig_main.params.a(11) = get(hObject,'Value');
    set(hfig_control.edit_a11, ...
        'String', num2str(hfig_main.params.a(11)));
```

edit_a12_Callback

```
%-------------------------------------------------------------------
function edit_a12_Callback(hObject, eventdata, handles)
global hfig_main
global hfig_control
global hfig_graphics


    hfig_main.params.a(12) = str2num(get(hObject,'String'));
    hfig_main.params.a(12) = edit_control(hfig_main.params.a(12), ...
                        hfig_control.slider_a12, ...
                        hfig_control.edit_a12);
```

slider_a12_Callback

```
%-------------------------------------------------------------------
function slider_a12_Callback(hObject, eventdata, handles)
global hfig_main
global hfig_control


    hfig_main.params.a(12) = get(hObject,'Value');
    set(hfig_control.edit_a12, ...
        'String', num2str(hfig_main.params.a(12)));
```

slider_a2_Callback

```
%----------------------------------------------------------------------
function slider_a2_Callback(hObject, eventdata, handles)
global hfig_main
global hfig_control


    hfig_main.params.a(2) = get(hObject,'Value');
    set(hfig_control.edit_a2, ...
        'String', num2str(hfig_main.params.a(2)));
```

slider_a3_Callback

```
%----------------------------------------------------------------------
function slider_a3_Callback(hObject, eventdata, handles)
global hfig_main
global hfig_control


    hfig_main.params.a(3) = get(hObject,'Value');
    set(hfig_control.edit_a3, ...
        'String', num2str(hfig_main.params.a(3)));
```

slider_a4_Callback

```
%----------------------------------------------------------------------
function slider_a4_Callback(hObject, eventdata, handles)
global hfig_main
global hfig_control


    hfig_main.params.a(4) = get(hObject,'Value');
    set(hfig_control.edit_a4, ...
        'String', num2str(hfig_main.params.a(4)));
```

slider_a5_Callback

```
%----------------------------------------------------------------------
function slider_a5_Callback(hObject, eventdata, handles)
global hfig_main
global hfig_control


    hfig_main.params.a(5) = get(hObject,'Value');
    set(hfig_control.edit_a5, ...
```

```
                    'String', num2str(hfig_main.params.a(5)));
```

edit_a1_Callback

```
%------------------------------------------------------------------------
function edit_a1_Callback(hObject, eventdata, handles)
global hfig_main
global hfig_control
global hfig_graphics

    hfig_main.params.a(1) = str2num(get(hObject,'String'));
    hfig_main.params.a(1) = edit_control(hfig_main.params.a(1), ...
                        hfig_control.slider_a1, ...
                        hfig_control.edit_a1);
```

slider_a1_Callback

```
%------------------------------------------------------------------------
function slider_a1_Callback(hObject, eventdata, handles)
global hfig_main
global hfig_control

    hfig_main.params.a(1) = get(hObject,'Value');
    set(hfig_control.edit_a1, ...
        'String', num2str(hfig_main.params.a(1)));
```

edit_control

```
%------------------------------------------------------------------------
function param = edit_control(param, hSlider, hEdit)

    smax = get(hSlider, 'Max');
    smin = get(hSlider, 'Min');

    if param > smax
        param = smax;
        set(hEdit, 'String', num2str(param));

    elseif param < smin
        param = smin;
        set(hEdit, 'String', num2str(param));
```

```
        end

        set(hSlider, 'Value', param);
```

edit_a2_Callback

```
%-----------------------------------------------------------------------
function edit_a2_Callback(hObject, eventdata, handles)
global hfig_main
global hfig_control

    hfig_main.params.a(2) = str2num(get(hObject,'String'));
    hfig_main.params.a(2) = edit_control(hfig_main.params.a(2), ...
                           hfig_control.slider_a2, ...
                           hfig_control.edit_a2);
```

edit_a3_Callback

```
%-----------------------------------------------------------------------
function edit_a3_Callback(hObject, eventdata, handles)
global hfig_main
global hfig_control

    hfig_main.params.a(3) = str2num(get(hObject,'String'));
    hfig_main.params.a(3) = edit_control(hfig_main.params.a(3), ...
                           hfig_control.slider_a3, ...
                           hfig_control.edit_a3);
```

edit_a4_Callback

```
%-----------------------------------------------------------------------
function edit_a4_Callback(hObject, eventdata, handles)
global hfig_main
global hfig_control

    hfig_main.params.a(4) = str2num(get(hObject,'String'));
    hfig_main.params.a(4) = edit_control(hfig_main.params.a(4), ...
                           hfig_control.slider_a4, ...
                           hfig_control.edit_a4);
```

edit_a5_Callback

```
%---------------------------------------------------------------------
function edit_a5_Callback(hObject, eventdata, handles)
global hfig_main
global hfig_control

    hfig_main.params.a(5) = str2num(get(hObject,'String'));
    hfig_main.params.a(5) = edit_control(hfig_main.params.a(5), ...
                        hfig_control.slider_a5, ...
                        hfig_control.edit_a5);
```

5.3   Custom GUI Control Styles

Although MATLAB provides UIControls for most graphical control elements that are standard for GUI operating systems, you may desire to create unique GUI controls or graphical interface styles for your application that requires custom development. Here are some examples of custom controls you may want to add to your application:

- Click Tab Controls
- Custom Sliders
- Toggle Switches
- Dials
- Advanced Navigator Controls
- Animated Controls

There are a few techniques that you can use to create custom controls by using common **HG Objects** provided in MATLAB. This section discusses one common technique for creating custom controls and provides an implementation example.

5.3.1   Image Mapped Controls, IMCs

One powerful technique commonly used to develop custom GUI interfaces is referred to in this text as Image Mapped Controls, IMCs. The concept is quite straight forward:

- First, layout your GUI controls in terms of the pixel regions they will cover in the application
- Next, create icon images of the correct size for each control style and state you wish to implement in your design based on your layout
- Read the images into your application upon startup and display them in their appropriate location
- Last, map each GUI control image to a respective callback function that initiates an action when the user clicks a mouse button or moves the mouse over the region of the control

The following figure show a simple application that uses image mapped controls:

Figure 5.13: Example GUI with image mapped controls

The application shown above uses IMCs as button controls for allowing the user to control the application by clicking on each image. The control images shown above are created such that their background color matches the figure background color to provide a blended, smooth appearance.

Although the concept of using IMCs is straight forward, implementation requires some up-front planning and vision in terms of the overall style you wish to achieve for your application. In general, image mapped controls are used for applications that you plan to deploy to a large audience where style can become an important aspect for the GUI. Also, there are some control styles that simply are not sufficient to provide the user with the appropriate interaction with the application. In this case, image mapped controls may be the only answer.

5.3.2   Image Mapped GUI Layouts

IMC layouts may be constructed using two common approaches: The first approach is to use an **Axes Object** for each image control that you wish to use and the second approach is to use a single **Axes Object** with multiple control images mapped within a single image.

One advantage of using a separate **Axes Object** per control is that separate **Image Objects** may be used for each control image. Since each control image is a unique object, the **ButtonDownFcn** property callback function may be used to detect mouse button clicks for each control. Also, the **Position** property of each **Axes Object** may be used in a figure's *WindowButtonMotionFcn()* callback to detect if the mouse pointer is within an image control boundary. This information may then be used to properly route the GUI control actions. We will focus on using the multiple **Axes Object** approach since it is simpler to implement.

5.3.3   IMC Callbacks

As mentioned above, separate **Image Objects** may be used along with the **ButtonDownFcn** callback property to create an IMC. The following code shows you how to initialize an IMC in the *OpeningFcn()* function and assign a **ButtonDownFcn** to an **Image Object**:

Example 5.4: Image Mapped Controls, IMCs

OpeningFcn

```
function imc_OpeningFcn(hObject, eventdata, handles, varargin)
global hfig

        % initialize play button control
        hfig.img_play = imread('play.jpg', 'jpg');
        hfig.img_play_sel = imread('play_select.jpg', 'jpg');
        image(hfig.img_play, 'Parent', hfig.play, ...
                    'ButtonDownFcn', @play_ButtonDownFcn);
        hfig.play_pos = get(hfig.play, 'Position');
        set(hfig.play,    'XTick', [], ...
                        'YTick', [], ...
                            'XColor', bg_color, ...
                            'YColor', bg_color);
```

play_ButtonDownFcn Callback

```
function play_ButtonDownFcn(hObject, eventdata)
global hfig

    % perform play button task

    .

    .

    .
```

5.3.4   Highlighting IMCs Based On Mouse Pointer

Often it is useful to change the state of an image for an IMC to show the user the mouse is within the region of the control. The following code segment demonstrates a simple method of highlighting an image control when the mouse pointer moves over the image's **Axes Object**:

```
function figure1_WindowButtonMotionFcn(hObject, eventdata, handles)
global hfig

    pos = get(hfig.figure1, 'CurrentPoint');

    if pos(1) > hfig.play_pos(1) & ...
       pos(1) < (hfig.play_pos(1) + hfig.play_pos(3)) & ...
       pos(2) > hfig.play_pos(2) & ...
       pos(2) < (hfig.play_pos(2) + hfig.play_pos(4))
        set(get(hfig.play, 'Children'), 'CData', hfig.img_play_sel);
    else
        set(get(hfig.play, 'Children'), 'CData', hfig.img_play);
    end
```

The above code uses a figure's *WindowButtonMotionFcn()* to detect the mouse position and compare it with the position of a variable called *hfig.play_pos* that holds the axes position for the play button IMC. If the mouse is within the bounds of the play button axes, then a highlighted version of the play button image, *hfig.img_play_sel*, is displayed in the axes *hfig.play*. If the mouse is not within the axes boundary, then the normal play button state image, *hfig.img_play*, is displayed.

The following example steps you through the process of implementing a GUI using IMCs:

Example 5.5: Image Mapped Controls: AVI Video Player

For demonstrating the design of an image mapped control GUI, we will develop a simple GUI interface that may be used playback an AVI movie file using MATLAB's *aviread()* and *aviinfo()* functions. The goal is to use IMCs to create the following buttons that will be used to control the playback of the video file:

- Play
- Stop
- Forward
- Reverse

Two images should be created for each image mapped control listed above: one image to show the control is in focus, or highlighted state, and another for the control in its normal state. There should also be a main axes object placed within the figure to display video data. The screen capture figure below shows an example layout for the buttons and main axes:

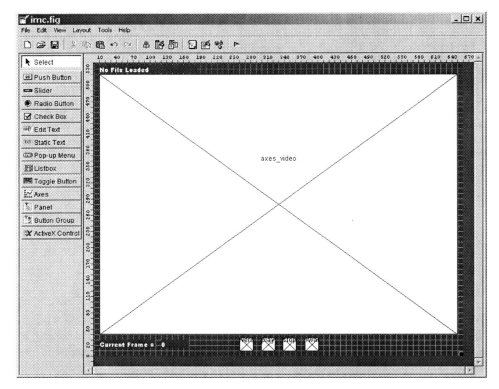

Figure 5.14: Example 5.5 layout in GUIDE, image mapped controls

There are a few important axes properties that should be modified to ensure the axes boundaries and tick marks will not interfere with the image control that is displayed:

```
set(hfig.axes_control,      'XTick', [], ...
                            'YTick', [], ...
                            'XColor', get(hfig.figure, 'Color'), ...
                            'YColor', get(hfig.figure, 'Color'));
```

Setting the **XTick** and **YTick** properties to empty matrices removes the ticks from the axes while setting the **XColor** and **YColor** properties to the background color of the figure ensures that the boundaries of the axes will not be visible.

Example 5.5 Code for imc

imc Main Function

```
% -----------------------------------------------------------------
function varargout = imc(varargin)
    gui_Singleton = 1;
    gui_State = struct('gui_Name',        mfilename, ...
                       'gui_Singleton',  gui_Singleton, ...
                       'gui_OpeningFcn', @imc_OpeningFcn, ...
                       'gui_OutputFcn',  @imc_OutputFcn, ...
                       'gui_LayoutFcn',  [] , ...
                       'gui_Callback',   []);
    if nargin && ischar(varargin{1})
        gui_State.gui_Callback = str2func(varargin{1});
    end


    if nargout
        [varargout{1:nargout}] = gui_mainfcn(gui_State, varargin{:});
    else
        gui_mainfcn(gui_State, varargin{:});
    end
```

imc_OpeningFcn

```
% -----------------------------------------------------------------
function imc_OpeningFcn(hObject, eventdata, handles, varargin)
global hfig

hfig = handles;

    % read GUI control images and display in axes objects
    bg_color = [0 51/255 108/255];

    % reverse button control
    hfig.img_reverse = imread('reverse.jpg', 'jpg');
    hfig.img_reverse_sel = imread('reverse_select.jpg', 'jpg');
    image(hfig.img_reverse, 'Parent', hfig.reverse, ...
                        'ButtonDownFcn', @reverse_ButtonDownFcn);
    hfig.reverse_pos = get(hfig.reverse, 'Position');
    set(hfig.reverse,    'XTick', [], ...
                         'YTick', [], ...
                         'XColor', bg_color, ...
                         'YColor', bg_color);
```

```
% play button control
hfig.img_play = imread('play.jpg', 'jpg');
hfig.img_play_sel = imread('play_select.jpg', 'jpg');
image(hfig.img_play, 'Parent', hfig.play, ...
                     'ButtonDownFcn', @play_ButtonDownFcn);
hfig.play_pos = get(hfig.play, 'Position');
set(hfig.play,    'XTick', [], ...
                          'YTick', [], ...
                          'XColor', bg_color, ...
                          'YColor', bg_color);


% stop button control
hfig.img_stop = imread('stop.jpg', 'jpg');
hfig.img_stop_sel = imread('stop_select.jpg', 'jpg');
image(hfig.img_stop, 'Parent', hfig.stop, ...
                     'ButtonDownFcn', @stop_ButtonDownFcn);
hfig.stop_pos = get(hfig.stop, 'Position');
set(hfig.stop,    'XTick', [], ...
                          'YTick', [], ...
                          'XColor', bg_color, ...
                          'YColor', bg_color);


% forward button control
hfig.img_forward = imread('forward.jpg', 'jpg');
hfig.img_forward_sel = imread('forward_select.jpg', 'jpg');
image(hfig.img_forward, 'Parent', hfig.forward, ...
                     'ButtonDownFcn', @forward_ButtonDownFcn);
hfig.forward_pos = get(hfig.forward, 'Position');
set(hfig.forward,    'XTick', [], ...
                          'YTick', [], ...
                          'XColor', bg_color, ...
                          'YColor', bg_color);


% initialize video framerate timer and default to 15fps
hfig.frame_count = 1;
hfig.video_timer = timer( 'TimerFcn', ...
                          @video_timer_Callback, ...
                          'ExecutionMode', 'fixedRate', ...
                          'Period', round(1/15*1000)/1000);


% Choose default command line output for imc
handles.output = hObject;
```

```
    % Update handles structure
    guidata(hObject, handles);
```

imc_OutputFcn

```
% ---------------------------------------------------------------------
function varargout = imc_OutputFcn(hObject, eventdata, handles)
    varargout{1} = handles.output;
```

figure1_WindowButtonMotionFcn

```
% ---------------------------------------------------------------------
function figure1_WindowButtonMotionFcn(hObject, eventdata, handles)
global hfig

    % get current mouse position in figure
    pos = get(hfig.figure1, 'CurrentPoint');

    % check if mouse is over the reverse button and hightlight if true
    if pos(1) > hfig.reverse_pos(1) & ...
       pos(1) < (hfig.reverse_pos(1) + hfig.reverse_pos(3)) & ...
       pos(2) > hfig.reverse_pos(2) & ...
       pos(2) < (hfig.reverse_pos(2) + hfig.reverse_pos(4))
        set(hfig.image.reverse, 'CData', hfig.img_reverse_sel);
    else
        set(hfig.image.reverse, 'CData', hfig.img_reverse);
    end

    % check if mouse is over the forward button and hightlight if true
    if pos(1) > hfig.forward_pos(1) & ...
       pos(1) < (hfig.forward_pos(1) + hfig.forward_pos(3)) & ...
       pos(2) > hfig.forward_pos(2) & ...
       pos(2) < (hfig.forward_pos(2) + hfig.forward_pos(4))
        set(hfig.image.forward, 'CData', hfig.img_forward_sel);
    else
        set(hfig.image.forward, 'CData', hfig.img_forward);
    end

    % check if mouse is over the play button and hightlight if true
    if pos(1) > hfig.play_pos(1) & ...
       pos(1) < (hfig.play_pos(1) + hfig.play_pos(3)) & ...
```

```
    pos(2) > hfig.play_pos(2) & ...
    pos(2) < (hfig.play_pos(2) + hfig.play_pos(4))
      set(hfig.image.play, 'CData', hfig.img_play_sel);
else
    set(hfig.image.play, 'CData', hfig.img_play);
end


% check if mouse is over the stop button and hightlight if true
if pos(1) > hfig.stop_pos(1) & ...
    pos(1) < (hfig.stop_pos(1) + hfig.stop_pos(3)) & ...
    pos(2) > hfig.stop_pos(2) & ...
    pos(2) < (hfig.stop_pos(2) + hfig.stop_pos(4))
      set(hfig.image.stop, 'CData', hfig.img_stop_sel);
else
    set(hfig.image.stop, 'CData', hfig.img_stop);
end
```

menu_open_avi_Callback

```
% ------------------------------------------------------------------
function menu_open_avi_Callback(hObject, eventdata, handles)
global hfig

    % open file browser to select AVI file
    [filename, pathname] = uigetfile( ...
    {'*.avi','AVI Video File (*.avi)'; ...
    '*.avi',  'AVI Video File (*.avi)'}, ...
    'Open AVI Video File');

    % check if OK button pressed
    if ~isequal(filename,0) & ~isequal(pathname,0)
        [pathstr,name,ext,versn] = fileparts([pathname filename]);
        ext_size = size(ext');
        if ext_size ~= 4
            errordlg('Invalid Image File Extension');
        else
            if ext == '.avi'

                % read AVI video file
                hfig.movie = aviread([pathname filename]);

                % read AVI video file info
```

```
            hfig.movie_info = aviinfo([pathname filename]);


            % format axes for width/height of video frames
            set(hfig.axes_video, ...
                'XLim', [0 hfig.movie_info.Width], ...
                'YLim', [0 hfig.movie_info.Height], ...
                'YDir', 'Reverse', ...
                'NextPlot', 'ReplaceChildren');


            % create an image object for displaying video frames
            % and show the first video frame
            hfig.mov_img = image('Parent', hfig.axes_video, ...
                    'CData', hfig.movie(1).cdata);


            set(hfig.text_file, 'String', filename);


            % update frame count text
            set(hfig.text_frame_count, 'String',
num2str(hfig.frame_count));


        else
            errordlg('Invalid Image File Extension');
        end
    end
end
```

play_ButtonDownFcn

```
% --------------------------------------------------------------------
function play_ButtonDownFcn(hObject, eventdata)
global hfig


    % check if an AVI file has been opened
    if  isfield(hfig, 'movie_info')
        % start the video and reset the frame count if at the end
        if hfig.frame_count < hfig.movie_info.NumFrames
            start(hfig.video_timer);
        else
            % reset frame count if video at last frame
            hfig.frame_count = 1;
            start(hfig.video_timer);
        end
    end
end
```

stop_ButtonDownFcn

```
% -------------------------------------------------------------------
function stop_ButtonDownFcn(hObject, eventdata)
global hfig
    stop(hfig.video_timer);
```

reverse_ButtonDownFcn

```
% -------------------------------------------------------------------
function reverse_ButtonDownFcn(hObject, eventdata)
global hfig

    frame = hfig.frame_count;

    % check if an AVI file has been opened
    if  isfield(hfig, 'movie_info')
        % decrease frame count by 1
        if frame > 1
            frame = frame - 1;
            % render current frame
            set(hfig.mov_img, 'CData', hfig.movie(frame).cdata);
        end
    end

    % update frame count text
    set(hfig.text_frame_count, 'String', num2str(frame));

    hfig.frame_count = frame;
```

forward_ButtonDownFcn

```
% -------------------------------------------------------------------
function forward_ButtonDownFcn(hObject, eventdata)
global hfig

    frame = hfig.frame_count;

    % check if an AVI file has been opened
    if  isfield(hfig, 'movie_info')
        % increase frame count by 1
        if frame < hfig.movie_info.NumFrames
```

```
        frame = frame + 1;
        % render current frame
        set(hfig.mov_img, 'CData', hfig.movie(frame).cdata);
    end
end


% update frame count text
set(hfig.text_frame_count, 'String', num2str(frame));


hfig.frame_count = frame;
```

video_timer_Callback

```
% --------------------------------------------------------------------
function video_timer_Callback(timer_object, eventdata)
global hfig

    frame = hfig.frame_count;

    % check if frame count is at the end of the video
    if frame <= hfig.movie_info.NumFrames

        % render current frame
        set(hfig.mov_img, 'CData', hfig.movie(frame).cdata);

        % increase frame_count to next frame
        frame = frame + 1;
    else
        % stop video timer when last frame is reached
        stop(hfig.video_timer);
    end

    % update frame count text
    set(hfig.text_frame_count, 'String', num2str(frame));


    hfig.frame_count = frame;
```

figure1_CloseRequestFcn

```
% --------------------------------------------------------------------
function figure1_CloseRequestFcn(hObject, eventdata, handles)
global hfig
```

```
% make sure video timer object is deleted before closing
delete(hfig.video_timer);
delete(hObject);
```

5.4   Creating Stand-Alone Executable GUIs

In chapter 1, the concept of creating stand-alone executable applications was mentioned as one of the capabilities of the MATLAB Compiler. Deployment of your GUI application as a stand-alone executable allows a wider audience to utilize the application since they are not required to run a MATLAB session. This section discusses the basics of using the MATLAB Compiler to generate an executable version of your GUI.

5.4.1   Requirements and Limitations

The most important requirement is that you must purchase or have access to the MATLAB Compiler add-on tool since this is not included with the base version of MATLAB. Another important requirement for the MATLAB Compiler is that it must be version 4 or higher. Version 4 contains support for all MATLAB functions including graphics and math functions. Previous versions required the MATLAB C/C++ Math and Graphics Library to compile GUI applications. The following list outlines the important requirements and limitations for generating stand-alone executable GUI applications:

- Must have MATLAB Compiler version 4 or higher OR MATLAB Compiler plus the MATLAB C/C++ Math and Graphics Library

- Must have either MS Windows or Linux operating system since MATLAB Compiler version 4 currently only supports these

- Must have MATLAB 7 (Release 14) to install MATLAB Compiler version 4

- The MATLAB Compiler version 4 does not speed up your GUI application, it will run the same speed when run in a MATLAB session

- Code that depends on interpreting M-file statements, such as running a script M-file, will cause an error since a MATLAB session is not available to create workspace variables, etc ...

You can convert script M-files to functions to avoid this problem.

- Some toolboxes will not compile, it is recommended that you check The MathWorks website for current information regarding compiling toolboxes

- Predefined GUIs included in MATLAB and toolboxes, such as examples, will not compile

- Functions that depend on the MATLAB session, such as help or edit, are not supported

You are encouraged to browse the help for the MATLAB Compiler for more details regarding limitations are restrictions. Also, www.mathworks.com will contain up to date information regarding what functions and toolboxes are supported by the MATLAB Compiler.

5.4.2   M-file Only Executable Generation

The MATLAB Compiler may be used to convert M-file scripts to C code or generate COM Objects although using it to create stand-alone executables using only M-files is our primary concern since all the GUI designs discussed throughout are built purely from M-file code. Creating an executable program from your M-files is quite simple, the following command demonstrates how to generate an executable program from a single M-file:

```
>> mcc -m my_mfile.m
```

The *mcc* command invokes the MATLAB Compiler The *-m* option allows you to compile and link the M-file *my_mfile.m* into *my_mfile.exe*. If your application has multiple M-files then you need to include each file after the *-m* option to ensure they are incorporated into the executable. For example, if you have several files:

```
>> mcc -m main.m f1.m f2.m f3.m
```

To compile and link GUI applications you do not need to include *.fig files in the *mcc* command line although adding them does not cause an error. Both an executable file and a CTF file are created when the *mcc* command is successful. The CTF file, *main.ctf* for the example above, is an archive file that stores all the information and additional files used by *main.m*. This file must be included when deploying your executable application.

5.4.3   Command Window

Once you have generated your executable file you can start your GUI application outside the MATLAB session. Stand-alone executables first popup a command window that emulates the MATLAB session text output. This window must remain open while your GUI application is running. If the command window is closed then it will also close all your GUI windows as well. The following figure shows the command window that comes opens and remains active:

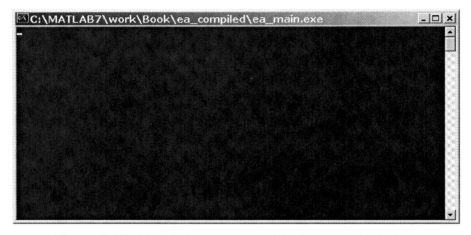

Figure 5.15: Stand-alone executable Command Window

If your application doesn't output any text to the command line, then the command window will not display any information. Most GUI applications that do not have command line output would rather not have this command window open since it conflicts with the overall appearance of your GUI however there doesn't seem to be way to suppress displaying the command window.

5.4.4   Deploying Your GUI Application

After compiling your application using the MATLAB Compiler *mcc* command and the executable and CTF files are generated, your application is ready to distribute! It is important to check the licensing conditions set by The MathWorks, located on their website, before you release your application.

The following example shows the command used to compile example 5.3.4 and the files generated:

Example 5.6: Compiling Stand-alone Executables

Compile

```
>> mcc - m imc
```

PC Files Generated After Compiling

The MATLAB Compiler generates C files as an intermediate step during the compiling and linking process. Only the executable and CTF files are required to deploy your application:

imc.exe

imc.ctf

imc_main.c

imc_mcc_component_data.c

Bibliography

1. The MathWorks, *Release 14 Help*, www.mathworks.com, Natick, MA, 2005-2006.

2. Cleve B. Moler, *Numerical Computing with MATLAB*, Siam, Philadelphia, 2004.

3. Patrick Marchand and O. Thomas Holland, *Graphics and GUIs with MATLAB, Third Edition*, Chapman & Hall/CRC, Boca Raton, FL, 2003.

4. D. C. Hanselman and B. L. Littlefield, *Mastering MATLAB 7*, Prentice Hall, 2004.

5. Foley, Van Dam, Feiner, Hughes, and Phillips, *Introduction To Computer Graphics*, Addison-Wesley Publishing Company, 1994.

6. The MathWorks Training Services, *MATLAB For Building Graphical User Interfaces*, 2004.

7. Eugene Hecht, *Optics, Second Edition*, Addison-Wesley Publishing Company, 1990.

8. Jim Krause, *Color Index: Over 1100 Color Combinations, CMYK and RGB Formulas, For Print and Web Media*, HOW Design Books, Cincinnati, OH, 2002.

9. J. C. Sprott, *Strange Attractors: Creating Patterns in Chaos*, New York: Henry Holt, 1993.

300

Printed in the United States
104640LV00003B/7-12/A

9 781598 581812